*Oracle Press*™

Oracle Exalogic Elastic Cloud Handbook

 *Oracle Press*™

Oracle Exalogic Elastic Cloud Handbook

Tom Plunkett
TJ Palazzolo
Tejas Joshi

New York   Chicago   San Francisco
Lisbon   London   Madrid   Mexico City
Milan   New Delhi   San Juan
Seoul   Singapore   Sydney   Toronto

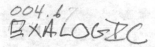

Cataloging-in-Publication Data is on file with the Library of Congress

004.6
EXALOGIC

McGraw-Hill books are available at special quantity discounts to use as premiums and sales promotions, or for use in corporate training programs. To contact a representative, please e-mail us at bulksales@mcgraw-hill.com.

Oracle Exalogic Elastic Cloud Handbook

1 2 3 4 5 6 7 8 9 0   QFR QFR   1 0 9 8 7 6 5 4 3 2

ISBN   978-0-07-177828-2
MHID   0-07-177828-4

Sponsoring Editor Paul Carlstroem	**Technical Editors** Paul Done Jeff Savit	**Composition** Cenveo Publisher Services
Editorial Supervisor Patty Mon	**Copy Editor** Lisa Theobald	**Illustration** Cenveo Publisher Services
Project Manager Sandhya Gola, Cenveo Publisher Services	**Proofreader** Claire Splan	**Art Director, Cover** Jeff Weeks
Acquisitions Coordinator Ryan Willard	**Indexer** Ted Laux	**Cover Designer** Pattie Lee
	Production Supervisor James Kussow	

We dedicate this book to our families.

About the Authors

Tom Plunkett is a senior consultant with Oracle. Tom has taught graduate-level computer science courses for Virginia Tech's computer science department and has authored several books on topics related to Big Data, Cloud Computing, Java, and Service-Oriented Architecture. Tom has spoken internationally at over thirty conferences and delivered hundreds of presentations worldwide on the subjects of Big Data, Cloud Computing, Java, and Service-Oriented Architecture. Previously, Tom worked for IBM and the United States government, and practiced patent law for a law firm. Tom has a B.A. and a J.D. from George Mason University, and an M.S. in Computer Science from Virginia Tech.

TJ Palazzolo is a senior principal curriculum developer with Oracle University. He is the lead curriculum developer for Exalogic Elastic Cloud, WebLogic Server, and Oracle's virtualization products. He develops classroom and online training materials on these and other Oracle Fusion Middleware products. He is also responsible for maintaining the Exalogic rack installations used by Oracle University to deliver education. Prior to working for Oracle, TJ created and delivered training on Java and WebLogic for BEA Systems.

Tejas Joshi is a technical director with Oracle Consulting in the United Kingdom. He has worked on many high-profile multi-million-dollar solutions during the past fourteen years in both the public and private sectors, drawing recognition from both Oracle and customers through numerous awards including Consultant of the Year 2012 for Western Continental Europe. Tejas is a recognized Oracle design authority for numerous Oracle customers in the United Kingdom and represents Oracle on their respective design boards and steering committees, while reporting directly to CxOs of these organizations. Tejas specializes in delivering IT transformation roadmaps for consolidation, cloud computing, and Fusion Applications. He is a frequent and prominent speaker on many events such as Cloud academy, Oracle Services events, Oracle networking events, and Oracle Product launch events. Tejas is a member of a number of strategic programs within Oracle that work on influencing the future directions of the Oracle products and offerings.

About the Technical Editors

Paul Done is a Technical Director for Exalogic at Oracle, a contributing author to the book, Professional Oracle WebLogic Server (Wiley, 2009), and the lead developer of the DomainHealth open source monitoring tool for WebLogic.

Jeff Savit has more than 25 years of experience in operating systems, virtualization, and performance on multiple platforms and is a principal sales consultant at Oracle Corporation specializing in these areas. He was previously a principal engineer at Sun Microsystems with a similar focus. Before joining Sun, Jeff was a vice president at Merrill Lynch, where he held roles in development, systems management, market data, and web applications. He also managed a department responsible for the firm's virtual machine systems, wrote market data portions of Merrill Lynch's Internet trading applications, and created one of the Internet's first stock quote web sites. Jeff has a patent for a computer system workload manager and is the author of *Sun Blueprint Energy Efficiency Strategies: Sun Server Virtualization Technology* and the virtualization chapter of the *Datacenter Reference Guide Blueprint*. Jeff has written and coauthored several books, including *Oracle Solaris 10 Virtualization Essentials, Enterprise Java, VM and CMS: Performance and Fine-Tuning*, and *VM/CMS Concepts and Facilities*, and his work has been published in *SIGPLAN Notices*, a journal of the Association of Computing Machinery. He has a master's degree in computer science from Cornell University.

Contents at a Glance

Contents

xiii

PART II
Administration and Deployment for Oracle Exalogic Elastic Cloud

Acknowledgments

This project has taken a considerable effort. We would like to thank our families for putting up with the burden. We would like to thank Oracle and the members of the Exalogic mailing list, especially Michael Palmeter and Brad Cameron, for their support of this project. We would like to thank our technical reviewers, Paul Done and Jeff Savit, for their many comments and feedback. From Oracle Press and McGraw-Hill Professional, we would like to thank everyone on the editorial and production team, especially including Paul Carlstroem and Ryan Willard. Finally, there are far too many people to name them all individually, so we would like to thank everyone that we have not thanked yet.

Additional Acknowledgments from Tom Plunkett

I'd like to thank Laura, Daniel, and Daphne, and my other family members for putting up with this additional drain on my time. I would also like to thank my co-authors, my reviewers, my co-workers, my management team, my editors, and everyone else who assisted with this effort. In particular, I would like to thank Rizwan Jaka, Mark Comishock, Ken Currie, Peter Doolan, and Mark C. Johnson for their support and encouragement. I would also like to thank Mark A. Johnson for his feedback on deploying packaged applications on Exalogic.

Additional Acknowledgments from TJ Palazzolo

In addition to those mentioned by Tom, I would also like to thank my family for their patience during the many hours I was locked away in the office, including my wife Amber and my children, Maverick and Catalina. I would especially like to thank my wife and best friend for providing much-needed inspiration and motivation during this project and throughout my entire career.

I can't count the number of times I'd still be glued to the couch without her encouragement. I would also like to thank my parents for the loving, stable household that undoubtedly contributed in no small part to my success in work and life. See, I told you that all of the hours tinkering with the computer would pay off! I should also acknowledge the great Exalogic community within Oracle, many of whom are willing to answer questions and troubleshoot problems at a moment's notice. Great communities like this one usually emerge due to talented leadership, so I wish to reiterate our thanks to Michael Palmeter. Despite the complexity and learning curve, I truly believe that Exalogic is an amazing innovation and has some great new capabilities on the horizon. Technology is always a moving target, and I look forward to working on the next edition after a much-deserved break.

Additional Acknowledgments from Tejas Joshi

I would like to thank my wife, Diggu, and my son, Dhruv, for their support and patience during countless weekends and late evenings that I spent on this project. I would like to thank Diggu for being a constant source of inspiration and encouragement in my life and especially during many hours I spent at a stretch locked inside the study room. I promise to my little one to make up for all the lost time. I would also like to thank my parents for their unconditional love and guidance that played a big part in shaping my success in life. I would like to thank my brother, Sid, and sister, Tamanna, for always believing in me. I would also like to thank Paul Done for offering me the opportunity to write this book. I would also thank my co-authors, editors, and publishers for their support and patience in putting up with my constant changes and delays. Finally, I would like to thank my Oracle management team Hasan Rizvi, Senior Vice President; Maurizio Bobbio, Senior Vice President; Malhar Kamdar, Vice President; Phil, Head Vice President; and Ana Perez, Senior Practice Director; without their support and encouragement this project would not have been possible.

Introduction

Oracle Exalogic Elastic Cloud is the world's first integrated cloud machine—hardware and software engineered to work together to provide a "cloud in a box." Exalogic is Oracle's first engineered system for Java. Exalogic is designed to revolutionize data center consolidation and enables enterprises to bring together large numbers of performance-sensitive workloads into a single machine. Complex applications can be executed with results not achievable with typical servers used in today's data centers.

Oracle Exalogic Elastic Cloud Handbook is intended as a handbook for anyone with an interest in Exalogic, including architects, administrators, and developers. As a broad overview, this book will remain relevant for future versions of Exalogic. Although many books on cloud computing, Java, and WebLogic are available, this is the first book to focus on Exalogic. This is a technical book that assumes some prior knowledge of Java Enterprise Edition but does not assume any prior knowledge of Exalogic. This book includes screenshots, diagrams, and photographs when relevant.

Several members of the author team have responsibilities with regard to Exalogic. The team has extensive experience with cloud computing, Java, Service-Oriented Architecture (SOA), and WebLogic Server. Further details on the author team are provided in "About the Authors" section at the beginning of this book.

About This Book

The following section provides short descriptions of the chapters of this book.

Chapter 1, "Architecting the Foundation for Cloud Data Centers," provides an overview of Oracle Exalogic Elastic Cloud, an overview of Oracle Exadata Database Machine, and an overview of how Exalogic and Exadata can be combined to create the foundation for a cloud data center to provide Infrastructure as a Service and Platform as a Service. This chapter describes how the history of Oracle, BEA, and Sun led to the development of this product. Also provided is a description of some of the key business drivers that are creating a market for this product. It includes a general description of the product's benefits and the roles and responsibilities for those who interact with it. Chapter 1 also includes a description of some of the technology trends that have enabled the creation of the product and the standards on which some of the components are based.

Chapter 2, "Exalogic Hardware Architecture," describes Exalogic hardware, which is deployed in rack units that each consist of standard processing, storage, network, and power components. These components have been engineered to provide exceptional levels of performance, high availability, and serviceability. There is redundancy at all levels, including disks, network paths, power, and cooling. Racks are available in eighth, quarter, half, and full configurations. Exalogic's internal networking is based on InfiniBand, an increasingly popular technology for connecting data center components and for delivering much greater throughput than Ethernet.

Chapter 3, "Exalogic Software Architecture," describes Exalogic's high performance and throughput for Java and JVM-based applications, particularly for those built on Java EE and Oracle Fusion Middleware. The Exalogic software architecture consists of several layers, from the OS, to the JVM, to the Java EE container, WebLogic Server. Fusion Middleware then runs as applications and services on WebLogic. The latest releases of WebLogic have been specifically engineered to run on Exalogic. Coherence provides a distributed caching solution for very data-driven applications. Finally, you can manage and monitor all of these different software layers and processes from a single interface with Oracle Enterprise Manager.

Chapter 4, "Exalogic Solution Architecture," describes vertical and horizontal scaling topologies for Exadata and Exalogic. This chapter also describes best practices for disaster recovery and high availability. Finally, this chapter describes how to provide multi-tenancy for deployed applications.

Chapter 5, "Deploying Exalogic," provides a walk-through of how to deploy Exalogic in a data center. Deploying Exalogic involves a significant amount of planning, including space, weight, power, cooling, and network requirements. This chapter discusses planning worksheets and software utilities that are provided for the configuration process. The Exalogic Configuration Utility is used to input network specifications into a supplied spreadsheet; this tool will then update the corresponding network settings on each node to match these specifications. Some additional network configuration tasks must be performed manually. After the network setup is complete, additional configuration tasks include using the storage appliance to define projects, shared files systems, and access rights. Additional deployment steps are required if multiple racks are installed together.

Chapter 6, "Exalogic Administration," describes day-to-day administration of applications that are deployed on Exalogic using Integrated Lights Out Manager (ILOM) and Grid Control. Preceding chapters explained how to deploy Exalogic Machines in a data center; Chapter 6 focuses on understanding how to administer the Exalogic system. A number of tools are available to manage and monitor the Exalogic machine. This chapter tries to organize these tools and how to use them based on the task you would like to perform.

Chapter 7, "Building Private Cloud Applications," covers how to take advantage of performance optimizations offered by Exalogic during development and administration of applications. Building applications on Exalogic can enable organizations to support application development by ensuring that all the environments are identical and deployed by a click of a button. Chapter 7 also discusses how to deploy a private cloud based on Exalogic.

Chapter 8, "Packaged Applications on Exalogic," describes deploying different application workloads on the Exalogic platform. Applications described in this chapter include Oracle E-Business Suite, Oracle PeopleSoft, and SAP. This chapter includes sample application deployment topologies that include both Exadata and Exalogic. Descriptions of examples and benchmarks are also provided.

The back of the book includes an appendix of information that is not appropriate for individual chapters, a list of references, and an index intended to enable this book to be more easily accessible.

Roles and Responsibilities

Although anyone could benefit from reading this entire book, different sections of this book are intended for different roles.

Architects

Chapters 1 through 4 are targeted at architects. Architects could also benefit from reading the remainder of the book.

Administrators and Developers

Chapters 5 through 8 are targeted at administrators and developers. Administrators and developers could also benefit from reading the remainder of the book.

PART
I

Oracle Exalogic
Elastic Cloud
Architecture

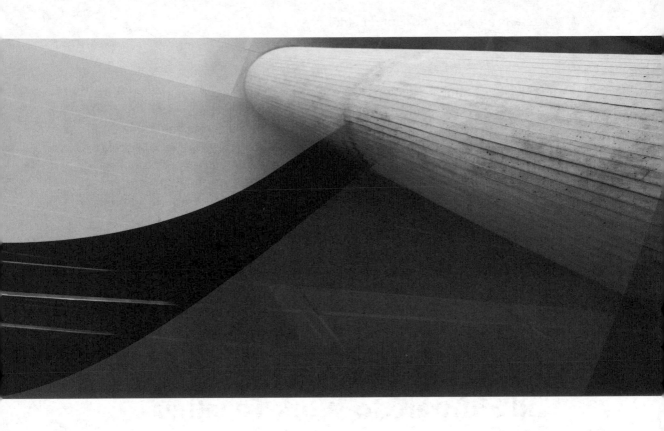

CHAPTER
1

Architecting the Foundation for Cloud Data Centers

racle Exalogic Elastic Cloud is Oracle's first engineered system for enterprise Java. Hardware and software are engineered together to optimize extreme Java performance. Exalogic is designed to revolutionize data center consolidation, enabling enterprises to bring together large numbers of performance-sensitive workloads into a single machine. Complex applications can be executed with results not achievable with the typical servers and complex software stacks used in today's data centers.

Cloud computing is an emerging *disruptive technology* (a new technology that unexpectedly displaces an established technology) that will be discussed at length in this chapter, particularly the value of engineered systems to cloud data centers. This chapter is also the first technical chapter in this book and serves as a technical introduction, as many of these topics are described in greater detail throughout the book.

Engineering Hardware and Software to Work Together

Once upon a time, two boys each received a gift.

The first boy opens his present and discovers a box containing a model car. The label on the box indicates that some assembly is required. The box contains plastic and wooden parts, several wheels, and metal axles. Tools, paint, and adhesives are not provided, and have to be obtained separately from other retailers. It will take time and effort for the boy to collect the necessary tools, and he will need to spend additional time and effort assembling the model car. It is possible that the model car will never be fully assembled—or even if it is fully assembled, it may lack functionality due to incorrect tools being used in the assembly process or inadequate instructions provided.

The second boy opens his present and discovers a box containing a preassembled model car. The second boy can immediately use the fully functional model car.

For many years, traditional information technology (IT) systems have been assembled using a process similar to the first model car example. Various layers of hardware and software components were obtained separately. In some cases, the complexity of integrating the acquired components was such that the purchased components were never used (giving rise to the term "shelfware"). Even when the components were assembled together to function correctly, the assembled solution often exhibited poor performance, chronic reliability problems, and major difficulties to manage and maintain. There are many reasons why a do-it-yourself platform may suffer from problems, including reasons due to project management, application development, unmanaged specification changes, and complexity.

In an effort to overcome these problems, the IT industry is moving toward appliances and engineered systems, which are preassembled systems that combine software and hardware that is optimized, packaged, tested, and deployed together. These systems arrive preconfigured and fully assembled, and they can be placed into operation in a single day. Engineered systems are necessary to overcome the problems of the past. These systems are also necessary to overcome the problems of the future, and the ever increasing amount of information that must be managed.

Furthermore, a common centralized platform for hosting software services provides businesses with benefits such as a reduced total cost of ownership and a faster time to market.

Figure 1-1 illustrates the example steps that a traditional IT customer might follow when developing a platform to host its software solutions.[1]

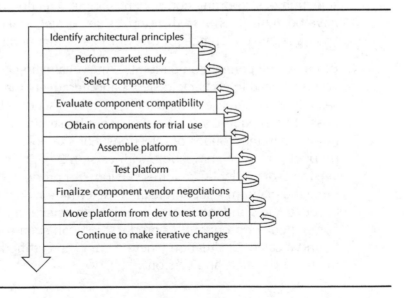

FIGURE 1-1. *Iterative platform development process from a Fortune 500 IT organization (simplified to fit on one page)*

An *iterative platform development process* looks like this:

1. Identify architectural principles and/or platform requirements. In some cases, only architectural principles are known at the start of this process. In other situations, actual requirements have already been determined. Example architectural principles include support for open standards, a preference for integrated product suites, a preference for single-vendor–integrated stack solutions, service orientation, and so on. Platform requirements, on the other hand, will be application focused in terms of functional and nonfunctional requirements. Example requirements include specific capabilities, response times, quality of service, service-level agreements, and so on.

2. Perform market study and rate different technologies and products. During this step, different products are evaluated by the architecture team. Evaluation procedures vary but may include recommendations from analysts such as Forester and Gartner, previous experience with the products by team members, and testing the products in a lab environment.

3. Select software and hardware components. Note that this may be an iterative process, as selection of some components may compel selection of supporting components. Some selections may already have been made prior to this step, as key project stakeholders may have a strong preference for one or more components.

4. Evaluate component compatibility. After evaluating compatibility, you may need to go back to step 3 and iteratively make additional selections to increase compatibility. The first set of selections (and possibly subsequent selections) may not be sufficiently compatible, requiring further rounds of selections. For example, version 1 of product A may be compatible with version 2 of product B, but version 2 of product C requires version 2 of product A. This will force the platform selection team to determine which version of product A to standardize on, requiring the selection of a substitute component for product B or product C. It can even become possible to find a catch-22 situation where there is no certified line through a matrix of products and versions.

5. Obtain components from vendor(s) for trial use. Some vendors make software components available for free download for evaluation. (Oracle makes virtually all of its software components freely downloadable for trial use.) However, other vendors may require a nondisclosure agreement (NDA) or provide only a time limited or trial license. Furthermore, hardware components are often further restricted.

6. Assemble hardware and software components. In the case of limited access to hardware components, it may be acceptable to utilize a virtual machine environment such as Oracle VM to emulate the hardware environment for platform testing purposes.

7. Test the platform. If defects are identified, determine the root cause if possible. If the defect is caused by a product or (more likely) a combination of products, work with the vendor(s) to obtain fixes for the defects. If a single vendor is being utilized for the combination of products, it can make it easier to obtain a fix. (When multiple vendors are involved, one may blame another for any problems.) Once fixes are obtained, continue to test until platform is stable.

8. Finalize vendor price negotiations. Note that component selection may change at this point if price considerations are sufficient to cause a change of component.

9. Move the platform from development through test to production. Additional changes to the platform may result in response to new requirements and/or new incompatibilities discovered during this process.

10. Continue to make iterative changes when requirements change or when product changes, including the challenge of patching or updating the system of components over time (security patches, bugs, and so on).

The overall complexity of the list of steps is apparent after reviewing the list. Of course, different companies will have different versions of this list of steps. Many companies might not perform all of the steps, particularly in repetitive scenarios; however, the general pattern will be similar.

After reviewing the example list of steps, it becomes apparent that the original comparison of a box of parts of a model car to a preassembled model car does not truly capture the differences between traditional IT platform development and optimized engineered solutions. Instead, a more apt comparison may be the car that you buy from a car dealer versus the car that the protagonist assembled in the Johnny Cash song "One Piece at a Time."[2]

In the song "One Piece at a Time," the protagonist builds a car from parts selected from 1949 to 1973. The transmission is from 1953, the motor is from 1973, and there are many other mismatched parts. The protagonist ends up with two headlights on the left side of the car and one headlight on the right side. In some places, holes are missing bolts; in other places, there are no holes for the bolts. We may laugh along with the protagonist in the song at the resulting automobile, but we may shed tears when considering the results of traditional IT platform development. Some IT platforms are terminated after spending billions of dollars on development without ever providing value to the organization that paid for the system. That said, many traditional IT projects involve substantial local development and project management, and root cause determination for the cause of the failure is difficult. Purchasing a prebuilt platform such as Exalogic avoids the risk of a do-it-yourself platform.

One of the key advantages of optimized engineered solutions is that such systems enable customers to avoid processes such as those mentioned. Some organizations have hundreds of people involved in processes to develop standard platforms and test all of the components together. The staff resources spent on engineering the platform is far from free and doesn't provide competitive advantage. Engineered systems enable the enterprise of the future to skip the platform development process and instead focus on the applications that matter for the enterprise's core business. For these reasons and more, engineered and highly performance optimized systems are the future of the IT industry.[3]

Engineered systems yield many benefits, including the following:

- Removes the costs and risks of integration engineering
- Includes pretuned stacks for optimized performance
- Allows for single management and administration view
- Provides support from a single vendor

- Offers a consistent application to a disk patching mechanism provided by the vendor

- Reduces time to deployment.

TIP
If requirements do not mandate that you design your own application platform, you should consider an engineered system such as Oracle Exalogic Elastic Cloud. A prebuilt engineered system such as Exalogic will perform faster and will cost less to purchase, run, and maintain than a custom-designed application platform.

Exabytes of Information

Exadata and Exalogic received their names because of the exabytes of information that the data centers of the future will be required to handle. Our society is becoming increasingly inundated with digital information. Today, information is broadcast from satellites and transmitted over the airwaves, cables, fiber networks, and through other means. In 2004, monthly Internet traffic exceeded 1 exabyte, the equivalent of 1000 petabytes. In 2010, monthly Internet traffic exceeded 20 exabytes.[4]

An *exabyte* is a unit of information or computer storage equal to 1 quintillion bytes. One kilobyte equals 1000 bytes. One megabyte equals 1000 kilobytes. One gigabyte equals 1000 megabytes. One terabyte equals 1000 gigabytes. One petabyte equals 1000 terabytes. One exabyte equals 1000 petabytes. See Table 1-1 for a visual representation of the size of information from byte to exabyte.

Integrated Machines vs. Appliances

Some of the characteristics of engineered solutions, such as the preconfigured assembly of components, are similar to appliances. Appliances do not have configuration options and are designed to perform a simple task, such as a toaster that heats bread to a certain temperature. Exadata and Exalogic are not true "appliances," however. Instead, they are engineered platforms that have

Name (SI symbol)	Power of 10	Number of Bytes
Byte (B)	0	1
Kilobyte (KB)	3	1000
Megabyte (MB)	6	1,000,000
Gigabyte (GB)	9	1,000,000,000
Terabyte (TB)	12	1,000,000,000,000
Petabyte (PB)	15	1,000,000,000,000,000
Exabyte (EB)	18	1,000,000,000,000,000,000

TABLE 1-1.   *Sizes from Byte to Exabyte*

been optimized to run application servers and databases. Hence, many of the traditional rules for managing application servers and databases continue to apply.

In the "One Day Installation Challenge" video on YouTube (www.youtube.com/watch?v=aWHPC188tus), Oracle demonstrates how to install an Exalogic machine in less than ten hours. In contrast, a company following the do-it-yourself platform development approach described earlier might spend more than six months to integrate and deploy a comparable platform.

With traditional IT systems, when a customer calls the support desk, before a problem can be diagnosed, a support team asks a customer numerous questions. These questions ask about the specific component vendors and versions used in the host environment, including operating system, hardware, network, storage, firmware, and patch levels. All must be determined before the actual process of diagnosing the problem can begin. Furthermore, the customer support organization for the specific component will not typically have access to an identically configured environment, especially if some of the elements are supplied by a different vendor. There are limitless combinations of how such components can be configured together. Indeed, during the issue resolution process, it may transpire that the root cause is actually related to a different element of the system belonging to a different vendor. When this occurs, the customer will need to begin this whole support issue process again, with the other product vendor, thus prolonging the issue resolution time.

In contrast, with integrated machines, you simply tell the customer support person the machine model you are using. Furthermore, the customer support desk has access to an identically configured machine, making it easy to replicate the problem that the customer has encountered and dramatically simplifying the troubleshooting process.

Oracle Exadata Database Machine

Although the focus of this book is the Exalogic machine, you'll also find it useful to have a basic understanding of its close cousin, Exadata. There is value in comparing and contrasting their architectures, and you need to keep in mind that both will often be used together.

The Oracle Exadata Database Machine is an integrated software and hardware platform that has been designed for data warehouses, Online Transaction Processing (OLTP), and database consolidation. The Exadata machine's InfiniBand fabric enables extremely fast input/output (I/O) communication between the storage server and the database server. (InfiniBand is also used within Exalogic for high performance I/O and is described in detail in Chapter 2.) Oracle Exadata includes intelligent storage server software that considerably increases the performance of data warehouses by reducing the amount of information that needs to be communicated between the data warehouse server and the storage server.

Exadata uses dedicated servers, or nodes, for storage and processing. The ratio of storage nodes to compute nodes in the Exadata machine is based on an understanding of the business problems that Oracle's customers are attempting to solve. (Compute nodes for Exalogic will be described in detail in Chapter 2.) The Exadata machine that is intended for data warehouses has a ratio that differs from the Exadata machine that is intended for OLTP applications. Both types of Exadata machines rely on the InfiniBand fabric to enhance performance between the database server and the storage server.

The database servers can utilize Oracle Linux or Oracle Solaris as the operating system. (Both operating systems are available for Exalogic, and are described in Chapter 2.) The storage servers use only Linux, and the ZFS Storage Appliance runs Solaris. Oracle 11*g* Release 2 is the current version of the Oracle database that runs on Exadata.

Appliances and similar solutions have been involved with data warehousing for a long time. Exadata, however, has optimizations that existing data warehouse appliances do not have. Furthermore, Exadata also provides the first optimized solutions for OLTP.

Exadata performance enhancements have focused on eliminating unnecessary communication between the database server and the storage server and speeding up communication between the database server and the storage server.

Oracle Exalogic Elastic Cloud

Oracle Exalogic Elastic Cloud is an engineered hardware and software machine designed to provide a platform for a customer's entire application portfolio. Exalogic includes hardware connected by an internal InfiniBand network fabric. An Exalogic machine can be connected with additional Exadata and Exalogic machines. Oracle's market-leading Java Enterprise Edition (Java EE) application server, WebLogic Server, has been reengineered for deployment to Exalogic and uses specific performance enhancements when running on Exalogic. The InfiniBand network fabric offers extremely high bandwidth and low latency, which provides major performance gains with respect to communication between the application server and the database server, and with respect to communication between different application server instances running with in the Exalogic system. Physically, Oracle Exalogic Elastic Cloud can be viewed as a rack of physical server machines plus centralized storage, which all have been designed together to cater to typical high-performance Java application use cases. Figure 1-2 shows the front view of an Exalogic machine.

In summary, Exadata is the database machine for the data tier and Exalogic is the middleware machine for the application tier.

Why Would an Organization Adopt Exalogic?

Why would an organization adopt the Oracle Exalogic Elastic Cloud machine? Just because Exalogic is an extremely high-performing Java solution, it does not mean that it is the perfect solution for every organization. Some organizations have architectural considerations that counsel adoption of alternative solutions. Further chapters will dive into these architectural considerations in greater detail, but the next few paragraphs describe some of the areas for which customers may find great value in adopting Oracle Exalogic Elastic Cloud. The next step is to understand Exalogic's hardware architecture in greater detail.

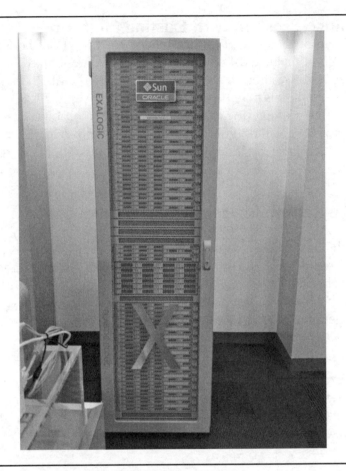

FIGURE 1-2. *Exalogic front view*

New Platform

If your organization is designing a platform for new applications based on Java technology, then Oracle Exalogic Elastic Cloud may provide great performance for a low cost. Cost savings with Exalogic come from a shorter time to production (the ability to install the system in a day), and the ease of managing the preconfigured appliance and maintaining and patching the system. Cost savings also come from the enhanced performance characteristics, which enable customers to reduce the amount of hardware and software that is necessary for a particular application. Exalogic is particularly relevant if the organization is interested in providing a private cloud from its data center (as discussed later in the section "Architecting Private Cloud Data Centers").

Performance Problem with Existing Platform

If the organization's current IT architecture is suffering from performance problems, migrating the existing applications to Exalogic may alleviate the performance issues without having to redesign and rewrite the applications. To a certain extent, this may be tempered by the specific versions of the applications that are suffering from the performance problems, as not all applications will benefit equally from deployment on to an Exalogic platform. Performance can be tremendously accelerated if the organization adopts both Exalogic and Exadata.

Hardware Refresh for Existing Platform

Most organizations refresh their existing hardware platform every three to six years with the next generation of hardware technology. If the organization is planning on replacing the existing hardware platform with next-generation hardware technology, this is an ideal time to consider Oracle Exalogic Elastic Cloud, and the dense high-performance computing hardware it employs, as the next-generation platform for the organization.

Oracle Workload

If the organization has already deployed Oracle technology in the data center, there will likely be significant performance benefits to moving the existing Oracle investment onto Oracle Exalogic Elastic Cloud, where Exalogic is explicitly tested, validated, and optimized for running such host applications.

TIP
If you currently use Oracle technology in your data center, you should consider adopting Oracle Exalogic Elastic Cloud the next time you do a hardware refresh. If you are currently suffering from performance issues, consider adopting Exalogic at your earliest opportunity. Your application performance should improve considerably while yielding a significant reduction in running costs.

Hardware Architecture

Oracle's Exalogic engineering staff conducted extensive testing on a wide range of hardware configurations to arrive at the optimal configuration for middleware type deployments. Design considerations included high availability, compute density, state-of-the-art components, balanced system design, field serviceability, centralized storage, and high-performance networking.

Exalogic includes Sun hardware connected by an internal InfiniBand network fabric. An Exalogic machine comes in several supported rack configurations. Up to eight of these racks can be connected together with the internal switches that are provided; more than eight can be connected together with additional external InfiniBand switches. Processing is performed by 30 Sun Fire X4170 M2 compute nodes; each compute node has two 64-bit Intel processors with six cores each (12 cores in total per compute node). A full rack has 30 compute nodes, a half-rack has 16 compute nodes, a quarter-rack has 8 compute nodes, and a one-eighth rack has 4 compute nodes. Shared storage is provided by a built-in Sun ZFS Storage 7320 appliance, which is accessible by all the compute nodes. InfiniBand and Ethernet switches enable network communication. Figure 1-3 shows the rear view of an Exalogic machine, including the InfiniBand cabling.

Figure 1-4 shows the Exalogic Hardware architecture. Chapter 2 explores Exalogic's hardware architecture in more detail.

Exalogic is accompanied by a set of software tools, including the Exalogic Configuration Utility (previously known as OneCommand). This utility configures the networking for the system to be accessible via the customer's wider data center network. (For the YouTube video, Oracle product development engineer Ram Sivaram was videotaped unwrapping and installing an Exalogic machine in ten hours.[5])

InfiniBand is a networking technology similar to Ethernet and is used as an alternative for high-performance computing within a data center. InfiniBand Technology is a critical component within both Exalogic and Exadata. The InfiniBand Trade Association (IBTA) was founded in 1999 and is led today by Oracle, Intel, IBM, Mellanox, QLogic, and Voltaire. The goal of the IBTA is to standardize a communication link for high-performance computing systems such as Exadata and Exalogic. Applications can take advantage of the low network latency and high performance provided by

FIGURE 1-3. *Exalogic rear view including InfiniBand cabling*

InfiniBand (IB) through protocols such as Sockets Direct Protocol (SDP) or Internet Protocol over InfiniBand (IPoIB). "Exalogic-ignorant" applications work by virtue of implicitly using IPoIB, and IB-aware applications can explicitly use IB's native SDP to reduce latency further—an example of software engineered for specific hardware. Exalogic utilizes 40-gigabit InfiniBand technology to accelerate performance, in comparison to 1-gigabit

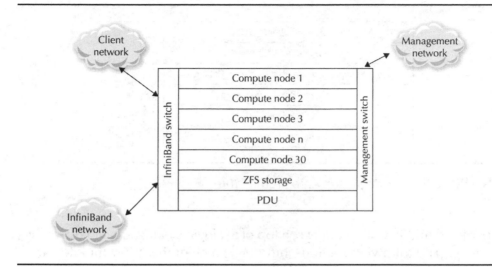

FIGURE 1-4. *Exalogic hardware architecture*

or 10-gigabit Ethernet networks used in typical systems. InfiniBand technology is continuing to evolve and future generations will be even faster.

Software Architecture

Several operating systems can be run on each compute node in an Exalogic system. Either Oracle Linux 5.5 or Solaris 11 Express, for x86-64 based processors, can be run on each compute node, with the restriction that all compute nodes must run the same type of operating system. Any vendor's software that is supported by the vendor for the above mentioned operating system is also supported to be deployed on Exalogic.

If you're running Solaris 11 on Exalogic, you can use operating system–level virtualization to help run applications on multiple instances of Solaris on a single compute node (including versions of Solaris such as Solaris 10). This virtualization technology in Solaris is called Solaris Zones. Refer to Chapter 4 for more details on virtualization.

Of course, just providing a enhanced operating system to run optimally on Exalogic is not enough. The real power of the engineered hardware and software combination comes from running Oracle's Exalogic-aware and

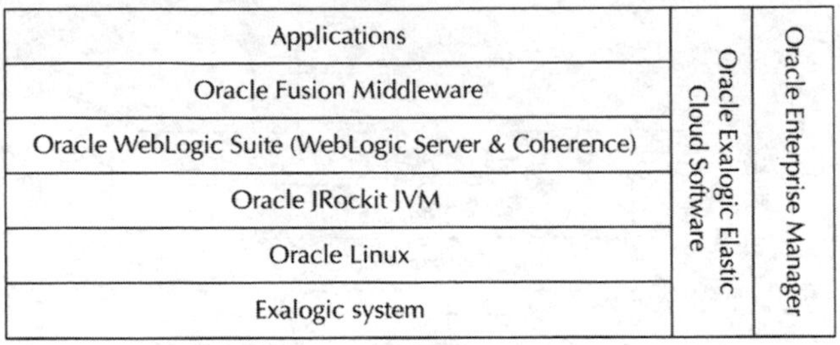

Applications	Oracle Exalogic Elastic Cloud Software	Oracle Enterprise Manager
Oracle Fusion Middleware		
Oracle WebLogic Suite (WebLogic Server & Coherence)		
Oracle JRockit JVM		
Oracle Linux		
Exalogic system		

FIGURE 1-5.   *Exalogic software architecture*

optimized middleware products on top of Exalogic's hardware and operating systems. The following sections introduce some of these key middleware components, including Oracle WebLogic Server, Oracle Coherence, plus the Oracle's management toolset for Exalogic, Oracle Enterprise Manager. See Figure 1-5 for a graphic representation of Oracle Exalogic Software architecture.

An alternative architecture based on Sun Solaris and the HotSpot Java Virtual Machine (JVM) is shown in Figure 1-6.

Version 2.1 and subsequent versions of Exalogic include Oracle Virtual Machine, as shown in Figure 1-7.

Chapter 3 will explore this software architecture in greater detail.

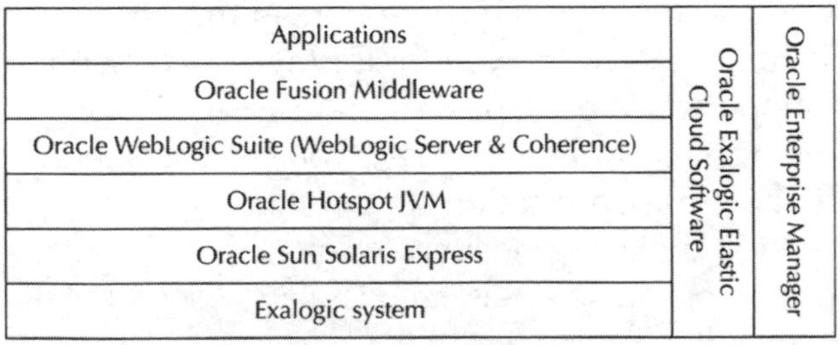

Applications	Oracle Exalogic Elastic Cloud Software	Oracle Enterprise Manager
Oracle Fusion Middleware		
Oracle WebLogic Suite (WebLogic Server & Coherence)		
Oracle Hotspot JVM		
Oracle Sun Solaris Express		
Exalogic system		

FIGURE 1-6.   *Exalogic software architecture*

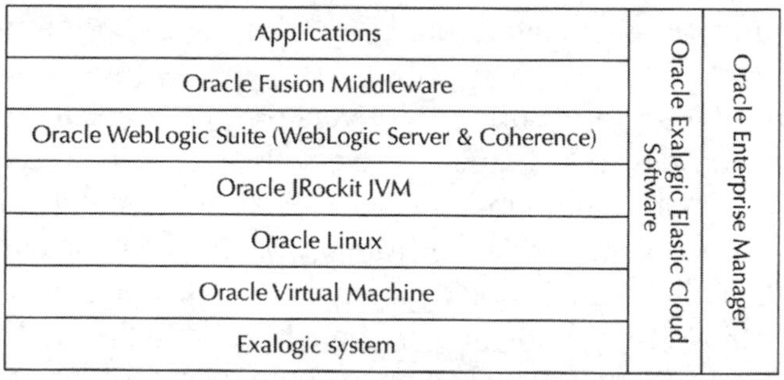

Applications		
Oracle Fusion Middleware		
Oracle WebLogic Suite (WebLogic Server & Coherence)		
Oracle JRockit JVM	Oracle Exalogic Elastic Cloud Software	Oracle Enterprise Manager
Oracle Linux		
Oracle Virtual Machine		
Exalogic system		

FIGURE 1-7. *Exalogic software architecture*

Oracle WebLogic Server

Oracle WebLogic Server (WLS) is the market leading Java EE Server. (Java EE is discussed in greater detail in subsequent sections and in Chapter 3.) WLS can be installed and run on many operating systems and hardware platforms. WLS is used to run mission-critical systems and applications, especially where reliability, availability, scalability, and performance are requirements.

WebLogic, Inc. (the company) was founded in 1995 with the goal of producing the world's first web application server (called Tengah). In 1998, BEA acquired the San Francisco startup WebLogic, Inc., and the application server was renamed WebLogic Server and became one of the main inspirations for Sun Microsystems' subsequent Java EE specification and industry standard. In 2008, Oracle acquired BEA, including WebLogic Server. Oracle has positioned WebLogic Server at the core runtime for its Middleware and Application products, Fusion Middleware.

Oracle is the market leader in the enterprise application servers market with more than 43 percent of the market. Gartner has published its application server market share numbers for 2010 based on total software revenues. According to Gartner, Oracle holds more market share than its four closest competitors and grew at a rate of 17.8 percent, faster than the industry average of 12.1 percent.[6]

Oracle WebLogic Server has set numerous world records for performance, including achieving the highest EjOPS/core of any SPECjEnterprise2010 result.

WLS also holds the world record for the jAppServer2004 results. More details on these specifications are available by consulting the references in the appendix.[7]

Oracle WLS 10.3.4 (and subsequent versions) contains the engineered optimizations necessary to leverage all the capabilities of the Exalogic hardware components, especially InfiniBand. If WLS 10.3.4 is running on a non-Exalogic system, it will be unable to take full advantage of these optimizations. Previous versions of WLS will run on Exalogic (if they are certified to run on Oracle Linux 5.5 or Solaris 11, generally) but will not be able to take full advantage of the Exalogic-specific software performance enhancements that appear in later versions of WebLogic.

Java Enterprise Edition

Java EE (formerly J2EE) is the industry standard for enterprise Java computing. Java EE is actually a collection of related specifications that have evolved over time. The Java EE standard adhered to by middleware vendors enables developers to create Java applications that leverage common capabilities while avoiding being locked into a specific vendor's Java EE product. Applications that rely upon the Java EE standard can be easily migrated to another Java EE platform.

Java is a programming language that was developed by Sun and released in 1995. It is an object-oriented language similar to C and C++, but with a simpler object model and automated garbage collection (memory deallocation). As a result, using Java typically results in less error-prone and more productive application development, compared with its programming language predecessors. Java employs the concept of a virtual machine that C++ does not, enabling developers to write Java code that is compiled into a file that could be deployed onto any platform that includes a JVM, regardless of what type of operating system and processor the platform runs on.

Sun's slogan of "write once, run anywhere" was based on this virtual machine concept. Soon after the initial release of Java, major web browsers added a JVM plug-in, enabling Java programs contained in HTML web pages (called *applets*) to run in the browser. Java became very popular because of the Java Applets technology; in the late 1990s, this was the first browser-based technology to support dynamic rich content. Figure 1-8 shows a graphic representation of Java client-side technology.

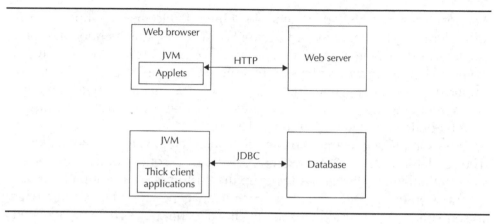

FIGURE 1-8. *Java client-side technology*

In the first example shown in Figure 1-6, a Java applet is displayed running in a web browser. As a security precaution, applets can communicate only to the web server they were downloaded from and cannot, for example, read or change the contents of files on the browser's local file system. In the second example, a Java thick client application running in a JVM on a client-side machine can communicate to a database server using Java's database connection API (JDBC).

However, the Java Standard Edition did not have all of the capabilities that enterprises sought for building long-running server-side applications. This led to the development of several technologies that were bundled together in the Java Platform for the Enterprise.

The original goal for the Java Platform for the Enterprise was to provide support for web applications where dynamic content is created on the server side (using Java Servlets and JavaServer Pages) and to provide support for running business logic components on the server (Enterprise Java Beans).

The initial Java Platform for the Enterprise in 1998 included specifications for Enterprise Java Beans (EJB 1.0), Java Servlets (2.1), JavaServer Pages (JSP 1.0), Java's database connectivity API (JDBC 1.1), and Java Naming and Directory Interface (JNDI 1.0) API.

Java Servlets

Java Servlets is a technology designed to generate dynamic web page content on a server that is streamed back to the web browser as HTML pages, ready to be rendered by the browser in a human-readable form.

Servlets are a multithreaded technology intended to improve upon many of the drawbacks that other server-side HTML-generating technologies of the late 1990s suffered from, such as the Common Gateway Interface (CGI), commonly used in web servers of the time. Servlets are deployed in an application server container that provides services that the servlet can rely upon, reducing the amount of software coding that is required to create a web application. Figure 1-9 shows Java servlets.

An example servlet might be an application created for online banking. The servlet in Figure 1-9, for example, receives a request for a customer's account balance. The servlet looks up the customer's current balance information using JDBC and then dynamically generates a HTML web page to send back to the customer, showing the account balance and associated account information.

JavaServer Pages

The JavaServer Pages technology was created to simplify the process of creating a web application using Java servlets, to reduce the amount of coding required. A JSP page appears similar to an HTML page, except that it includes special JSP tags that are used to generate bits of content dynamically on the server mixed in between the fragments of static HTML. This processing might include retrieving information from a database to populate a generated web page, for example. The generated HTML page is then sent from the server to the web browser. The JSP page itself is never seen by the user of the web browser, only the resulting generated HTML is seen.

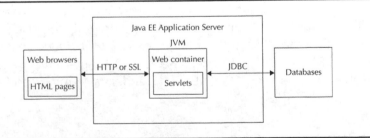

FIGURE 1-9. *Java servlets*

The advantage of JSP is that the technology separates the presentation logic from the business logic in a server-side application, thereby enabling different developer roles to handle the creation of different types of software logic. So presentation developers who understand HTML but do not understand Java can easily see how these pages will be displayed and can concentrate on getting the look, feel, and flow of a web page just right (unlike with traditional servlets, which are composed of pure Java code). Java developers can be responsible for the business logic, which is generated by special tags or in JavaBeans that are referenced from the JSP. Figure 1-10 shows how a JSP page returns a response page after receiving a request.

In Figure 1-10, a web browser sends a request for a JSP page. The web container (shown as the servlet/JSP container in the figure) recognizes that the request is for a JSP page and compiles the JSP page, generating a servlet. The servlet is then executed to generate the HTML response page. The HTML response page is then sent back to the web browser that sent the original request. Future requests to the same JSP will not incur the startup time of compiling the JSP and generating the servlet, as the JSP has to be compiled only once, regardless of how many different clients request it. Using the banking application example, the JSP version will have the same functionality as the servlet version, except that the bank can employ a user interface specialist who does not understand Java, but is more skilled in creating visually appealing and usable web pages, while freeing the Java developer to write the code for retrieving the customer account information from the database.

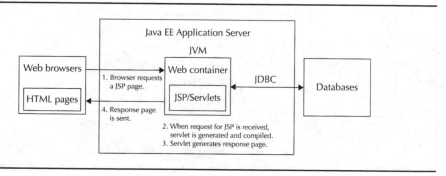

FIGURE 1-10. *Java Server Pages returning a response page after receiving a request*

TIP
We recommend separating the business logic from the presentation layer. JavaServer Pages are ideal technologies for separating the presentation layer from the business logic layer.

Enterprise JavaBeans

Enterprise JavaBeans (EJB) is a server-side component architecture for modular construction of the business logic for enterprise applications. The standard provides a pure-Java component architecture that is similar in concept to the Common Object Request Broker Architecture (CORBA) industry standard that emerged in the early-1990s and is in some ways an unofficial successor to CORBA, albeit for Java-based applications only. The EJB components are deployed into a container, in a similar manner to how Java Servlets and JSP pages are deployed into a container. However, EJB technology is far more complex than Servlet or JSP technology, and, with the benefit of hindsight, was deemed too complex. The EJB standard has been simplified in subsequent versions. Figure 1-11 shows an example of the EJB container along with the web container.

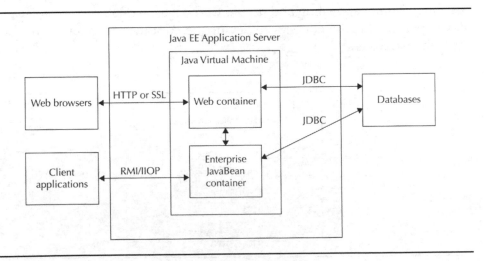

FIGURE 1-11. *EJB and web containers*

In a banking example, EJBs are used for transactions management and enabling easier persistence and retrieval of data from relational databases. Transactions management is important if the application is doing anything more than just displaying current data. For example, if the banking application allows the customer to change the account balance via a transfer, EJBs and transaction management should be used to ensure that a withdrawal from one account and the deposit to the other account is executed atomically as a single operation. Otherwise, during error conditions, money may go missing or duplicate deposits may occur.

TIP
If there is a need for transactions management,
consider using Enterprise JavaBeans.

A Little Java History

In December 1999, version 1.2 of the enterprise Java standard was released. Java had been renamed Java 2 in December 1998. The Java Platform for the Enterprise was subsequently renamed Java 2 Enterprise Edition (J2EE). J2EE version 1.2 added incremental changes to the previous components of J2EE (servlets, JSPs, EJBs, and so on) and also added support for transactions and messaging. Java Message Service (JMS) provided capabilities for asynchronous and synchronous messaging and support for publish/subscribe models. (JMS was a standard for messaging; the predominant proprietary technology that led to the development of JMS was Message Oriented Middleware and IBM's MQ Series product.) Another type of EJB was introduced, called Message-Driven Beans. Transaction support was provided through a container-based Java Transaction Service (JTS, based on the Object Transaction Service from CORBA, which itself was based on the X/OPEN standard) and a Java Transaction API (JTA) for writing code to interact with the JTS.

In September 2001, J2EE version 1.3 was released. In addition to including incremental changes to previous components of J2EE, this version added support for the Java Connector Architecture (JCA) and XML (Java API for XML Processing, or JAXP). JCA is a Java-based technology solution for connecting application servers and enterprise information systems. JDBC is used to connect JEE applications to databases, and JCA is a more generic architecture for connection to legacy systems. XML is becoming of increasing importance to Java development. Almost all enterprise Java programs involve XML at this point.

In November 2003, J2EE version 1.4 was released. This version added support for web services. J2EE 1.4 was delayed while waiting for the Basic Profile 1.0 web services to be completed. The Basic Profile was developed by a consortium that focused on interoperability conformance for the different web services standards.

In May 2006, Java EE version 1.5 was released. (Java 2 had been renamed Java, and hence J2EE had been renamed JEE.) JEE version 1.5 simplified the EJB persistence model.

In 2009, Oracle acquired Sun and committed to continue to support the Java EE standards. Subsequently in December 2009, Java EE 6 was adopted. This version is supported in the latest version of WLS. Java EE 7 and Java EE 8, which have not yet been released, are focused on adding additional capabilities for cloud computing into the JEE standard.

Java EE applications deployed on Exalogic may use all of the preceding technologies, as shown in Figure 1-12.

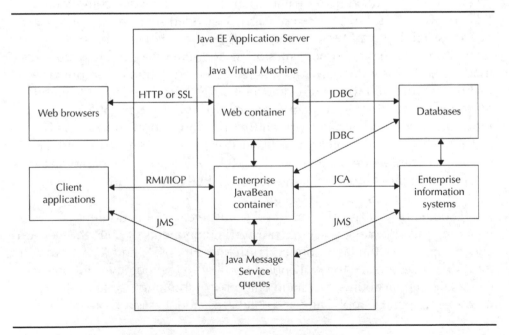

FIGURE 1-12. *Example Java EE application*

Oracle WebLogic Suite

Oracle WebLogic Suite is the name for a collection of related Oracle products. In addition to Oracle WLS Enterprise Edition, it also includes Oracle Coherence Enterprise Edition, Oracle WebLogic Real Time (JRockit), Oracle Virtual Assembly Builder, Oracle Web Tier, and two Oracle Enterprise Manager add-ons: Diagnostics Pack for Java and Management Pack for Coherence.

NOTE
Oracle Enterprise Manager: Diagnostics Pack for Java, which includes Advanced Diagnostics for Java (AD4J) and JRockit Mission Control, is discussed in the separate section that follows. Oracle Coherence and the management pack for Coherence are also discussed in a separate section.

Oracle WebLogic Real Time is a real-time solution for Java based on JRockit's real-time features. This solution is typically used by applications that have a requirement for deterministic scheduling with specified timing bounds. Java implements real-time solutions by providing deterministic control of the JVM garbage collection thread. Customers interested in real-time solutions include Wall Street banks (high-frequency traders, and so on), military command and control systems, and other applications where microseconds are critical.

Oracle Web Tier includes components that interact with end users through HTTP requests and responses. Capabilities include security gateways, support for a DMZ in front of the application server tier, load dispatching, and so on. Products include the Oracle iPlanet Web Server, the Oracle iPlanet Web Proxy Server, Oracle Traffic Director, Oracle Web Cache, and Oracle HTTP Server (an Apache-based server).

Oracle Virtual Assembly Builder (OVAB) is designed to help organizations configure multi-tier applications and provision them onto virtual machines. For example, a web server, an application server, and a database can be packaged and deployed as a single unit onto Oracle VM. OVAB structures the process of combining the components, deploying the components, and configuring the components. Virtualization enables organizations to separate the application from the underlying hardware infrastructure and operating system. Many organizations are investing considerable resources into virtualization to achieve greater agility and cost reductions.

Oracle Enterprise Manager: Diagnostics Pack for Java, which includes Advanced Diagnostics for Java (AD4J) and JRockit Mission Control, provides capabilities to perform JVM diagnostics. This package is included with WebLogic Suite and is an Enterprise Manager component. JVM Diagnostics is important whenever an administrator is trying to discover the root cause of a production problem.

Oracle Enterprise Manager (OEM) is Oracle's administrative console for the enterprise. OEM enables organizations to monitor all of their applications across the Oracle stack, from the application tier through the middleware and the database down into the hardware with OEM Ops Center. The particular Enterprise Manager packs mentioned so far are commonly required for enterprise Java deployments using WebLogic Suite.

Oracle Coherence

Oracle Coherence is an in-memory distributed data grid designed for clustered applications and application servers. Coherence provides distributed data caching on top of a scalable peer-to-peer clustering protocol. The advantage of using Coherence is that the data is located close to the processing applications while the Coherence data grid handles the data persistence functionality. This offers the benefit of scalability, with additional servers being able to handle an increased capacity of data without impacting response time.

Oracle Coherence is useful when you need to reduce the amount of time it takes to retrieve persistent data from a data source. Instead of a client application needing to communicate across the network to the data source and wait for the data source to process the request and compute a result, the result information is cached in the Coherence data grid for quick retrieval. This performs especially well when the data cache is on the same server with the client application. Coherence maintains the relationship between the data in the distributed cache and the original data source.

Coherence can reduce latency for application servers by reducing the time it takes to generate responses. Coherence provides high availability by transparently failing over the clustered services and redistributing cached data when necessary. When a new server is added, it automatically joins the cluster and Coherence fails back services to it, transparently redistributing the cluster load. Figure 1-13 illustrates the Coherence data grid.

As shown in Figure 1-13, several application servers are utilizing data stored in a clustered Coherence grid. The application servers are located near the data cache that they are utilizing.

Some optimizations for Exalogic have already been added to Coherence. For example, Coherence includes an Elastic Data feature that increases performance when used in conjunction with the local 100GB solid state drives (SSDs) in the Exalogic compute nodes. The Elastic Data feature has been optimized to prioritize RAM availability to store the primary copies of data, by moving backup copies to or from RAM to flash. The feature also triggers its internal garbage collection as its remaining RAM capacity approaches zero; alternatively, when RAM is plentiful, the internal garbage collection feature will be less likely to trigger. Other optimizations include increased concurrency when overflowing to flash devices, and more are planned for future releases.

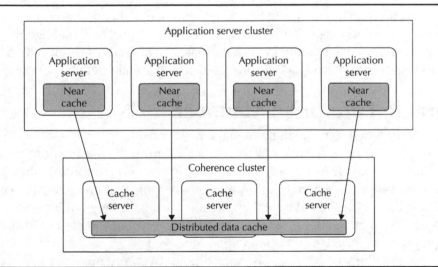

FIGURE 1-13. *Coherence in-memory data grid*

Oracle Fusion Middleware and Fusion Applications

Many of the Oracle Fusion Middleware 11*g* components run on WLS and can therefore take advantage of the InfiniBand-based and other performance enhancements that are present in WebLogic when running on Exalogic.

Oracle Fusion Middleware includes best of breed products such as Oracle WebLogic Suite, Oracle WebCenter Suite, Oracle SOA Suite, Oracle Identity Management, Oracle Service Bus, Oracle JDeveloper, and so on. These middleware products provide capabilities for business process management, enterprise and legacy systems integration, content management, data integration, business intelligence, event driven architecture, SOA governance, business transaction management, and transaction processing.

Oracle Applications includes applications such as PeopleSoft, JD Edwards, Siebel, ATG, Flex, E-Business Suite, and a new suite of applications known as Oracle Fusion Applications. Oracle Fusion Applications are architected to run on Oracle Fusion Middleware and will be able to take advantage of the capabilities of Exalogic. Oracle Fusion Application areas include customer relationship management; financials; governance, risk, and compliance; human capital management; procurement; project portfolio management; supply chain management; and other areas. Advantages of running Oracle Fusion Applications on Exalogic are discussed in greater detail in Chapter 8.

Oracle Enterprise Manager

OEM is designed to be a single management console that can manage all the levels of today's complex IT infrastructure, from the application layer to the hardware layer. As organizations move into cloud computing, they'll find it no longer sufficient to use management tools that are designed for a single layer or a single vertical application. Instead, they will need access to a tool set that can be used to manage the enterprise. Oracle Enterprise Manager is intended to offer that capability.

Oracle Enterprise Manager is composed of two core management tools: Grid Control and Ops Center. Grid Control is used to manage and provision software. Ops Center is used to manage and monitor the hardware and the network. Other optional management packs add capabilities to Oracle Enterprise Manager.

Exalogic Performance Enhancements

Exalogic performance enhancements enable applications to take full advantage of InfiniBand's fast networking infrastructure. In addition to IB-based enhancements, there are also enhancements to the JDBC driver, JVMs, and other features. These performance enhancements fall into three general categories: enhancements to increase communication performance between the application server and the database server; enhancements to increase communication performance among application servers; and general enhancements to WLS. In addition to performance enhancements to WebLogic, performance enhancements are being made to many other products in the Oracle Fusion Middleware platform, including Oracle Coherence. Layered products running on SOA Suite, WebCenter, and so on, will then implicitly take advantage of these optimizations.

Communication between WLS instances on Exalogic and database server instances on Exadata can take full advantage of performance enhancements provided by InfiniBand. There are also improvements to integration between WebLogic and Oracle RAC.

Application Server cluster communication is improved by InfiniBand. For example, web applications can keep track of the current state of end user interactions using an HTTP session object managed by the application server. WLS can automatically replicate session data from the primary server to a secondary server in the cluster each time session data changes. However, session replication incurs a performance cost if a large amount of user data is being held. For Exalogic, WLS's replication mechanism is improved to utilize the 40 Gb/s I/O bandwidth provided by InfiniBand for interprocess communication between servers.

WLS (and the underlying JVM) includes additional general enhancements, such as network request handling, memory, and thread management. These enhancements yield better response times, better throughput, and other benefits that are described later in this book. These enhancements are specific to Exalogic because they alleviate bottlenecks that would otherwise materialize on dense computing resource environments.

Architecting Private Cloud Data Centers

The term "cloud computing" dates back to the days in which a cloud was drawn on a whiteboard to abstract away the network details. Today, cloud computing means much more than just an abstraction to simplify concepts on a whiteboard.

Sometimes referred to as a "Cloud in a Box," Exadata and Exalogic provide the necessary application platform and information management capabilities that can be the foundation for a private cloud. While platform capabilities for information management and application platforms are a necessity, these capabilities alone are an insufficient condition for a private cloud. Also required for a private cloud is the ability to perform provisioning of resources, metering, and charge back for services that are used. Oracle Enterprise Manager can provide the necessary management capabilities to create a private cloud leveraging Exadata and Exalogic.

NIST Definition of Cloud Computing

Although there are several competing definitions of cloud computing in the industry, the National Institute for Standards and Technology (NIST) has provided the most accepted and comprehensive definition. NIST defines cloud computing as "a model for enabling convenient, on-demand network access to a shared pool of configurable computing resources (e.g., networks, servers, storage, applications, and services) that can be rapidly provisioned and released with minimal management effort or service provider interaction" (NIST Draft Definition of Cloud Computing v15).[8]

The NIST model includes five essential characteristics:

- **On-demand self-service** Consumers want to be able to access cloud resources without having to ask IT for access.

- **Resource pooling** To provide resources that can scale up to meet the consumer self-service demand, resources should be pooled.

- **Rapid elasticity** Consumers should be able to use the resources they need when they want them; resources should scale up and scale down as necessary to meet demand.

■ **Measured service**   Because resource usage will scale up and scale down as driven by demand, resource usage can be unpredictable. Therefore, resource usage should be measured to provide the ability to charge based on usage. Measured service proposes a metering system for IT (similar to how utilities bill for electricity or water usage) as opposed to the traditional approach where you pay for the system regardless of how much or how little you use it (the industry average for server utilization is under 30 percent).

■ **Broad network access**   To serve a wide range of consumers with a wide range of needs, it will be necessary for cloud providers to offer broad network access to cloud resources.

The NIST model describes three service models:

■ **Infrastructure as a Service (IaaS)**   IaaS providers typically offer virtual machine images that are either a base operating system or perhaps with some additional software deployed on the image. IaaS enables organizations to abstract out and enable allocation of compute resource, storage, network, and so on, on demand through the use of virtualization. Dynamic provisioning enables organizations to scale up and down as necessary. Typical IaaS providers include Amazon.com (public IaaS), Oracle VM (private IaaS), and other providers that offer virtualized machine images.

■ **Platform as a Service (PaaS)**   PaaS providers typically offer a platform upon which cloud consumers can build applications; this platform typically has an API and provides a variety of services to support the applications. Examples could include middleware as a service, database as a service, identity management as a service, and so on. A platform providing these services could then be dynamically provisioned on demand depending on the user's requirements. Typical PaaS providers include Oracle Exalogic Elastic Cloud (for private PaaS), Google App Engine (for public PaaS), Force.com (public PaaS), and other platforms on which cloud consumers can create applications.

■ **Software as a Service (SaaS)**   SaaS providers typically offer a multitenant application that can be configured to meet the application user's requirements. With multitenancy, multiple users (or organizations) share the application, but the application is configured so that user or organization has access only to their own data. Typical SaaS providers includes Oracle On Demand, SalesForce.com, Google Apps, and other applications that are provided in the cloud.

Finally, the NIST model includes four deployment models:

■ **Public cloud**   Public cloud providers offer their cloud resources to the general public over the Internet. Amazon, Google, and SalesForce.com are examples of public cloud providers.

■ **Private cloud**   Private clouds are built for a single organization and provide cloud resources to their internal departments and lines of business. Private clouds are built primarily when an organization wants greater controls than public clouds can offer (including performance guarantees, location of data, security, and so on). Numerous large organizations are building private clouds for their internal customers.

■ **Community cloud**   Community clouds are related to private clouds, with similar security and governance considerations that can leverage each other's resources to scale elastically. An example would be multiple private clouds developed for the U.S. Department of Defense that could leverage each other's resources to scale elastically while meeting Department of Defense security requirements.

■ **Hybrid cloud**   Hybrid clouds are a combination of private clouds and public clouds. In this case, an organization builds a private cloud for the control that the private cloud offers but makes use of public clouds when there is a need for greater elasticity than the private cloud can provide. An example would be an organization that needs to scale up resources on Super Bowl Sunday to handle a peak in consumer response after showing a Super Bowl ad.

Oracle Exalogic Elastic Cloud is an ideal building block to enable an organization to create a private cloud with a PaaS capability. Exalogic and Exadata can be combined in a PaaS offering, with Exadata providing Database as a Service capabilities and Exalogic providing Application Serving as a Service.

OEM can provide the capabilities for on-demand self-service and measured service, with Exalogic and Exadata providing the capabilities for resource pooling, rapid elasticity, and network access.

TIP
If your data center is planning to offer private cloud–based application resources and database resources, you should consider a private PaaS with Exalogic and Exadata as the foundation for your cloud data center. OEM can offer provisioning, metering, and charge-back services for your private cloud.

Public Clouds and Private Clouds

In August–September 2010, the Independent Oracle User Groups (IOUG) surveyed its members regarding enterprise cloud initiatives.[9] As of the fall of 2010, only 13.8 percent of respondents were using public clouds. However, the introduction of the Oracle Cloud and other public clouds designed for enterprise customers should increase this adoption rate.

Private clouds are of primary interest to many enterprise customers today. According to the 2010 IOUG survey referenced above, 28.6 percent of respondents have private clouds that are either in production or in a pilot. There is a two to one ratio when comparing the percentage of respondents who indicated that their organization is pursuing a private cloud to the percentage that is pursuing a public cloud (28.6 percent versus 13.8 percent). The disparity between private cloud adoption and public cloud adoption is driven by several factors, as indicated in the survey. Security concerns were the number one reason why respondents selected a private cloud effort over a public cloud. The number two issue was quality of service concerns: the ability to define an enterprise Service Level Agreement (SLA) for a private cloud instead of being forced to accept a public cloud's mandatory terms for an SLA. As the survey shows, private clouds in 2010 were still an immature technology and a number of issues remained to be resolved. That said, private clouds do avoid some of the key issues of public clouds—namely the security and SLA issues.

Why Use Exalogic in a Private Cloud Data Center?

Oracle Exalogic Elastic Cloud helps organizations achieve the opportunities and benefits that private clouds offer. It provides the high-performance computing power necessary for a private cloud. Exalogic, when combined with OEM's management capabilities, makes an excellent private cloud platform.

OEM helps provide the necessary capabilities that organizations require for provisioning server and storage capacity. OEM also provides support for metering and charge-back to enable organizations to create the business case and funding model for their private cloud. OEM also provides capabilities for managing service levels and providing visibility and control over applications and other resources.

Future versions of Exalogic will offer even greater support for private clouds.

Summary

If you are running Oracle middleware or applications, Oracle Exalogic Elastic Cloud is an extremely fast engineered system for running Oracle middleware and Oracle application workloads. Anyone who is considering improving performance for an existing system, refreshing a current hardware platform, or considering a new project should seriously consider choosing Exalogic as the platform of choice.

The value of engineered systems to cloud data centers was described in this chapter. It was also the first technical chapter in this book and served as a technical introduction to the rest of the book, as many of these topics are described in greater detail throughout.

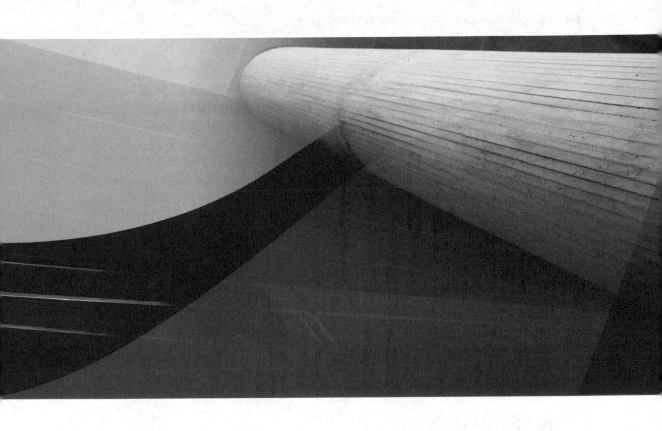

CHAPTER
2

Exalogic Hardware
Architecture

hat exactly does Exalogic look like? When it's delivered to your data center, what should you expect to find? What are the different pieces and how are they connected? This chapter describes the different hardware components of an Exalogic rack and their capabilities. More importantly, this chapter discusses some of the motivations behind the hardware architecture, from processors and memory, to storage and cabling. As you might expect, we'll pay particular attention to networking, including Exalogic's InfiniBand fabric.

Hardware Requirements

When evaluating any data center computing hardware solution, you should look for certain qualities. Performance and scalability are no-brainers—those apply to any deployment architecture. In fact, these traits are often the major considerations for a consolidated data center architecture. Other characteristics, however, are just as important, if not more so, but are often overlooked.

Redundancy

Today's businesses expect application downtime that is measured in hours per year—or sometimes even less. As you will see in the next chapter, Oracle's middleware solution is designed for high availability with features such as *clustering* and *migration*. However, these software capabilities provide the greatest value when the underlying hardware is also highly available.

It's no accident that a human being has two lungs and two kidneys. Eventually, an organ can fail, and when it does, the other picks up the slack to avoid certain death. The same applies to computer hardware—fans, power supplies, RAM, disks, and circuit boards are not immortal. It's not a question of "if it fails"; a much more interesting question is "what happens when it fails."

Certainly you want reliable hardware, but it's still your job to plan for the worst. When it comes to hardware availability, the key factor is *redundancy*. Each type of component is part of a pool of components of the same type. In other words, when PART_X_1 fails, PART_X_2 is ready to take over, automatically and transparently.

An Exalogic system has been specifically designed with many levels of redundancy. It can handle all kinds of potential failures—both minor (a fan failure) and major (the failure of an entire switch). Several sections in this chapter describe the specific redundancy characteristics for each type of hardware component in Exalogic.

Maintainability

Even if the hardware and the application can recover from a failure, it's still crucial that the problem be corrected, such as replacing a part, as soon as possible. The most important reason for doing so is to restore the original level of recommended redundancy. For example, a cooling fan might fail on a device that supports two redundant fans. Or two disks might fail on a server that originally contained four. In these scenarios, however, you can expect a minimal, if any, degradation in performance or throughput. But what about the rare occurrences in which an entire server or switch fails? Your applications may remain available, but you may no longer be able to meet your service levels. Again, the ability to correct an issue swiftly and easily is a key requirement for any data center.

The first step in maintainability is identifying a failure and its root cause. All of Exalogic's hardware components include a multitude of sensors that are actively monitored and that can trigger alerts. For example, an administrator may receive an e-mail alerting her about the loss of a hard disk. Later chapters will discuss tools such as Integrated Lights Out Manager (ILOM) and Ops Center to assist you in identifying hardware failures and locating the corresponding parts.

As you probably know from trying to maintain a home PC or especially a laptop, it's practically impossible to replace parts without powering off the whole device. Good enterprise-grade data center components, on the other hand, should be designed to be *hot-swappable* or to use *hot spares*. In this context, "hot" generally refers to the ability to remove and replace something without cycling power. As you will see in subsequent sections, most power supplies, fans, and disks in Exalogic support this capability.

A component may support hot replacement, but if it's not readily accessible when running in the data center, the component is still not easily maintainable. Most Exalogic components are front-mounted and easily removable, usually with just a press of a button. And for those components that must be replaced from the rear of the device, Exalogic's cabling is designed to allow for this type of maintenance.

Another often neglected aspect of maintenance is patching. At any given time, there is likely a patch available for at least one Exalogic component. Patching sometimes involves taking components offline, so it's not always feasible to apply them individually and frequently. Instead, Oracle offers a patch deployment service, which is performed several times a year (quarterly, for example). This service ensures that all hardware and software pieces are optimally maintained, and that all patches are applied together and have previously been tested and validated together by Oracle.

Engineered and Tested

Exalogic is not intended to be a completely customizable solution. You cannot make arbitrary hardware modifications to the system, such as the following:

- Putting an extra server inside the rack

- Upgrading server memory or disk space

- Adding a Peripheral Component Interconnect Express (PCIe) card to a server

- Installing a custom InfiniBand switch

Instead, you must select from one of four different rack or machine configurations. This approach is limiting, but it's implemented for a very important reason. Oracle can specifically engineer its software for these known hardware and OS configurations and can also rigorously test the software against them. For example, you won't have to worry about your PeopleSoft installation's stability and performance when you migrate it to Exalogic, because Oracle has already gone through this validation. This also allows Oracle to specify power and cooling requirements accurately for the data center hosting Exalogic.

If, instead, you engineer your own custom hardware and OS configuration, you would be responsible for properly testing and validating your middleware against it. This means addressing possible incompatibility issues between versions of the hardware, firmware, OS, and so on. In addition to reducing deployment problems, Oracle's engineered system strategy should allow Oracle to provide more accurate and timely support and services as well.

Hardware Topology

Recall that Exalogic is engineered for typical middleware workloads. This means highly available, shared storage along with a high-bandwidth, low-latency network.

Before this chapter provides detailed hardware specifications for each component in Exalogic, you will learn about the overall system architecture at a high level. This section introduces key concepts such as the different types of Exalogic nodes and networks.

Data Center Rack

Exalogic hardware is sold and deployed in standard data center rack units, as shown in Figure 2-1. These are also referred to as Exalogic "machines." The machine shown in Figure 2-1 is referred to as a "full rack" configuration.

Now let's look at what's inside an Exalogic rack.

FIGURE 2-1. *An Exalogic machine*

Compute Node

Oracle uses the term "node" to describe a processing component in Exalogic. Specifically, a node is a rack-mounted server. And like any server, it consists of CPUs, memory, disks, network ports, and so on. However, the configuration of each type of node is optimized for a specific type of processing.

The first type is the *compute node*. An Exalogic compute node resembles traditional server hardware and is designed to be a general-purpose processing unit, although its hardware and software have been specifically constructed and tuned to run Java-based middleware software. As you will see in Chapter 3, you are free to run any type of application you want on a compute node, so as long as it is supported on the operating system.

In other words, Exalogic is not a mainframe or supercomputer system. It is built from general-purpose components and runs standard operating systems such as Linux or Solaris. You can access and manage these servers using familiar tools such as Secure Shell (SSH), for example. This also means that neither Oracle applications nor any custom applications need to be ported to some specialized environment.

Like any good data center server, compute nodes strive to balance high performance with high density. *Density* is generally a measure of computing power within a given amount of floor space in a data center. For example, suppose that you can fit 30 compute nodes within a standard data center rack, and that each of these can run 10 instances of your application. Contrast this with a more powerful compute node that supports 20 application instances, but that is physically much larger in size so that only 14 of them fit within the same rack hardware (same square footage). The first option ($30 \times 10 = 300$) therefore provides higher density than the second ($14 \times 20 = 280$).

Storage Node

The second type of Exalogic node is the *storage node*. Its hardware configuration is designed for a much narrower scope than the compute node. The storage node is optimized to process remote disk access. This means accepting requests to write data to a file system, and to then read that data at a later point. A storage node supports various remote file system protocols, including File Transfer Protocol (FTP), Network File System (NFS), and Web-based Distributed Authoring and Versioning

(WebDAV). Alternatively, it also supports block-level remote storage protocols such as Internet Small Computer System Interface (iSCSI), although in general Oracle recommends the use of NFS for most Exalogic deployments. A group of storage nodes is backed by a shared array of disks.

Compute nodes also include their own storage devices, but these are designed primarily to host the operating system and not application binaries, configurations, and other critical business files. Therefore, the majority of your data will be managed centrally by these dedicated storage nodes. This approach also eliminates the need to back up the local storage of each compute node individually and therefore makes the process of backup and recovery much simpler.

As with compute nodes, Exalogic includes multiple storage nodes within each rack for redundancy and high availability.

As you will see, these storage nodes are far more sophisticated than a simple set of disks. They also support features such as RAID, flash acceleration (caching), and replication.

Networks

Exalogic includes a set of switches to connect the compute nodes and storage nodes to each other (via their network adapters) as well as to the outside world. It might go without saying, but this networking hardware is designed to provide very high performance, meaning very high bandwidth and very low latency. After all, because of the increasing speeds of microprocessors and disks these days, enterprise applications are limited most often by the network. So Oracle has paid particular attention to tuning the network, from the hardware, to the drivers, to the operating system, and finally to the middleware stack.

Exalogic includes two separate physical networks. One is intended to be linked to your existing external or client network, while the other can be connected to an existing management network. Not only does this approach allow you to isolate client and administrative traffic, but it gives you the ability to monitor and maintain your hardware remotely while at the same time disallowing client access. Figure 2-2 depicts these different networks.

Because of the critical nature of the client network and its availability, you will find redundant switches in Exalogic. Additionally, each compute and

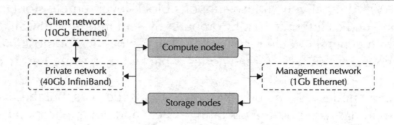

FIGURE 2-2. *Exalogic physical networks*

storage node has redundant links to these switches. At the physical layer, the management switch is based on Ethernet, which most administrators are familiar with. However, the remaining switches are instead based on InfiniBand technology, which will be covered soon in the section titled "InfiniBand."

Power Distribution

Power distribution units (PDUs) do what their name suggests: they supply and distribute power to all of the components in the Exalogic system, including compute nodes, storage nodes, and network switches. Practically speaking, they function similar to a power strip that you might use in your office, but they are able to monitor power consumption and handle disturbances or spikes in available power as well. PDU monitoring and diagnostics is done via an Ethernet interface that is built into each PDU and that is connected to your management network.

TIP
Exalogic machines are designed so that they can be quickly upgraded to support greater capacities, while also minimizing downtime. However, it is often challenging to upgrade PDUs without some loss in service. Therefore, if given a choice, consider purchasing the 24-kVA option to avoid this upgrade scenario altogether.

Although Exalogic hardware has been selected and engineered to minimize costs associated with power consumption, the hardware and therefore these PDUs are able to handle much greater source inputs than what's available in a typical home or office. An Exalogic machine includes a set of redundant PDUs and, depending on your selected rack configuration, you can choose from either 15-kVA or 24-kVA units. Full rack configurations always require 24-kVA PDUs.

TIP
When considering the total costs of an Exalogic deployment, be sure to include power and cooling requirements. Older data centers might not offer 15-kVA or 24-kVA inputs or might not meet Exalogic's cooling and circulation requirements. These may not be trivial upgrades.

InfiniBand

The InfiniBand Trade Association (IBTA) was founded in 1999. It is led today by Oracle, Intel, IBM, Mellanox, and others. The IBTA is responsible for the advancement of the InfiniBand specification, which prescribes a communication link suitable for use in high-performance computing systems.

Why the need for a different networking hardware architecture? The theoretical bandwidth limit for high-speed Ethernet is 10 Gigabits per second (Gb/s), while InfiniBand's bandwidth can be much larger. Exalogic hardware supports Quad Data Rate (QDR) InfiniBand, whose theoretical maximum bandwidth is 40 Gb/s.

Exalogic's switches include InfiniBand transceivers that are capable of processing QDR InfiniBand. Specifically, they use quad small form-factor pluggable (QSFP) transceivers. The compute and storage nodes include InfiniBand network adapters, which are also referred to as host channel adapters (HCAs). In addition, the operating system images shipped with Exalogic are bundled with a suite of InfiniBand drivers and utilities called the OpenFabrics Enterprise Distribution (OFED). OFED is a core component of what Oracle refers to as the Exalogic Elastic Cloud Software. The Exalogic Elastic Cloud Software also includes optimizations that have been engineered into Oracle Fusion Middleware and that leverage OFED to provide higher performance over InfiniBand.

An InfiniBand network offers a great improvement over traditional networks, but you should consider some complexities with regards to software interoperability. OFED provides an implementation of the InfiniBand Sockets Direct Protocol (SDP), in which network communication is done over the "raw" InfiniBand protocol. SDP essentially bypasses the standard TCP/IP stack of the operating system and consequently yields the best performance. As you will learn in later chapters, several Oracle products including the database and WebLogic Server can take advantage of SDP, but most other applications do not support it. To fill this gap, OFED provides, in addition to SDP support, an IP-compatible implementation of InfiniBand, which is referred to as IP over InfiniBand (IPoIB). IPoIB provides an important level of compatibility between IP-based software and the underlying InfiniBand hardware. It allows you to move existing applications onto Exalogic without modification.

There's also another compatibility scenario to consider. Although the hardware within Exalogic utilizes an InfiniBand fabric, the rest of your data center, along with the outside world, still speaks only Ethernet. This includes your application clients, such as web browsers, as well as legacy enterprise information systems, which components running within Exalogic may need to communicate with. Exalogic's switches and nodes enable this communication through the Ethernet over InfiniBand (EoIB) protocol. As the name suggests, EoIB gives InfiniBand devices the ability to emulate an Ethernet connection using IB hardware. Figure 2-3 illustrates these different network interfaces within Exalogic.

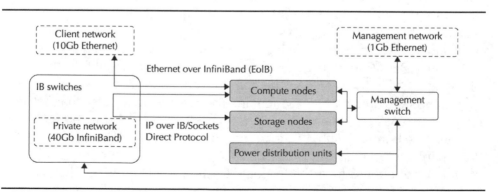

FIGURE 2-3. *Exalogic networks*

Finally, keep in mind that the use of InfiniBand is not limited to Exalogic. Oracle Exadata is an engineering system similar to Exalogic, but it's optimized for hosting Oracle Database clusters instead of middleware applications. Like Exalogic, Exadata's internal network is based on the InfiniBand architecture and hardware. Therefore, you can easily link Exalogic and Exadata together and ensure a very high-speed connection between your middle and data tiers.

Rack Configurations

As you just learned, Exalogic is a collection of different hardware components that have been engineered to work together:

■ Compute nodes

■ Storage nodes and disk array

■ Network switches

■ PDUs

Every organization, however, needs to weigh capital outlay costs against initial and future capacity needs. Consequently, Exalogic is not designed to be a "one-size-fits-all" solution and instead provides some flexibility. You can grow your Exalogic infrastructure as needed and as funds permit. For example, your capacity needs might first dictate a quarter Exalogic rack, but you can easily upgrade this to a half or full rack as your business grows and requirements change. As mentioned, Exalogic is designed to be field-upgradable and without incurring downtime.

Exalogic utilizes the Sun Rack II model cabinet. Prior to installing the rack, verify its space, access route, power, grounding, and air flow requirements. You can find these specifications in the *Exalogic Machine Owner's Guide*, which is part of the online documentation.

Eighth

An eighth (1/8) rack is the smallest supported Exalogic configuration. It consists of the following:

■ Four compute nodes

■ Two storage nodes (60TB raw storage)

- Two InfiniBand gateway switches

- One Ethernet management switch

- Two PDUs (15, 22, or 24 kVA)

The IB gateway switches support direct IPoIB connectivity between the nodes and also act as gateways between this IB network and your existing Ethernet client network (EoIB). The detailed specifications and capabilities of these components will be covered later in this chapter.

Quarter

When you upgrade from an eighth- to a quarter-rack configuration, the component inventory remains virtually the same. The quarter rack consists of twice as many compute nodes:

- Eight compute nodes

- Two storage nodes (60TB raw storage)

- Two InfiniBand gateway switches

- One Ethernet management switch

- Two PDUs (15, 22, or 24 kVA)

Half

When you upgrade from a quarter- to a half-rack configuration, once again the main difference is the number of compute nodes:

- Sixteen compute nodes

- Two storage nodes (60TB raw storage)

- Two InfiniBand gateway switches

- One InfiniBand spine switch

- One Ethernet management switch

- Two PDAs (15, 22, or 24 kVA)

With a half rack, you also receive an additional IB switch called a "spine" switch. The difference between these switches will be addressed in more detail later in the section "NM2-36P" but in general, a spine switch is required when there is a need to link multiple Exalogic racks together.

Full

The "big enchilada," a full rack, is filled to its physical capacity:

■ Thirty compute nodes

■ Two storage nodes (60TB raw storage)

■ Four InfiniBand gateway switches

■ One InfiniBand spine switch

■ One Ethernet management switch

■ Two PDUs (22 or 24 kVA only)

Notice that a half rack is not exactly half the computing power of a full rack (16 versus 30). This is due to the physical dimensions of the rack unit. Given the much larger number of compute nodes, it should not be surprising that more switches are needed to link them all together. A single management switch is still sufficient, however. Figure 2-4 shows the placement of these hardware components within a full rack.

Multi-Rack

A full rack offers an immense amount of processing power in a small data center footprint and should be sufficient for most applications. However, as you consolidate more and more of your applications into your Exalogic data center, you may require a multi-rack configuration. The spine switches found in the half and full racks enable you to connect multiple racks together quickly so they share the same InfiniBand network fabric. However, keep in mind that even these spine switches have a physical limit. Currently, you can link up to eight full Exalogic racks together using the embedded spine switches. Beyond eight, you will need to purchase and

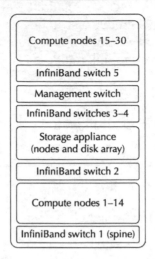

FIGURE 2-4. *Full-rack layout*

mount additional IB switches in the data center. These switches will be external to the racks themselves.

Sun Fire X4170 M2 Compute Nodes

Currently, Exalogic compute nodes are Sun Fire X4170 M2 rack-mount servers. This model has been specifically engineered to optimize the performance of multithreaded Java applications such as Oracle WebLogic Server and Oracle Fusion Middleware. As you might expect, particular emphasis is placed on processing and memory speed. At the same time, this model is relatively compact and energy efficient. Like any server hardware, the X4170 consists of processors, cores, memory, disks, fans, power supplies, and network interfaces. Figure 2-5 depicts the placement of these compute node hardware components. Both the front and rear panels are shown.

The following sections describe these components in more detail.

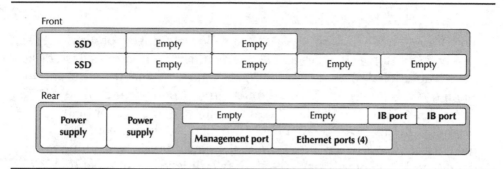

FIGURE 2-5.   *Compute node schematics*

Processors and Memory

Each compute node hosts dual 3.06GHz Intel Xeon processors (5600 series). Each processor consists of 6 cores for a total count of 12 cores per compute node. The processors utilize Intel's hyper-threading technology, which provides two CPU compute threads per core. This means that each compute node provides 24 parallel hardware threads, which allows highly concurrent workloads to execute efficiently.

The X4170 also contains 18 double data rate (DDR3) DIMM module slots. When delivered as part of an Exalogic deployment, these slots are equipped with 96GB of RAM. In terms of computing density, this means that an Exalogic full-rack configuration has a total memory capacity of 2.8TB. Note, however that 96GB is not the maximum amount of RAM supported by the X4170. Of these 18 DIMM slots, only 12 are filled at the factory. This is done intentionally. 96GB is the maximum amount of RAM permitted before the memory clock speed is reduced from a maximum value of 1333 MHz. As mentioned, memory speed is a critical part of Exalogic's value. It is essential for the optimal performance of the Java middleware applications for which Exalogic is designed. Even though you might be tempted to fill these empty memory slots under certain circumstances, remember that doing so would be in breach of any Exalogic hardware support contract that you have purchased.

Local Disks

Each compute node contains two 100GB solid state drives, or disks, (SSDs). These types of storage devices are also sometimes referred to as flash disks. Unlike a traditional spinning hard disk, SSDs have no moving parts and in general use less power and provide much greater performance. The X4170 also includes a RAID controller that mirrors these two SSDs for high availability. In other words, as changes are made to the primary disk, the same changes are also synchronized on the backup disk. So although each compute node technically has 200GB of raw disk space, the real usable space is 100GB. Just as with the RAM scenario described earlier, this server model actually has storage bays that can support up to eight disks. But in Exalogic deployments only two are occupied, to reduce heat output and costs and also due to the availability of shared storage.

It's true that 100GB is not a lot of disk space when it comes to running large enterprise systems, but Exalogic is designed so the large majority of your files are stored on the storage appliance and not on the compute nodes themselves. In fact, these SSDs are generally intended to serve three main purposes:

- Store the base operating system's root file system (including Exalogic-specific OS software) to enable a compute node to boot as fast as possible

- Provide high-performance local swap space

- Use with Oracle Coherence for a high-speed, clustered data cache

TIP
Oracle recommends that you do not use compute node SSDs to store product installation binaries, server configurations, or application files.

The X4170 storage drives are hot-pluggable, meaning that you can safely add and remove them while the server is running, but with one important caveat: To remove a disk, you must first take it offline so the RAID controller can direct running processes to the backup disk. You can use tools such as Oracle ILOM or Oracle Enterprise Manager Ops Center to take a drive offline. They can also trigger alerts to notify you when disks and other hardware components fail. The storage drives are removable from the front of the storage node.

Power and Cooling

The X4170 includes two redundant power supplies and two redundant fan modules. Like SSDs, the power and fan units are hot-swappable, but they do not require any additional configuration changes. This means that you can safely install and remove them while the server is running, without performing any other administrative actions. Obviously, one exception to this rule is the removal of all of the power supplies or fans. A server cannot function without at least one power supply and fan.

Although power supplies can be added and removed from the rear panel, which is normally accessible to data center administrators, fan modules are accessible only from the top panel of the compute node. Therefore, you will need to partially remove the server from the rack to replace a failed fan. Fortunately, Exalogic racks are assembled to handle this scenario without losing power to compute nodes and interrupting your applications.

Network Ports

The rear panel of each compute node has three PCIe 2.0 slots. Two are empty and the third hosts a dual-port InfiniBand HCA. This allows the compute node to interface with the InfiniBand switches and fabric within Exalogic. Two ports are used to provide redundant IB connections; each is connected to a different switch within the fabric.

At the OS level, these two IB ports are represented by two separate network interfaces. On Linux, for example, these interfaces are named ib0 and ib1 by default. Applications can certainly open sockets against these raw ports, but then the applications would be responsible for failing over to one port when the other becomes unavailable. Instead, a separate bonded interface is configured so that the IB ports appear as a single channel (and a single IP address) to your applications. The bond is configured in active-passive mode, meaning that only one of the IB ports is used as a time. On Linux, this bonded interface is named BOND0 by default. On Solaris, this same capability is referred to as IP multipathing (IPMP). This bonding configuration is illustrated in Figure 2-6. The next chapter, "Exalogic Software Architecture," will explore the Exalogic OS network setup in more detail.

In addition to IB connectivity, the X4170 also has five traditional 1Gb Ethernet ports. In an Exalogic installation, however, only one of these is used. It is connected to the rack's management switch so that the OS can access your data center's management network. This port is also used by the node's service processor. More on this service processor in a moment.

Operating System Support

A standalone X4170 M2 server model supports a variety of different operating systems, but within the context of Exalogic, you must run one of the following:

- Oracle Linux operating system

- Oracle Solaris operating system

- Oracle VM hypervisor (running Oracle Linux as a guest OS)

Why the limitation? Remember that these software environments have been specifically configured and engineered for Exalogic's hardware to achieve optimal middleware performance. They have also been rigorously

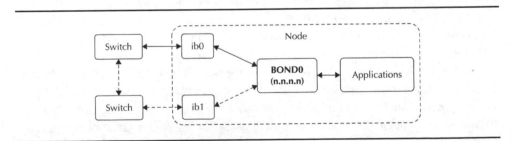

FIGURE 2-6. *Bonded network interfaces*

tested and certified against Oracle middleware products. Documentation exists to help you migrate other operating systems to either Oracle Linux or Oracle Solaris.

At the factory, the compute nodes are preloaded with the Exalogic Oracle Linux base image, but the other OS images are available for download. The base image includes the OS kernel (tuned for the Exalogic hardware) as well as the OFED drivers and tools.

NOTE
As of the time of this writing, Oracle does not support a heterogeneous OS setup, meaning that you must run the same OS on all compute nodes within the same rack.

Service Processor

Both compute and storage nodes contain an additional, separate CPU beyond those mentioned. This is called the *service processor* and is dedicated to monitoring the server's hardware and enabling remote hardware management. Each compute node includes an array of sensors to measure the availability and effectiveness of all the hardware components. These sensor readings are made available through the service processor.

The service processor also hosts the Integrated Lights Out Management (ILOM) tool, which is accessible remotely via SSH or HTTP. ILOM allows these hardware sensors to be monitored remotely, allows alerts to be triggered when hardware errors occur, and lets administrators remotely power the node on or off. "Lights-out" refers to the fact that these capabilities are all remotely accessible and do not require physical access to the server. ILOM is also available regardless of the state of the primary CPUs and the host operating system.

Each compute node's service processor in Exalogic is configured to use the same physical 1Gb Ethernet management network that is used by the operating system running on the compute node's other processors (although typically on a different subnet). Recall that this network is routed through a dedicated management switch and not through the InfiniBand network.

NOTE
You may notice that Exalogic nodes include a dedicated 10Base-T management port in addition to the other four Ethernet ports. This management port is wired directly to the service processor and thus gives you the ability to have a dedicated ILOM network if you want. This configuration is referred to as "out-of-band" management. However, these management ports are unused in an Exalogic configuration. Instead, Exalogic uses this "sideband" configuration to avoid the need for an additional switch, to simplify network cabling, and to reduce the initial number of required IP addresses.

Sun ZFS Storage Appliance 7320

All Exalogic rack configurations include two storage nodes along with a 60TB disk array. Together these three components are referred to as the "7320 storage appliance," which is mounted in the center of the rack. As the name "appliance" suggests, this hardware (and its embedded software) is intended to be treated as a "black box" device, which is ready to use and requires only minimal configuration. However, the appliance's administrative interface allows you to customize its storage characteristics, to define new access points, and to enforce access control. This interface is accessible from the rack's management network and also includes an impressive array of monitoring and analytic capabilities.

The storage appliance uses Exalogic's InfiniBand connectivity to enable remote disk access. The clients of the storage appliance are all of the compute nodes located on the same IB fabric. Compute nodes can remotely access the shared storage using one of several supported block-level or remote file system–level protocols, although the recommended protocol for Fusion Middleware is the NFS protocol. The storage is not directly accessible from the external EoIB client network.

Traditionally, this type of storage hardware would be mounted in the data center at a location that differs from that of your servers, and it would be shared by all of your different server hardware. However, the Exalogic architecture promotes the use of this shared storage found within the racks themselves. The primary motivation for this approach is performance; it allows the servers and storage to be located on the same high-speed IB network.

Architecture

The two storage nodes in the 7320 (also referred to as storage "heads") are interconnected and run in an active/passive configuration. This means that all client traffic is directed to one of the storage nodes and, in the event of the storage node failure, traffic is redirected to the other storage node without an interruption in service (although there may be a brief delay).

Both nodes are connected to the shared disk array using Serial Attached SCSI (SAS) cables. These disks are set up in a mirrored configuration to allow fast and automatic failover when a disk fails or is taken offline. Furthermore, some disks are not used and instead act as "hot" spares. During a disk failover, one of the spare disks is also chosen as the new backup and is synchronized via a background task. The contents of these disks can also be replicated to other remote locations to support backup and disaster recovery requirements, as discussed in Chapter 4, "Exalogic Solution Architecture."

Even though Exalogic will generally not be used to host very disk-intensive applications such as relational databases, disk I/O can still become a performance bottleneck. The 7320 disk array is intentionally made up of traditional disks to reduce hardware costs, but it also employs two levels of flash-based caching—one for disk reads and one for writes. These caches are implemented using low-latency SSDs.

Storage Nodes

At first glance, the 7320 storage nodes might appear similar to the X4170 compute nodes. Both are x86, enterprise-grade servers. But there are some important distinctions. Overall, these servers are not designed to host customer software and consequently you do not have direct access to its operating system kernel. They also do not require quite as much processing power as the compute nodes.

Figure 2-7 shows some of the differences in the hardware configuration. Once again, both the front and rear panels are shown. On the rear panel in particular, note the presence of the SAS host bus adapter (HBA) and the cluster interconnect. Also locate the cache SSDs on the front panel.

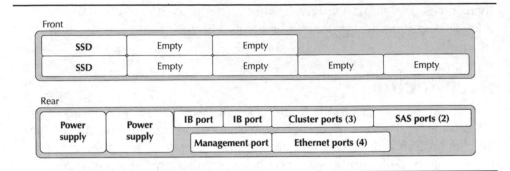

FIGURE 2-7. *Storage node schematics*

Cluster Interconnect

Similar to the compute nodes, each storage head supports up to three PCIe devices. One of these slots hosts the CLUSTRON device that provides high availability between the two storage nodes. It essentially creates a small, private "network" (there is no switch) between the two nodes that is used solely to facilitate failover. Regular heartbeat messages are sent between the CLUSTRON devices so that each can detect potential failures.

If you inspect one of these devices, you will notice that there is not just a single cable that connects the nodes, but three. Two of these are unidirectional serial connections and one is a bidirectional Ethernet connection. The serial cables are connected in a crossover fashion—the output port from one node connects to the input node on the other.

Processors and Memory

Each storage node hosts dual 2.4GHz Intel Xeon processors (5600 series). Each of these processors consists of two cores; therefore, the total core count for the entire appliance is eight. The 7320 also contains 12GB of RAM per node, although keep in mind that this RAM is simply used to run the appliance kernel.

Power and Cooling

Each storage node includes two redundant power supplies and fan modules, similar to the X4170 compute node. These components are also maintained in the same fashion as those found in the compute nodes.

Read Cache

Each storage node has two 2TB SSDs (4TB total), which together act as a read cache to increase performance. In response to a read request from a compute node, the storage node first checks to see if the requested data is found in its cache. If not, the data is retrieved from the disk array and cached in the SSDs. If the same data is later updated, it is removed from the read cache. And as you might expect, this is all done transparently to the client.

In the event of a storage node failure, the appliance will automatically fail over to the other node. You can expect an initial degradation in performance because all of the cached data on the failed node is gone, but this effect decreases as the new active storage node begins caching data in its own SSDs.

Disk Shelf

The storage appliance contains a single disk shelf, which is made up of 24 disk bays, two power/fan units, and two SAS HBA devices. Figure 2-8 depicts these hardware components. The disks can be replaced from the front of the appliance, and the power/fan units are accessible from the rear.

Each SAS HBA provides two, 4-channel mini-SAS connectors, the same as those found on the storage heads. This configuration enables two redundant

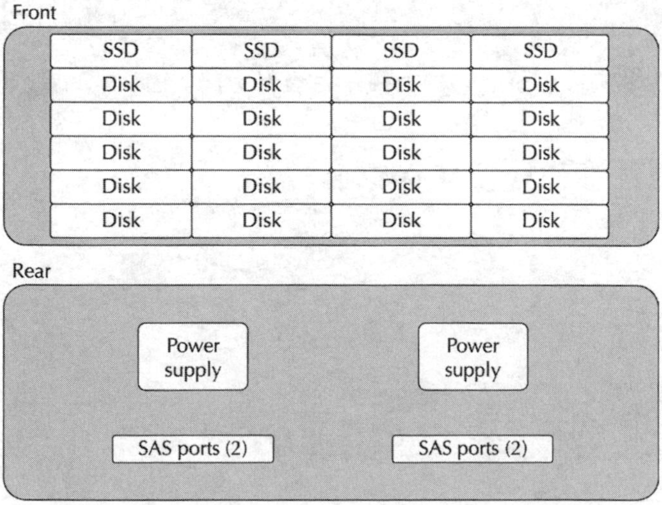

FIGURE 2-8. *Disk shelf schematics*

paths to the disk shelf, should an HBA fail. Both paths can access all of the disk drives.

Twenty of the twenty-four disk bays are occupied with hard disks, which make up the shared storage that is available to all compute nodes. However, only eighteen of these disks are active at a given moment. The remaining two are configured as hot spares and used only in the event of a disk failure. Given that each hard disk is 3TB in size and each disk is mirrored to another disk, the disk shelf provides a total of 60TB of raw disk space and 27TB of practical space. Data compression is available on the storage appliance, but 27TB uncompressed should be more than adequate for typical middleware product installations, application files, and logs.

Like compute node hardware, storage node hardware can be monitored via ILOM. But the disk shelf is configured, monitored, and managed from a separate storage appliance administration interface (shown in Figure 2-9). Use this tool to configure storage shares on the appliance and also to control access to them. These tasks will be addressed later in Chapter 5, "Deploying Exalogic."

Similar to ILOM, the storage appliance administration interface has both SSH and HTTP (web browser) versions. However, for convenience, most ILOM operations are also exposed through the storage appliance interface. For example, you can use this single interface to monitor SSD hardware on

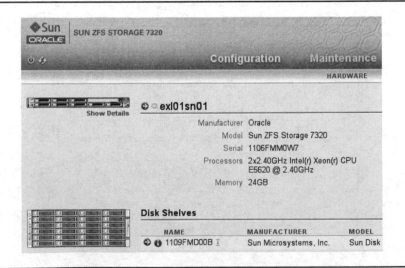

FIGURE 2-9. *Storage appliance browser interface*

both the storage node and disk shelf. You can also perform hardware tasks such as taking a disk offline for maintenance.

Write Cache

The remaining four bays on the disk shelf house 73GB SSDs (292GB total), which are used as a write cache, although this write cache functions more like a buffer or queue than a traditional cache. As synchronous write requests come into the storage appliance from clients, the clients do not actually wait for the write to be performed on one of the SCSI disks (and corresponding backup disk). Instead, these writes are added to the cache and quickly acknowledged. The disks are then updated asynchronously. In other words, the processing is done as a background task.

Sun NM2 InfiniBand Switches

Earlier this chapter introduced the two different types of InfiniBand switches included in Exalogic: spine and gateway. Spine switches support only InfiniBand networking and are generally used only when you need to connect multiple racks together. Full- and half-rack configurations contain a single spine switch, while the eighth and quarter racks do not include one at all. Gateway switches, on the other hand, support both 10Gb Ethernet and InfiniBand traffic. Put another way, these switches acts as a gateway to your existing data center client network. All compute and storage nodes within the same rack are linked together via these gateway switches.

NOTE
A spine switch is actually not required at all to connect eighth and/or quarter racks together. There are enough available ports on the gateway switches to meet the connectivity requirements. This cabling scenario applies both to Exalogic-to-Exalogic and Exalogic-to-Exadata installations.

From their exteriors, the two types of switches are virtually indistinguishable. Both gateway and spine switches contain the same number of redundant power supplies and fan modules. Both contain the same number of InfiniBand ports (36) and Ethernet management ports (2) as well, although only 32 IB ports are

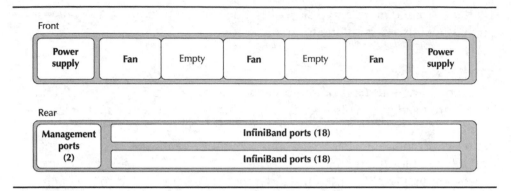

FIGURE 2-10. *InfiniBand switch schematics*

enabled on the gateway switch. Like most modern switch hardware, these IB switches utilize pluggable transceivers to allow for different types of cables and connectors. All Exalogic switches include QSFP InfiniBand transceivers, which support up to 40 Gb/s. Figure 2-10 shows the locations of these ports and other switch hardware components. Both copper and optical QSFP cables are available, depending on the lengths required.

Similar to the other hardware components in Exalogic, each IB switch has an ILOM management interface (both HTTP and SSH). In addition to standard hardware health monitoring features, the SSH interface also includes various network diagnostic utilities. Similar IB troubleshooting tools are found on each compute node as well. On the other hand, should you prefer a more sophisticated looking tool, try the fabric monitor found in the switch's web management interface, as shown in Figure 2-11. Or use a consolidated hardware management solution such as Oracle Enterprise Manager Ops Center.

NM2-GW

On the NM2-GW QDR InfiniBand Gateway Switch, two of its thirty-six QSFP ports serve a special purpose. They are capable of bridging high-speed (10Gb) Ethernet traffic to the rest of the IB network. These two gateway ports are located in the top-rightmost corner of the switch when viewing it from the rear. This means that with a single switch you can bridge up to two different 10Gb Ethernet networks to Exalogic. A full rack, which contains four gateway switches, can therefore support up to eight different external networks. Also note that the two bottom-rightmost ports on the gateway switch (directly below the gateway ports) must remain unconnected. To prevent the use of these ports, Exalogic gateway switches have these ports covered at the factory.

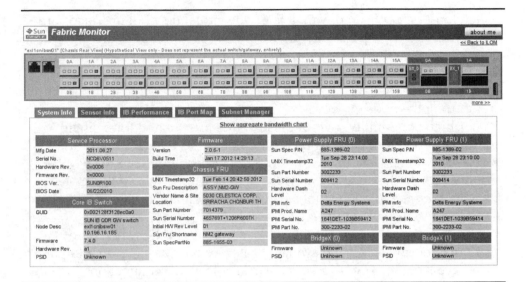

FIGURE 2-11. *InfiniBand switch web-based fabric monitor tool*

Remember that each quad-rate IB port supports 40 Gb/s, meaning that each of the two gateway ports can handle four times as much throughput as a single 10Gb Ethernet connection. Therefore, to make the most efficient use of the available bandwidth, Oracle provides special splitter cables. On one end of each cable is a single QSFP connector, which plugs into the IB switch. On the other end of each cable are four LC Small Form-Factor Pluggable (SFP+) fiber-optic connectors to link Exalogic to the client Ethernet network. Of course, this setup requires that your Ethernet switches have SFP+ transceivers.

NOTE
Older data centers may not be equipped with a 10Gb Ethernet network. What should you do if your client network is only 1GB Ethernet? Oracle does not offer QSFP splitter cables for 1GB Ethernet. Instead, you will need to provision an additional, intermediary switch that can bridge 10GbE and 1GbE networks.

Simply connecting these cables to your client network will not make the network available to the compute nodes. At the factory, compute nodes are configured to support only IPoIB and not EoIB. Consequently, each gateway switch must be configured with at least one virtual network interface card (vNIC) for each compute node that wants to use the EoIB network. These steps are most commonly performed using the switch's command line interface. The vNIC maps one of the 10Gb connections to a MAC address on a compute node. This MAC address does not map to a real physical port on the compute node, however.

For high availability, two of these vNICs are created for a single compute node, with each using a different 10Gb connection on the gateway switches. Just like with IPoIB, a network interface (or IPMP group) exists on the compute node that exposes these two vNICs as a single interface to applications by using a single IP address. This EoIB setup is illustrated in Figure 2-12.

For a balanced system, these pairs of configured vNICs should be distributed evenly across the available gateway switches (four in a full rack) and also distributed evenly across the available 10Gb connections. A vNIC configuration example will be covered in Chapter 5, "Deploying Exalogic."

NM2-36P

The Datacenter InfiniBand Switch 36, known as the spine switch in Exalogic, is simply used to route IB traffic between multiple racks. This includes Exalogic-to-Exalogic scenarios, as well as Exalogic to Exadata. Unlike the NM2-GW gateway switch, it consists of only 36 standard IB ports. There are no 10GbE gateway ports; otherwise, the hardware of the two switches is identical.

The "Machine Owner's Guide" in the Exalogic online documentation includes an appendix that describes the most common scenarios for using the spine switch. The "Multi-Rack Cabling Guide" then describes the general

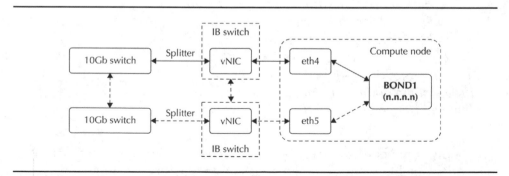

FIGURE 2-12. *vNICs in the gateway switches to support EoIB*

process that you (or an Oracle engineer) should use when connecting racks together with the spine switch.

Essentially, the spine switch in one rack is connected to at least one gateway switch in another rack. To provide complete redundancy and high availability, the spine switch is normally connected to all of the gateway switches. This practice ensures that a spine switch is not a single point of failure. Furthermore, to ensure that there are no performance bottlenecks in the network and to ensure a throughput of 40 Gb/s, multiple connections exist between any two switches in the IB fabric. Due to these considerations, there is a physical limitation in the number of Exalogic racks (eight full racks) that can be connected together by using only the switches found in the racks themselves.

Exalogic ships with a spare parts kit. To facilitate multi-rack environments, this kit includes 5-meter cables specifically for use with the spine switches. Enough cables are included to link together two full racks.

Power and Cooling

Networking hardware must be especially robust since it plays such a crucial role in your data center. However, components in these IB switches can still fail. Each switch contains two redundant power supplies and three redundant fan modules. And all of these parts are easily accessible and serviceable from the front of the rack.

Cisco Catalyst 4948

Up to this point most of this chapter has been devoted to the Exalogic InfiniBand networks (private and client). But don't forget about the management network. This 1GB Ethernet network is connected to every hardware component in the rack, from compute nodes and the storage appliance, to the switches and PDUs. It is intended for moderate administrative traffic created by various monitoring and diagnostic applications, such as Oracle Enterprise Manager. It should not be used to route client traffic or for any other business-critical applications.

Exalogic currently includes a Cisco Catalyst, 48-port management switch in each rack, which provides a network channel for ILOM and other data center management tools on all of the devices in the rack. Like the IB switches, this management switch has a dedicated management port as well as redundant power and fan modules. Although Oracle continues to innovate in InfiniBand technologies, Cisco is already a proven market leader in Gigabit Ethernet. This explains the choice to deviate from Oracle hardware in this one instance.

The management network also differs from the IB network in one other important way. Although the management switch itself has redundant components for high availability, there is only a single switch per rack. Additionally, each piece of hardware in the rack has only a single connection to the management switch. If the entire switch should ever fail completely, the management network would be unavailable until the unit could be repaired or replaced. This point emphasizes the role that Oracle intends for this network. You may temporarily lose the ability to monitor your hardware remotely, but your applications and clients will remain unaffected.

Summary

Exalogic hardware is deployed in rack units that each consist of standard processing, storage, network, and power components. These components have been engineered to provide exceptional levels of performance, high availability, and serviceability. You will find redundancy at all levels, including disks, network paths, power, and cooling. Solid state disks are also used over traditional hard disks in several places to increase system responsiveness. Manageability is addressed via dedicated service processors, administration ports, and tools such as ILOM.

Racks are available in eighth, quarter, half, and full configurations. Each varies in its number of compute nodes and switches, while all configurations contain a single ZFS (Zettabyte File System) storage appliance. Intel-based compute nodes are intended to run large middleware installations and business applications and are equipped with CPUs and RAM to meet these processing requirements. Compute nodes can host any custom application provided that the application supports either Oracle Linux or Solaris. The Exalogic storage appliance consists of two clustered storage nodes and a disk array. It provides 27TB of highly available, shared storage for use by the compute nodes. These storage nodes are able to read and write at high speeds due in part to the use of flash-based caching.

Exalogic's internal networking is based on InfiniBand, an increasingly popular technology for connecting data center components and for delivering much greater throughputs than Ethernet. All compute and storage nodes are linked via InfiniBand. However, Exalogic's IB switches also allow compute nodes to interface with your existing 10 GbE Ethernet client networks (EoIB). Gateway switches perform this service. Spine switches are used to scale out your Exalogic deployment to multiple racks or to connect your Exalogic system to an Exadata database machine.

CHAPTER
3

Exalogic Software
Architecture

his chapter describes the types of software deployments that Exalogic is intended to host. Special focus is given to the Oracle Fusion Middleware platform, which has been specifically tested and optimized for the Exalogic environment. Much of Fusion Middleware's deployment architecture is defined by the core runtime, WebLogic Server, so it is given particular emphasis. Lastly, this chapter describes how to monitor all of these middleware applications on Exalogic by using Oracle Enterprise Manager.

Target Applications

Generally speaking, Oracle supports any software on Exalogic that is certified to run on either Oracle Linux 5.5 or Solaris 11 (64-bit), the two operating systems that Oracle supports on the Intel-based Exalogic hardware. Consequently, you can use Exalogic to consolidate literally thousands of different software products, both Oracle and non-Oracle. It's important to keep in mind, however, that Exalogic was designed and engineered primarily to host Oracle middleware applications. For these deployments, there can be significant performance gains on Exalogic, assuming you follow the recommended deployment described in this chapter.

TIP
The performance of non-Oracle applications will likely benefit from the dense computing and network power of Exalogic. However, it is always wise to conduct an initial benchmark to compare the application's performance on Exalogic to the earlier hardware platform.

Java Enterprise Edition Review

For the past decade, the dominant force in the enterprise middleware space has been Java EE. This specification creates a contract between application developers and middleware software, freeing companies from being locked in to a specific vendor's products. More importantly, Java EE allows developers to focus on implementing business requirements (order processing, billing, claim processing, employee workflows, and so on) and spend less time worrying about infrastructure. Programmers no longer need to write code that manages threads and sockets, or code that handles load distribution and failover.

While there is no "typical" implementation of a custom application using Java EE, an example can help illustrate some of the burdens that Java EE attempts to remove from application developers. Suppose you need to build an auction system. First, you will likely need a web site that allows customers to find auctions, place bids, and configure notifications. In Java EE, the application code that generates a web site is referred to as a *web application.* Next, these auction tasks will need to be integrated into partners' web sites and systems. Java EE supports the creation of web service applications, which use XML and other standards to facilitate interactions with other Java and non-Java applications. Finally, to support auction notifications, you will need a third application that collects and processes the notifications as a batch process, perhaps every 30 minutes. With Java EE, the Enterprise JavaBean (EJB) and Java Message Service (JMS) standards provide a simple solution for this common use case. If you put all of these pieces together, your final auction system resembles Figure 3-1.

To host Java EE applications on Exalogic or any server platform, you require a compliant application server, or "container." Java EE containers supply applications with the necessary runtime infrastructure services, including support for various protocols, database access, messaging, security, and high availability. Oracle WebLogic Server is the recommended container for production Java EE applications. It performs and scales extremely well, particularly in Exalogic environments.

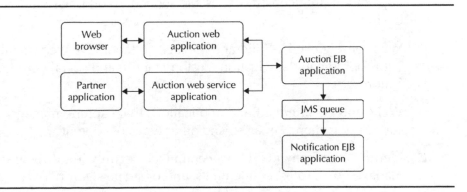

FIGURE 3-1.   *A Java EE auction system*

Oracle Fusion Middleware

Although Java EE certainly facilitates the creation of custom enterprise applications, it tends to concentrate on the low-level infrastructure. However, there are invariably additional application requirements that tend to arise over and over that Java EE does not directly address. Consider the following requirements:

- How do I turn our web site into a corporate portal that lets my end users customize the site and add their own web content to it?

- How do I create and orchestrate some corporate workflow, such as hiring a new employee? Can I even allow end users to customize this workflow?

- How do I implement a centralized security manager that provides account management, single sign-on, and access control to the rest of our applications?

Oracle Fusion Middleware includes several products to help address these challenges. These products essentially leverage Java EE capabilities, such as web applications, web services, EJBs, and JMS, to provide higher-level functions. Most Fusion Middleware products are organized and packaged into suites, although the individual component products can often be licensed and installed individually. These product suites include the following:

- **SOA Suite**   Build and manage distributed, service-oriented applications that consist of reusable services, workflows, and business rules.

- **WebCenter Portal**   Build and manage collaborative web portals with sophisticated navigation, customization, and social computing features.

- **WebCenter Content**   Build applications that capture, manage, and surface documents, images, and other types of content.

- **Identity Management**   Use a centralized security infrastructure to manage users, roles, entitlements, and/or single sign-on tokens.

Oracle Fusion Applications

You might be wondering why you should bother with application development
at all, when in many cases you can buy a complete, packaged software solution
that already meets your business requirements:

- Customer relationship management

- Risk management and compliance

- Supply chain management

- Human resources

- Financial analysis

- Procurement

Fusion Applications represents Oracle's latest evolution of its popular
packaged applications, including E-Business Suite, PeopleSoft, JD Edwards,
and Siebel. The primary difference between these older releases and
Fusion Applications is the reliance on Fusion Middleware. Most Oracle
Fusion Applications rely on multiple Oracle Fusion Middleware components,
such as SOA Suite and Identity Management.

WebLogic Server

As mentioned, WebLogic Server is Oracle's production-ready, Java EE
application server. It can host any Java EE–compliant application. But more
important, it is the only supported application server for most Oracle Fusion
Middleware components as well as for most Oracle Fusion Applications.
Therefore, understanding WebLogic's architecture and capabilities is a
critical part of understanding Exalogic's software architecture.

Servers and Machines

An instance of WebLogic Server is often simply referred to as a "server."
From the host operating system's perspective, a server is a running process
listening to one or more ports. Each server process can host multiple Java EE
applications along with other WebLogic resources that the applications
require, such as database connections or message queues.

WebLogic Server is itself a Java application and therefore running it requires a Java Virtual Machine (JVM). For running a server on Oracle Linux, both the Oracle JRockit and Oracle HotSpot JVMs are supported; however, JRockit is recommended because of its better performance and administrative capabilities. The HotSpot JVM is recommended for Solaris on Exalogic. When you install WebLogic, you indicate which JVM it should use by default.

A physical piece of hardware, such as an Exalogic compute node, is not limited to running a single server process. Especially in the case of Exalogic, you can expect to run many servers on each compute node to utilize all the available CPU cores and memory. WebLogic documentation and tools use the term "machine" to designate these physical hardware boundaries. As part of configuring a WebLogic server, you can explicitly associate it with a machine. Like servers, WebLogic machines are simply given arbitrary configuration names, such as "MachineA" or "el01cn01." Machine names need not map to a network host name. Put another way, a WebLogic machine is simply a logical collection of WebLogic servers running on the same physical device, as shown in Figure 3-2.

The definition of machines may seem unnecessary, and strictly speaking it is optional. However, several WebLogic capabilities rely on machine definitions, each of which will be addressed later in the "Node Manager" section of this chapter. Specifically, you must explicitly group servers using machines in order to use WebLogic's Node Manager feature and to support some of WebLogic's high availability features.

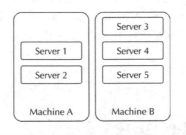

FIGURE 3-2. *WebLogic servers and machines*

TIP
*On Exalogic, a WebLogic machine maps to a
compute node. Define a separate WebLogic
machine for each compute node that will run
WebLogic servers.*

Domains

WebLogic servers are organized and grouped together through the
definition of machines and also through the definition of domains. A
WebLogic domain is a set of servers that is configured, monitored, and
managed as an administration unit. A server can belong to one domain
only. Keep in mind that this is only an administrative boundary, not a
functional one. A web application deployed in one domain can still, for
example, communicate with an EJB or web service application that is
deployed to another domain.

One (and only one) server in each domain is flagged as the domain's
administration server, as shown in Figure 3-3.

By default, the administration server in a domain is named AdminServer.
An administration server supports all the same capabilities supported by any
other server, along with some additional duties. To help distinguish the
administration server from other servers in the domain, the remaining
servers are often referred to as "managed" servers.

First, the administration server acts as the owner of the domain's
configuration files. These files describe all the functional aspects of each
server, including IP addresses, port numbers, application deployments,

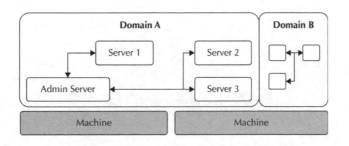

FIGURE 3-3. *A WebLogic domain*

database connections, message queues, and so on. As part of starting up, a managed server contacts the domain's administration server and requests the configuration. Each managed server also caches a copy of these files, should the administration server be unavailable at a later time.

TIP
Deploy your business applications on managed servers. Do not deploy applications to the administration server.

Second, the administration server automatically hosts a web application called the WebLogic Administration Console. It can be accessed from a browser using the URL http://*<adminserver>:<port>/* console. The console provides a GUI to configure, manage, and monitor all servers in this domain from a single location. As modifications are made to the domain's configuration, not only are the changes written to disk by the administration server, but they are also broadcast to all running managed servers. Figure 3-4 shows a typical interaction with the console—viewing the status of the servers in the domain.

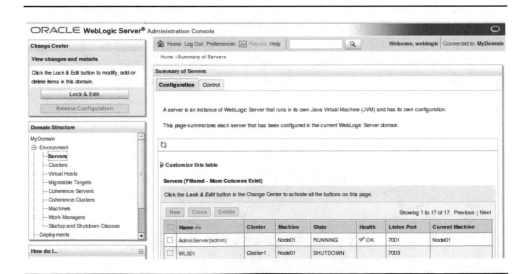

FIGURE 3-4. *The WebLogic Administration Console*

How many domains should you create in your Exalogic data center? For larger organizations, different applications, especially those in different business units, are often managed by distinct IT groups. In this scenario, it makes sense to configure a separate domain for each major business unit. For example, you would separate the HRDomain from the OrderProcessingDomain. Furthermore, even within a single business unit, we recommend that each project phase be associated with its own domain. For example, consider an application that is first deployed to HR-QADomain and then to HR-ProdDomain. As we shall see in later chapters, tools such as Oracle Enterprise Manager let you manage and monitor multiple domains from a single interface.

On Exalogic's shared file system, each domain is stored in a separate directory. The domain directory contains the domain's configuration files along with server logs and other runtime files such as transaction and message logs. A domain directory also contains shell scripts that you can use to start and stop the domain's administration server and managed servers. These scripts can be useful for initial domain testing and troubleshooting, but the preferred approach for starting and stopping servers is the WebLogic Node Manager, which will be discussed shortly.

TIP
Maintain each domain directory in a part of the file system separate from the location of the WebLogic Server product installation. Your product installation should effectively remain read-only and can be reused by many WebLogic domains.

Clusters

As a quick review, recall that you need to organize and group your WebLogic servers using two different constructs:

- **Domains**   Servers that are administered as a unit

- **Machines**   Servers that are hosted on the same hardware

A third way in which servers are grouped together is a *cluster*. A cluster defines a set of servers that work together to provide high availability for the applications and services deployed to the servers. Generally speaking, all servers in a cluster are configured identically (ignoring minor exceptions such as the listen address and listen port). Cluster members periodically communicate with one another via a heartbeat mechanism. Servers then know which other servers in the cluster are available and unavailable at any moment in time. Figure 3-5 illustrates the WebLogic cluster architecture.

Another important characteristic of a cluster is that it appears to clients as a single server. High availability is then transparent both to clients and the applications being accessed. Finally, clusters provide a method of scalability for applications, because a single WebLogic server supports a finite capacity. You can quickly create additional capacity by adding more members to the cluster.

TIP
In general, you can deploy WebLogic applications to a single server or an entire cluster. Always target applications to a cluster, even if it initially only consists of a single managed server. This helps avoid some of the challenges involved in upgrading a single-server environment to a clustered one.

High availability within a cluster falls into two general categories: load distribution and failover. The mechanisms by which cluster members provide these features vary according to the type of application. For example, when an EJB client remotely accesses an EJB within a cluster, the client transparently

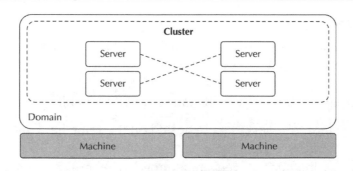

FIGURE 3-5. *A WebLogic cluster*

downloads and uses a WebLogic "stub" object that intelligently distributes requests across the cluster members, and the client also transparently fails over if a member becomes unreachable. The web and web service applications, on the other hand, rely on HTTP, where the option to use a WebLogic stub is not possible. Instead they need to include a proxy server between the client and the application hosted by WebLogic. This cluster-aware proxy performs similar behavior to that of the EJB stub. See Figure 3-6 to compare these two types of deployments in a cluster. Several hardware and software options are available to implement a WebLogic cluster proxy, including Oracle HTTP Server, Oracle iPlanet, and Oracle Traffic Director.

Failover can also take the form of data replication. Consider, for example, an EJB or web application that maintains a user's shopping cart in server memory. If the server that hosts that shopping cart fails, the shopping cart is lost. Although the user can automatically be redirected to another available server, the user will have to start over again to re-create his shopping cart. For many types of applications, the loss of this in-memory session data is unacceptable. Cluster members address this issue by replicating sessions, so that at any given moment there is no single point of failure. WebLogic supports replicating session data across members within the cluster, or replicating externally to a highly available file system or database.

Getting Started with WebLogic

After installing the WebLogic Server product, you are ready to create your first domain. The primary tool used to create a new WebLogic domain, and also to define the initial servers, machines, and clusters to be contained in

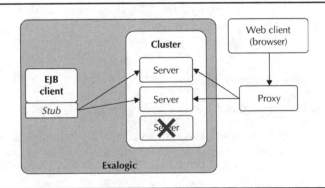

FIGURE 3-6. *Cluster load balancing and failover*

the domain, is the Fusion Middleware Configuration Wizard. It interactively guides you through the process of creating your domain's configuration. The output of the Configuration Wizard is a new domain folder on the shared file system. You are then free to start the domain's administration server and make further modifications to the domain (such as adding a new server) using online tools such as the administration console. As you get more proficient with WebLogic domains, if you want to improve automation of the domain provisioning process, you can employ tools such as the WebLogic Script Tool (WLST) or Oracle Enterprise Manager.

TIP
Remember that all product binaries, configurations, and applications should be placed on the ZFS storage appliance. This includes WebLogic installations and domain configurations. A recommended approach for organizing this shared storage is covered next in Chapter 4.

To create a new domain, you must select at least one template. Templates define the default topology, applications, and settings for the domain. A base WebLogic Server installation includes a few simple templates, and each separate Fusion Middleware product installation (WebCenter or Identity Manager, for example) will include additional templates. Figure 3-7 lists some of the FMW templates you may be asked to choose from while running the Configuration Wizard. Refer to the Deployment Guide for a specific Fusion Middleware product in the Oracle documentation to determine the template or templates you should choose in the Configuration Wizard.

The general tasks that you perform with the Configuration Wizard are as follows:

- Select one or more templates.

- Provide the destination on the file system.

- Enter credentials for the default administrative account.

- Confirm the JVM that should be used to run this domain.

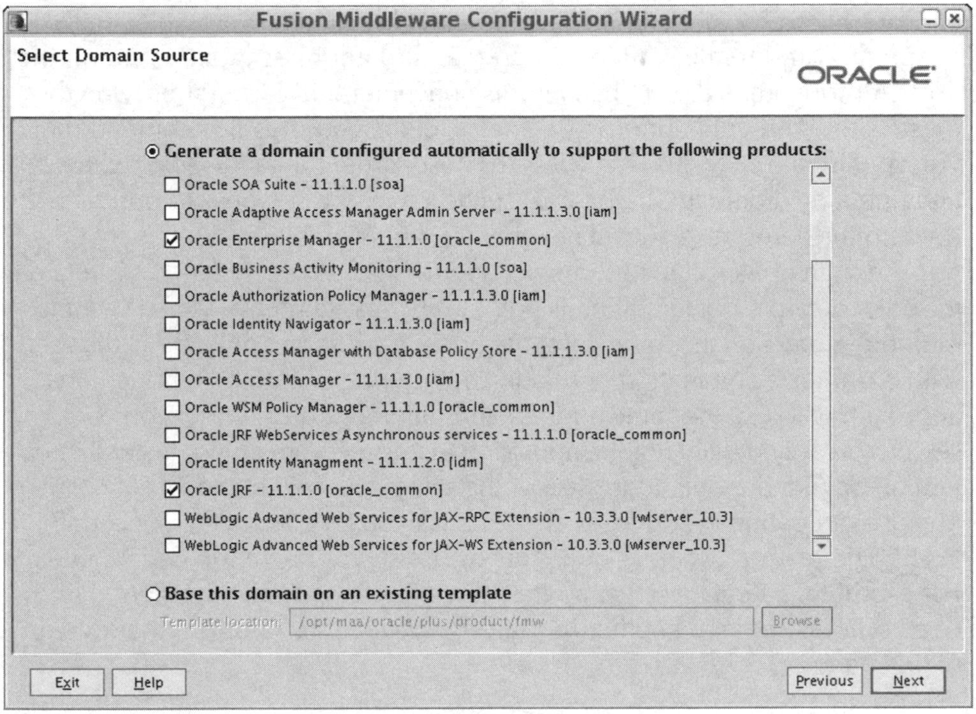

FIGURE 3-7. *Configuration Wizard templates*

- Enter the listen address and port of the administration server.

- Enter the name, address, and port of each managed server.

- Define any clusters and their member servers.

- Enter the name, node manager address, and node manager port of each machine, along with the target servers.

- Configure any template resources such as JDBC data sources or JMS destinations.

Notice that each server is initially configured with a single IP address and port number. But you may recall that an Exalogic compute node participates in multiple networks and is therefore assigned several IP addresses (BOND0, BOND1, eth0, and so on). So which should you choose? If you leave the Listen Address field blank, a server will actually attempt to bind to all available interfaces and addresses it can find on the host. Although this default behavior is convenient, it does not provide the most optimized configuration on Exalogic. Instead, it is recommend that you specify the BOND0 IP address (or host name) for each server when creating a new domain. In the next section, we will see how to optimize the domain further to take advantage of all of the available Exalogic networks.

Although not specific to Exalogic, another issue to consider that is related to server network configuration is port number assignments. When running multiple servers on the same compute node, each server must be configured with a unique combination of IP address and port number. Although one approach is to use the same address and different port numbers on each server, this is generally not the approach that is recommended. Instead, create virtual, or "floating," IP addresses for the same network interface (BOND0). The use of floating IP addresses also enables you take advantage of certain WebLogic features, such as node manager's server migration capability. For example, a floating server address could be temporarily transferred from one compute node to another in response to a failure or during hardware maintenance.

TIP
Use floating IP addresses for all server listen addresses.

Here is an example of configuring a floating IP address on Linux for BOND0:

```
ifconfig bond0:1 192.168.100.100 netmask 255.255.255.0 up
arping -U -I bond0 192.168.100.100
```

Optimizing for Exalogic

The performance of a standard WebLogic domain configuration will certainly benefit from the processing power, memory, and network bandwidth provided on the Exalogic hardware. In addition, the JRockit and HotSpot JVMs both include Exalogic-specific performance optimizations. However, you should also consider some simple modifications to your domain to take full advantage of the unique characteristics of Exalogic.

Server Memory (Heap)

The *heap* is the amount of memory available to the JVM for storing Java objects. The JVM itself also requires some memory of its own, but for application servers like WebLogic, the size of the heap is usually the critical consideration. When any JVM process is started, you can specify the starting heap size as well as the maximum heap size. The following example configures a starting heap of 100MB and a maximum heap of 1GB:

```
java -Xms100m -Xmx1g MyJavaProgram
```

As the current heap size approaches the maximum, the JVM must dedicate more and more CPU time to garbage collection—the discovery and cleanup of Java objects that are no longer in use. Worse still, if no heap is available at all during the creation of a new object, the JVM sends an "out of memory" error to the code that attempted to create the object. If this scenario occurs during execution of your application code, it may simply cause this one request to fail and not impact other users. But an "out of memory" error during WebLogic's internal processing can result in a server hanging or crashing.

By default, all WebLogic servers specify minimum and maximum heap sizes of 256MB and 512MB, respectively. However, many applications require significantly more RAM. Remember that each compute node runs a 64-bit OS and has 96GB of RAM. The optimal amount of heap for a given server is going to vary according to the types of applications it is hosting, the expected workload, and so on. As always, it is a good idea to determine the best heap size experimentally using JRockit Mission Control, Oracle Advanced Diagnostics for Java, or another software package designed for diagnostics and tuning. However, a good starting point is 4GB per server. Modify your domain's start scripts to change the default heap settings.

TIP
In almost all cases, you will see better performance results running a cluster of multiple servers with 4 to 8GB RAM each, rather than running a single huge server that is allocated almost all of the compute node's available RAM.

Network Channels

The servers within a domain support several different forms of communication along with various protocols. Consider these different scenarios:

- The server accepts an HTTP request for a web or web service application.

- The server accepts a T3 request for an EJB application.

- The server accepts a T3 request to publish or consume a JMS message.

- An application running on a server accesses a database by using JDBC and a database vendor–specific wire protocol.

- During startup, a managed server contacts the admin server by using T3 to obtain its configuration.

- While using the console to monitor the domain, the admin server communicates with managed servers using T3.

- Cluster members send heartbeats and data replications to each other.

- The admin server accepts a Simple Network Management Protocol (SNMP) request.

NOTE
T3 is a WebLogic-specific wire protocol that is used by default for JVM-to-JVM communication and applies to several of the preceding scenarios.

Initially, each of your servers has been configured with a single listen address and port. This is referred to as the server's *default channel.* Without any additional configuration, all of these scenarios are handled by this default channel. WebLogic is capable of accepting and multiplexing all the supported protocols via the same listen port. However, recall that an Exalogic machine includes different networks: private (BOND0), client (BOND1), and management. Ideally, each server should be configured so that it utilizes the Exalogic network that is best suited for every one of these scenarios. For example, you can use the client network for external application requests and use the private network for administrative and cluster communication. Figure 3-8 illustrates the recommended WebLogic network configuration on Exalogic.

WebLogic's network channel feature allows you to isolate different types of communication and assign them to specific addresses and ports. If a network channel is not explicitly created for a protocol, the default channel will be used instead. Earlier we recommended that you use a floating IP address on the private network as each server's default channel. Consequently, you need to create additional network channels only for scenarios that involve the Exalogic client or management networks. Network channels are created for each server individually. In the Administration Console, select a server and open the Protocols and then Channels tabs, as shown in Figure 3-9.

TIP
Create an HTTP network channel on a domain's administration server that is associated with the Exalogic management network. This will let you remotely access the Administration Console from a browser.

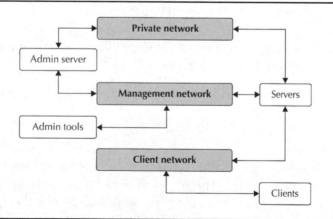

FIGURE 3-8. *Server communication and Exalogic networks*

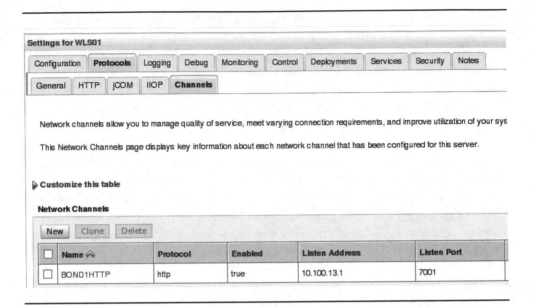

FIGURE 3-9. *Creating a network channel*

All the different communication scenarios can be implemented using a combination of the default channel and custom channels, with one exception. To identify a separate channel to use for data replication within a cluster, you must perform the following:

1. Create a T3 protocol channel on each cluster member; use an address on the private Exalogic network.

2. Update the cluster and specify the name of the channel to use for replication.

For the specific case of cluster replication on the private network, WebLogic can also take advantage of the Sockets Direct Protocol (SDP) as a faster alternative to TCP. The use of SDP reduces the latency involved in these server-to-server communications, which is especially significant for large session objects (a shopping cart with ten items, for example).

Enable this optimization on each server's replication channel individually, as shown next.

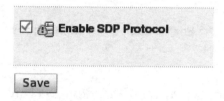

Finally, you can enable one more Exalogic-specific optimization for replication traffic. As it turns out, a single network channel is not able to utilize all the available bandwidth on the 40Gb InfiniBand network. Instead, Oracle recommends that you define multiple replication channels for each server, which the servers will then use in parallel to transmit data. Luckily, you are not required to create all of these additional channels manually on each server in the cluster. Instead, edit the cluster settings of each server (via the Configuration and Cluster tabs) and provide a range of ten port numbers, such as "7005-7015." Upon server restart, WebLogic will automatically start ten replication channels, all using the same IP address but different port numbers. This field is shown next.

Server Optimizations

WebLogic provides several more performance optimizations when running on Exalogic. These facilitate a great increase in server throughput, responsiveness, and scalability. Included are improvements to WebLogic's mechanisms for request handling, networking, memory management, and thread management. Although you can enable each of these optimizations individually and for each server, Oracle recommends that you simply enable all of them together, and for all servers in a domain. Within the Administration Console, select domain-wide settings (click your domain name) and locate the Enable Exalogic Optimizations checkbox, as shown next:

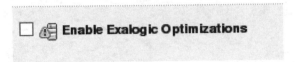

When this attribute is turned on and the servers are restarted, one of the first changes that takes place is in regard to threading. By default, WebLogic creates a fairly modest number of server threads and then increases this number as the workload on the server increases. In other words, a server dynamically optimizes its thread count. However, a server running on Exalogic has a much greater than average amount of processing power behind it, so it creates a much larger initial thread pool during startup. Similarly, if more threads are needed later, the server increases the size of the thread pool at a much faster rate. The process of creating threads is a relatively expensive one, so it makes sense to optimize sooner rather than later when the server is already busy handling application requests. Essentially, this optimization increases the default size of the initial thread pool and also increases the number of threads that are incrementally created when there is a need for additional threads.

The second group of optimizations relates to network I/O. On an InfiniBand network, the maximum transmission unit (MTU) is 64KB versus about 1.5KB for Ethernet. To take advantage of this throughput, the server's internal network I/O engine is optimized to use larger message buffers and to perform multiple reads and writes in parallel. Furthermore, in general the server optimizes its calls to the OS kernel based on the assumption that it in turn is using an InfiniBand driver. These WebLogic optimizations will be discussed in even greater detail in Chapter 7.

Node Manager

Configuring and optimizing the collection of servers in the domain is only a start. Now we must consider how best to manage the server lifecycle. In earlier sections, we mentioned that a domain is represented on the file system as a folder, and that its contents include shell scripts to start and stop servers in the domain. Therefore, you can certainly configure your host operating system so that these scripts are executed as the compute node boots and shuts down. However, this approach is not recommended, because it does not account for all possible scenarios in a server's lifecycle. For example, you may want to do the following:

- Remotely start or restart a server.

- Suspend or bring down a server for maintenance, without shutting down the entire operating system.

- Move or migrate a server from one host to another for maintenance purposes.

- Enable failed servers to be automatically restarted.

- Automatically kill and restart a failed or hung server.

Ideally, you should be able to perform all of these tasks from a single location. WebLogic's node manager fulfills all of these needs.

Node Manager Architecture

Similar to a WebLogic server, a node manager is a Java process that listens for requests on a specified address and port. However, the node manager is limited to handling remote server lifecycle requests. Consequently, it has a very negligible CPU and memory footprint compared to a server. For each machine (compute node) that will run at least one server, you run just a single node manager process. You need only a single node manager per machine (compute node), regardless of to which domains each of the host servers belongs. A node manager responds to remote requests to start, stop, suspend, resume, kill, or migrate a server. These lifecycle requests can be issued by a domain's administration server (via the Admin Console), Oracle Enterprise Manager, or by the WLST. The diagram in Figure 3-10 illustrates the node manager architecture.

Node manager can also be used to start administration servers remotely. However, since the administration server itself hosts the administration console, you are limited to using one of the other mentioned tools to issue the start command. It's also important to keep in mind that while node manager will, by default, automatically restart failed servers, it will monitor only the local server processes that it started. If, instead, a server is started through some other means such as a shell script, this process will remain outside of the node manager's control.

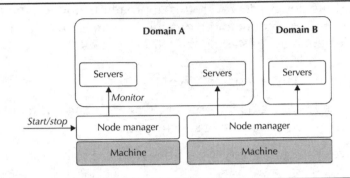

FIGURE 3-10. *Machines, servers, and node managers*

Node Manager Configuration

The node manager for each compute node must be configured individually. The overall setup process for each node manager is as follows:

1. Create a node manager home folder on the storage appliance.

2. Create a start script and register it with the OS init process.

3. Create and initialize a nodemanager.properties file.

4. Use WLST to enroll one or more domains with the node manager.

Regarding the storage of node manager files, a recommended convention is to create a separate home folder for each node manager and give it the name of the hosting compute node, such as "el1cn15" (rack #1, compute node #15). For convenience, a sample node manager start script is found in the WebLogic installation at /server/bin, which you can copy into each node manager home folder.

TIP
Maintain node manager home folders within a separate file system from that used for the corresponding WebLogic Server installation. Your product installation should effectively remain read-only.

Similarly, when you launch node manager the first time, if a properties file is not present, it will automatically generate one that lists all available properties and their default values. At a minimum, the properties file should configure a listen address and port, and also specify that the node manager start and stop servers by using the default domain scripts. With this file, you can also tune other parameters related to node manager logging, health monitoring, auto-restart, and security. By default node manager requires a Secure Sockets Layer (SSL) connection, but to avoid some additional setup you can disable this. Here is a simple nodemanager.properties example:

```
NodeManagerHome=/u01/SalesApps/nodemanager/el1cn15
ListenAddress=el1cn15
ListenPort=5056
SecureListener=false
StartScriptEnabled=true
StopScriptEnabled=true
```

If you plan to use the domain's administration server (via the WebLogic Admin Console) to start server processes remotely, you will also need to configure the connections between the administration server and each node manager. In the Admin Console, select the machine on which the node manager is running and click the Node Manager tab. Supply the host name and port of the node manager (the same values used in nodemanager.properties), and also disable SSL if applicable.

Finally, for each domain that includes servers that will be run on the target compute node, you must register, or enroll, the node manager with that domain's administration server. To accomplish this task, you can manually create and configure some additional node manager and domain files. Alternatively, you can run a WLST command from a terminal or script, which generates these files for you. The latter approach is generally preferred since it is less error prone, although it does require that your domain's administration server be running:

```
cd /u01/app/FMW/Middleware/wlserver_103/common/bin
./wlst.sh

connect('user,'password','10.100.10.100:7001')
nmEnroll('/u01/SalesApps/domains/SalesDomain',
    /u01/SalesApps/nodemanager/el1cn15 )
exit()
```

Remote Start

After node manager is configured and running on each compute node that participates in your domain, you can begin issuing commands to the node manager to start servers in that domain (and later stop, kill, or migrate servers). WebLogic gives you the ability to control individual servers, all servers in a target cluster, or all servers in the entire domain. If you prefer the command line, you can send remote requests to a node manager from the same WLST interface discussed earlier in the chapter. Alternatively, if the administration server is running, you may perform this same functionality from the Administration Console. In general, you can control server lifecycle through the Control tabs, which are found in various places throughout the interface. To view the screen in Figure 3-11, for example, first click the name of the domain.

Migration

At this point, you are able to bring your servers up and down from a single remote location. If any of these servers fail, the node manager running on the Exalogic compute node will automatically try to restart them, if desired.

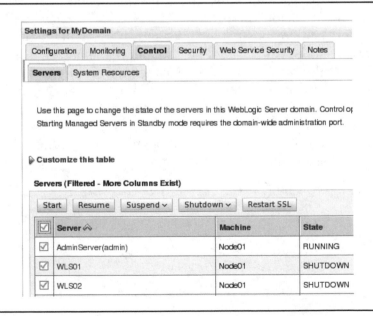

FIGURE 3-11.   *Start all servers in a domain using the console.*

But now consider a situation in which the entire compute node has failed or is being taken offline for maintenance. If other compute nodes have available capacity, why not restart or migrate the servers from the unavailable compute node? Even more important than the performance considerations of a lost compute node are scenarios in which the application can no longer function. For example, consider a server with pending insurance claim messages on a failed compute node.

Since all of our server resources utilize a shared storage appliance, any server can potentially run on any of the compute nodes. An advantage of using the node manager architecture is that it enables you to support migration in these cases, including both manual and automatic migration. Keep in mind that automatic server migration in WebLogic is available only to clustered servers. Specifically, cluster members monitor each other's availability, and, in response to a machine failure, an active member (called the cluster master) instructs the node manager on one of the remaining active compute nodes to restart the failed managed servers. The administration server does not directly participate in the migration process, although you can initiate a manual migration from the administration server (via the console or WLST). The WebLogic server migration architecture is illustrated in Figure 3-12.

To support this server migration architecture on Exalogic, you must perform the following additional configuration tasks:

1. Update nodemanager.properties to support address migration.

2. Enable automatic migration on an entire cluster or individual servers.

3. Provide a list of machines that can participate in migration.

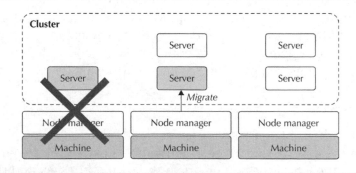

FIGURE 3-12. *Migrate a server across machines.*

As part of executing a migration, the node manager is responsible for ensuring that the IP addresses required by the target server are available on the host machine. In fact, migration is one of the primary motivations for using floating IP addresses in the first place. There is no guarantee that a server will always run on the same compute node. Although node manager can dynamically add and remove the required IP addresses for a server, it must also know the associated interface and subnet mask for these addresses. Provide these parameters using nodemanager.properties. For a given range of IP addresses, indicate the interface name and subnet mask, as shown in this example:

```
bond0=192.168.100.1-192.168.100.50,NetMask=255.255.255.0
bond1=10.0.0.1-10.0.0.50,NetMask=255.255.255.0
UseMACBroadcast=true
```

Coherence

Consider a typical application that retrieves persistent data, such as an order or a report, from a relational database or similar source. This type of interaction is often slow, so to increase performance, the application caches the retrieved data in memory to avoid unnecessary interactions with the database. In the case of WebLogic, applications can use server memory as a cache, but this approach has its limitations. Suppose the amount of data to be cached is significant (for example, gigabytes). Adding more application servers to your cluster may be a solution, but these servers are designed to perform complex application processing, not to be simply a memory cache.

Instead, Oracle offers a dedicated caching solution called Coherence. Coherence is similar to WebLogic in that they are both Java servers and both support a clustering solution to provide scalability. However, Coherence is not designed to host Java EE applications and all of the services required by these applications. It is instead optimized solely for the purpose of distributed, in-memory caching of data objects. A single product installer is available from Oracle that contains both WebLogic and Coherence, and a license for WebLogic Suite includes a license for using Oracle Coherence.

Coherence Clusters

Recall that with WebLogic, servers are explicitly defined as members of a cluster. And, unless overridden, cluster members communicate with each other through each of the server's default listen addresses and ports.

Coherence clusters, on the other hand, are defined more loosely and have a slightly more flexible topology. As Coherence servers start, they essentially search the network for other members of the same Coherence cluster. If a port is in use, the server will automatically try a different one. Furthermore, as data is sent to a Coherence server for caching, this data is automatically distributed, or partitioned, across the current cluster members to provide scalability and high availability. If a cluster member later becomes unavailable, the data is then repartitioned, similar to WebLogic session replication. Figure 3-13 depicts the basic Coherence architecture.

So who uses Coherence to cache data? In the context of a Fusion Middleware deployment, most Coherence "clients" are Java EE applications, but other custom Java or C programs can also utilize a Coherence cluster. However, unlike traditional client-server applications, Java programs that connect to a Coherence cluster are actually considered members of the cluster as well. In fact, they utilize the same protocol to discover Coherence servers on the network as the Coherence servers do themselves and automatically perform load balancing and failover. Additionally, these clients can be *storage-enabled*, meaning that they also participate in the maintaining and partitioning of cached data.

Within an Exalogic deployment, all Coherence cluster members (including clients such as WebLogic Server) are often co-located in the same data center, in which case it makes sense for these members to utilize the private InfiniBand (IB) network (BOND0) in their configuration settings. If, instead, certain cluster members are not on the IB fabric, then cluster members may instead bind to the client network. Another important consideration is Coherence's default use of

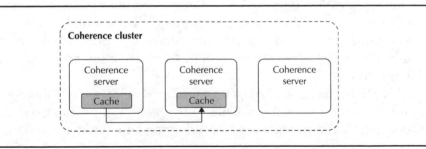

FIGURE 3-13.   *Cache partitioning within a Coherence cluster*

UDP multicast (WebLogic clusters do not use multicast by default). Your data center's existing 10Gb Ethernet service network may block multicast traffic, in which case you must configure Coherence to use TCP instead.

Coherence*Web

Originally we introduced the Coherence solution by contrasting this to an all-WebLogic architecture. Many Java EE applications are stateful in nature and store information in memory on behalf of the client. Consider a company store application that maintains a user's shopping cart. This server data is referred to as the client's *session*.

If your goal with Coherence is to implement a centralized, consolidated caching solution on Exalogic, it may also make sense to offload application sessions from WebLogic to Coherence. With this model, you can separately scale and tune your processing and caching tiers. A convenient way to accomplish this is through a WebLogic plug-in for Coherence called Coherence*Web. When deployed to a WebLogic server, the server essentially acts as a storage-disabled member of a specified Coherence cluster and is now able to leverage the Coherence cluster to hold session objects. Coherence*Web does not require any changes to your existing Java EE applications.

Coherence and WebLogic Domains

Each Coherence server's configuration is maintained in a set of files that are referenced when the server is started. Traditionally, these Coherence files were created and edited manually, and configured and managed independently from your WebLogic domain infrastructure. However, beginning with WebLogic 10.3.4, a domain can be used to administer both your Coherence and WebLogic configurations. For example, you may use the Administration Console or WLST to define new Coherence servers and clusters. Figure 3-14 shows how to view Coherence servers in a domain by using the console.

In addition, the node manager now supports managing Coherence processes. This includes the abilities to remotely start or stop Coherence servers, and to also perform health monitoring and automatic restart.

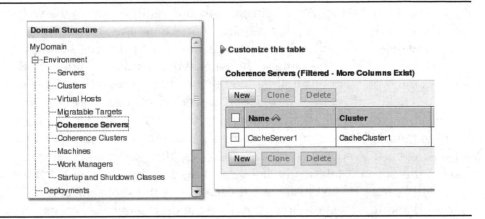

FIGURE 3-14.   *Creating a Coherence server with the WebLogic console*

Web Tier

Now let's return our attention to WebLogic Server clusters. Remember that the general purpose of a cluster is to provide transparent load distribution and failover. The clients of web applications are typically browsers and can't download and run stub code as a Java application can. Instead, web browsers must interact with the web application via some intelligent proxy layer that is capable of making load balancing and failover decisions. This proxy layer is referred to as the *web tier*, to differentiate it from the *application tier* (WebLogic and other Fusion Middleware) and the *data tier*. The diagram in Figure 3-15 illustrates the concept of a cluster proxy.

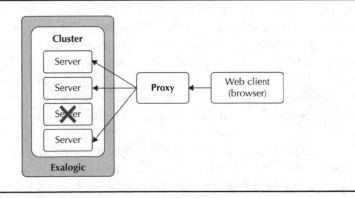

FIGURE 3-15.   *Web application access through a web tier proxy*

Generally speaking, WebLogic has only one requirement of the web tier, and technically it's not a strict requirement. Once a user establishes a session with a web application, subsequent requests from that same user should be directed to the same server whenever possible. In other words, a user should be "pinned" to the server that is hosting his or her data. This expected behavior is also referred to as *server affinity* or *session stickiness*. At this point you might ask the question, "Doesn't this introduce a single point of failure?" What happens to a user's shopping cart if the server she was using fails? WebLogic provides a feature called session persistence to handle this scenario. Basically, if a server fails and the proxy directs the user to another server in the cluster, a backup copy of the shopping cart is retrieved and used without interruption to the user. However, optimum performance is achieved when the web tier is able to pin users to their assigned servers during normal processing.

Web tier proxies come in a range of flavors. Many hardware and software solutions exist, and several of each are certified for use with WebLogic clusters. One solution is to use Oracle's Web Tier set of software utilities for this purpose. This brand includes the following:

- Oracle Traffic Director (OTD)
- Oracle HTTP Server (OHS), a derivative of the Apache web server
- Oracle (formerly Sun) iPlanet Web Server

Traffic Director

Oracle Traffic Director is the only option from the preceding list that is not a traditional web server. It cannot host web content or run scripts, for example. It is simply a high-performance HTTP load distributor that has been optimized for Exalogic's InfiniBand network fabric. Therefore, unlike a hardware load balancer, it is specifically engineered to run on Exalogic itself and to distribute traffic locally within the same data center. Traffic Director can perform simple round-robin load balancing, but it also supports more complex routing rules and priorities. It can also cache frequently accessed content to increase performance, similar to other popular load balancing products.

A Traffic Director server, or instance, is configured with one or more server pools, each of which is a collection of HTTP URLs to direct traffic to. These can be any HTTP-based servers, but in the case of Exalogic they are most likely to be WebLogic servers. Simply supply an initial list of servers in a WebLogic cluster to which Traffic Director will attempt to connect. Once Traffic Director is successfully connected to any one server, that server provides Traffic Director with the latest list of all running cluster members. This list is then dynamically updated with each response from the cluster.

The deployment architecture of OTD has many similarities to WebLogic Server. A group of instances is managed by a central administration server, which hosts a web-based administration console. Also a type of node manager is used to enable remote management capabilities for all instances on the same machine or node. OTD does not include a cluster configuration entity, however. Instead, two instances can be paired in an active/passive configuration for failover purposes. If the active instance fails, the backup instance will automatically bind to the same IP addresses that were previously in use by the failed instance.

Proxy Plug-ins

WebLogic Server supports several other cluster proxy solutions, including both Oracle and non-Oracle ones. Whichever product you choose, you will need to configure the WebLogic proxy plug-in. This plug-in understands how to communicate with WebLogic clusters and is responsible for orchestrating load balancing, sticky sessions, and failover.

For convenience, a copy of the plug-in comes packaged with Oracle HTTP Server. However, for other supported proxy server products you must explicitly install the plug-in. The exact installation and configuration steps vary slightly from proxy to proxy, but the overall process is the same. Following is an excerpt from mod_ohs_wl.conf, the file that's used in Oracle HTTP Server to configure the plug-in:

```
<IfModule weblogic_module>
    WebLogicCluster 192.168.56.151:7001,192.168.56.152:7001
</IfModule>

<Location /companyportal>
    SetHandler weblogic-handler
</Location>
```

Simply supply an initial list of WebLogic servers that the plug-in will attempt to connect to. Once the plug-in is successfully connected to a server, the server will respond with the latest list of all running members in the same cluster, similar to the behavior in Traffic Director. The plug-in then distributes additional application requests across the cluster in a round-robin fashion.

TIP
It is recommended that you run Oracle HTTP Server outside of the Exalogic machine on separate hardware, particularly to meet existing security and DMZ requirements. Proxy servers can connect to the application tier using the external EoIB network.

Enterprise Manager

As you may have noticed by now, a typical Exalogic environment contains a lot of moving parts. In addition to the server, storage, and networking hardware, there are all the operating system instances to consider. On top of these operating systems, you are likely to run dozens or maybe even hundreds of different application processes, including WebLogic servers, other Fusion Middleware products, and Oracle applications such as Siebel, E-Business Suite, and PeopleSoft. It can be a daunting task to administer, maintain, and monitor the health of all of these pieces.

Oracle's Enterprise Manager products provide administrators with a large-scale management infrastructure along with a comprehensive and unified interface for managing such a heterogeneous environment. Both of the products introduced in this chapter, Grid Control and Ops Center, use an agent-based infrastructure that allows you to perform most day-to-day management tasks from a remote location. These Enterprise Manager agents are deployed to each remote system that needs to be managed, and they accept commands from the central Enterprise Manager management server. Data is periodically gathered by the agents, published to the central Enterprise Manager repository, and then used to trigger alerts and generate reports. As you will see shortly, Grid Control focuses on software monitoring, diagnostics, and management, while Ops Center focuses on the same for hardware.

TIP
Although Enterprise Manager agents will be deployed to and run within Exalogic, Oracle recommends that you host the management servers and repositories outside of Exalogic. Management agents and servers can then communicate using the Exalogic management network. This approach lets you manage both the middle and data tiers together.

Generally speaking, Enterprise Manager is licensed separately from both the Exalogic hardware and software. In addition, the individual features of each Enterprise Manager product are often licensed separately as plug-ins called management packs.

Grid Control

With Oracle Enterprise Manager Grid Control you can perform any combination of the following tasks on your compute nodes, all from a single web-based console:

- Monitor operating system metrics and trigger alerts.

- Upload and execute scripts.

- Administer NFS mounts.

- Start, stop, and monitor all WebLogic Servers and Oracle applications.

- Monitor Java EE application availability and performance.

- Provision compute nodes to support specific applications.

- Validate compliance with known good configurations.

- Perform low-level JVM and WebLogic diagnostics.

This list represents just a subset of the functionality available through Grid Control. If you are also using Exalogic to host other Fusion Middleware products such as SOA Suite or Web Center, Grid Control provides additional administrative features that are specific to these products.

NOTE
Although this chapter refers to Grid Control, the latest version of the product has been renamed Cloud Control. The features described here are available in both versions.

Recall that each WebLogic domain has its own administration server that maintains its servers' configurations and hosts its own copy of the web console. However, cases do arise, particularly in an Exalogic environment, in which it would be convenient to perform some task across multiple domains. A common scenario is checking the availability of all of your servers. With Grid Control, you can easily manage and monitor multiple domains from a single user interface.

Grid Control supports its own organizational units as well. Any software that can be managed/monitored is called a target. Targets also have implicit relationships to other targets. For example, a WebLogic domain target can span multiple host (OS) targets and also deploy application targets. You can also group related targets together and even create a custom dashboard for your system with metrics and reports. In fact, once agents have been installed and started on your compute nodes, Grid Control can automatically discover targets that it is able to manage and then automatically register them with the management server. On Exalogic, the output of this operation is a system group that consists of all compute node hosts and WebLogic domains, and that you can customize as needed.

In addition to providing a unified view of your Exalogic deployment, Grid Control has some additional Exalogic-specific features:

- Provisioning firmware, operating system, middleware, and Oracle applications on compute nodes

- Cloning an Exalogic deployment to allow easy scaling and to help transition from testing to production

- Performing functional, nonfunctional, and load tests on Exalogic deployments

- Managing patches and tracking changes

Finally, keep in mind that Grid Control is not limited to middleware administration. If your management network consists of relational databases, either Oracle or non-Oracle, you can manage and monitor them with Grid Control as well. As you might expect, you can perform tasks such as provisioning a new database node, starting database processes, monitoring metrics, and executing SQL scripts.

Grid Control Deployment

Oracle Enterprise Manager Grid Control deployment requires an Oracle Enterprise Management Agent and the Oracle Management Service (OMS) installations. OMS is the central management control of Enterprise Manager and is normally deployed outside of Oracle Exalogic environment. The Management Agent is the software that is used to monitor each of the compute nodes. The deployment of a Management Agent that shares its software binaries, in this context, is called the Master Agent. In Exalogic, because access to the shared storage appliance is available to all compute nodes, only a single, full Oracle Enterprise Management Agent installation is required. Then you must run the Shared Agent Deployment Wizard tool on each compute node to configure the compute node to boot its agent from this shared installation. This remote agent deployment requires that some files be stored locally on the solid state disks of the compute nodes, but the majority of the agent binaries remain on shared storage.

In summary, setting up Oracle Enterprise Manager Grid Control in the Oracle Exalogic environment involves the following steps:

1. Install Grid Control Enterprise Manager System on an external system to Exalogic.

2. Install Oracle Management Agent on the Sun ZFS Storage 7320 appliance.

3. Install Oracle Management NFS Agents on each Exalogic compute node.

Ops Center

With Grid Control, you can manage the applications on your compute nodes. But how do you monitor and manage the underlying compute node hardware or your Exalogic storage and networks? For example, how can you assess the health of the InfiniBand network or update the firmware on the Exalogic switches? Or how can you coordinate an OS patch across all compute nodes?

These types of lower-level data center administrative tasks are addressed by Oracle Enterprise Manager Ops Center.

Similar to Grid Control, Ops Center can quickly discover your existing hardware and OS assets on your management network, given a range of IP addresses. Include the Integrated Lights Out Manager (ILOM) and management (eth0) addresses for the compute nodes as well as the management addresses for the storage nodes and switches. You will then be able to view the hardware specifications, sensor readings, and metrics for all of these components from a single, unified interface. Ops Center also has convenient shortcuts to launch the browser or command line interfaces for ILOM, a switch, or the storage appliance.

Arguably the most critical feature of Ops Center is its monitoring rules framework. Define conditions based on hardware or OS metrics that, when met, trigger alerts. A hardware fault is a common example. Furthermore, if you have an existing support contract with Oracle for these assets, these alerts can also trigger the creation of new support requests.

Summary

Oracle Exalogic is designed to provide high performance and throughput for Java- and JVM-based applications, particularly those built on Java EE and Oracle Fusion Middleware. This Exalogic software architecture consists of several layers, from the OS, to the JVM, to the Java EE container, WebLogic Server. Fusion Middleware then runs as applications and services on WebLogic. These WebLogic processes are grouped into administrative domains, which are then configured and optimized for Exalogic using the WebLogic Administration Console. The latest releases of WebLogic have been specifically engineered to run on Exalogic. Various network, I/O, and threading optimizations are available and require various levels of configuration.

A separate JVM process called the WebLogic node manager enables remote process management and also facilitates server migration. Migration is one of several clustering features in WebLogic, which allow your applications to scale and be highly available. A third type of JVM process is Coherence, which provides a distributed caching solution for very data-driven applications. Finally, you can manage and monitor all of these different software layers and processes from a single interface with Oracle Enterprise Manager.

CHAPTER
4

Exalogic Solution
Architecture

n this chapter, we will discuss different aspects of the Exalogic solution architecture including software and hardware topology, networking, security, high availability, backup and recovery, disaster recovery, and multi-tenancy.

The Exalogic and Exadata systems are building blocks for data center consolidation, cloud infrastructure, and software consolidation. They are designed to host business-critical applications that require elasticity to deal with increase in demand and scale-back during off-peak periods. Invariably, deployment of enterprise IT solutions include the need to host applications, middleware, and databases. You will typically host applications and middleware on Exalogic. The Exadata system is the choice to host Online Transaction Processing (OLTP) database and data warehouse systems.

Exalogic machines normally host large Oracle Fusion Middleware and Applications deployments; these systems are typically based on WebLogic Server. They leverage an extensive set of high availability features to reduce unplanned downtime, including process death detection and restart, server clustering, server migration, clusterware integration, Active GridLink, load balancing, fail-over, and easy backup and recovery. These enterprise deployments also help minimize planned downtime with support for rolling upgrades and rolling configuration changes. Exalogic and Exadata are engineered systems that leverage an internal InfiniBand (IB) fabric to connect all of their processing, storage, memory, and external network interfaces within these systems to form a single, large computing device.

As we learned in earlier chapters, Exalogic machines are available in a number of different configurations and computational capacities, as shown in Table 4-1. These different configurations can scale into a very large platform to meet the growing demands of the businesses.

Exalogic machines in these different configurations can be upgraded without requiring any downtime to the system, thus maintaining the design objective of engineered systems that have in-built resilience. For example, you may upgrade from an eighth rack to a full rack without experiencing any downtime. Consider an example of an online retailer hosting its e-commerce website on an eighth Exalogic rack. Due to expected high demand in the coming Christmas season, the retailer wants to double e-commerce capacity. In this case, the Exalogic eighth rack can be upgraded to quarter rack without interrupting the live service by following the upgrade procedure documented in the "Exalogic Owner's Guide."

	Full	Half	Quarter	Eighth
Compute Nodes, Cores, and RAM	30 nodes 360 cores at 3.06 GHz 2.9TB RAM	16 nodes 192 cores at 3.06GHz 1.5TB RAM	8 nodes 96 cores at 3.06GHz 768GB RAM	4 nodes 48 cores at 3.06GHz 384GB RAM
Dual Head ZFS Storage Appliance (20×3=60TB)	One	One	One	One
IB Gateway Switches	Four	Two	Two	Two
Datacenter IB Switch	One	One	None	None
Management Switch	One	One	One	One
Redundant PDUs	Two	Two	Two	Two

TABLE 4-1. *Exalogic 2.0 on Intel for Oracle Enterprise Linux 5.5+ and Solaris 11 Configurations and Capacities*

Exalogic Machine Topology

Exalogic contains clustered hot-swappable compute nodes connected to a high-performance ZFS 7320 network storage appliance. Every internal component in Exalogic shares redundant connections to the InfiniBand fabric. The network connections to other Exadata and Exalogic machines are through the same InfiniBand fabric. Figure 4-1 illustrates an example Exalogic machine topology.

Figure 4-1 shows an Exalogic machine connected to the rest of the (non-Exa*) systems in the data center through redundant 10GbE connections, which are provided by the Quad Data Rate (QDR) ports on the InfiniBand Gateway Switch. Each component in the system connects to two independent power distribution units (PDUs) for resilience. The management LAN (local area network) is used to manage and monitor every component in the Exalogic machine. All components have an Integrated Lights Out Manager (ILOM) system interface connected to the management LAN, which can be

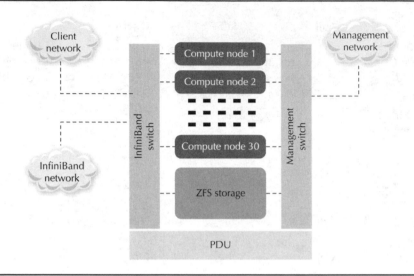

FIGURE 4-1. *Exalogic machine topology*

used for everything from rebooting servers to monitoring performance metrics of the system.

Software Topology

Oracle Exalogic Elastic Cloud Software includes optimizations and enhancements that are targeted at the core products within the Oracle WebLogic Suite. This includes Oracle WebLogic Server, Oracle Coherence, Oracle JRockit JVM, and Oracle HotSpot JVM. In addition to unique support for Java applications and Oracle Fusion Middleware, Exalogic also provides you with a choice of Oracle Enterprise Linux or Oracle Solaris operating systems. Figure 4-2 illustrates the Exalogic software topology to support your applications and middleware-based solutions. The following section describes every software component that forms the Exalogic ecosystem.

Exalogic Elastic Cloud Software

The Exalogic Elastic Cloud Software is a set of enhancements made to Oracle WebLogic Suite, which optimizes performance when running on Exalogic. This can be licensed on purchase of an Exalogic machine and activated (automatically for some, and manually for others) when WebLogic

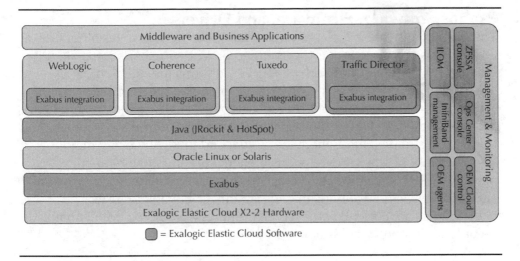

FIGURE 4-2. *Exalogic software topology*

Server is deployed onto Exalogic. The WebLogic Suite products that are enhanced include the WebLogic Application Server, the JRockit Java Virtual Machine (JVM) and the Coherence In-Memory Data Grid. The software optimizations address performance limitations that become apparent only when the software is running on Exalogic's high-density computing nodes connected to fast-networking InfiniBand switches. With these software optimizations, the WebLogic Suite products utilize the benefits of high-end hardware to the maximum, resulting in a well balanced hardware-software engineered system.

At a high-level, the key benefits provided by the optimizations can be grouped into the following:

- Increased WebLogic scalability, throughput, and responsiveness

- Superior WebLogic session replication performance

- Tighter Oracle RAC integration for more reliable database interaction

- Increased Coherence capability to use higher bandwidth of InfiniBand network

Exabus Software, Firmware, and Drivers

The Exabus software is the communication (I/O) fabric that ties all of the Exalogic system components together and provides the basis for Exalogic's reliability, scalability, and performance. It performs the function of extending and connecting the Peripheral Component Interconnect Express (PCIe)–based system bus used within each of the major system components. Exabus is based on QDR InfiniBand and consists of hardware, software, and firmware distributed throughout the system and involving every major system component. Exabus supports the creation of virtual local area networks (vLANs) within the Exalogic system itself as a means of providing application isolation, and it can transparently isolate inter-cluster communication to non-Ethernet subnets, thereby providing both enhanced security and improved cluster performance.

At the software layer, Exabus extends and enhances the OpenFabrics Enterprise Distribution (OFED). OFED is an industry standard open-source software toolkit for Remote Direct Memory Access (RDMA) and kernel bypass applications. OFED is widely used in high-performance InfiniBand-based computing systems that require maximum throughput, minimal latency, and a unified infrastructure for storage access, network virtualization, and cluster inter-process communication.

Exabus includes both kernel-level and user-level APIs and services for parallel message passing, sockets data exchange, storage, and file/database system access.

Exabus incorporates a number of reliability, management, and performance features exclusively for Exalogic and Exadata:

- Support for Exalogic's Ethernet-over-InfiniBand (EoIB) gateways

- Simplified management and monitoring with full ILOM and Oracle Enterprise Manager Ops Center integration

- Quality of Service (QoS) and enhanced IB partitioning configuration support

- High availability for Sockets Direct Protocol (SDP)

- IPv6 support for SDP, EoIB, and IP-over-InfiniBand (IPoIB)

- Automatic disabling of degraded physical links (autonomous port-level fail-over)

- Hundreds of separate design fixes and enhancements in the host stack and management stack, improving compliance, stability, efficiency, and performance

Integrated Lights Out Management

Exalogic components such as compute nodes, storage appliances, and switches are managed and monitored independently of the operating system through ILOM. The ILOM provides advanced service processor (SP) hardware and software that is dedicated and preinstalled on all the components. With ILOM, you can do the following:

- Monitor and understand hardware errors and faults in real time.

- Remotely power on or off compute nodes.

- View the current status of sensors and indicators on the system.

- Access hardware configuration information of the system.

You can configure ILOM to publish generated alerts about system events via either Simple Network Management Protocol (SNMP) traps or e-mail alerts. The ILOM SP runs its own embedded operating system and has a dedicated 1GbE port. In addition, you can access ILOM from the compute node's operating system. ILOM automatically initializes as soon as power is applied to the system. It provides a full-featured, browser-based web interface and has an equivalent command line interface (CLI). The ILOM management interface is also integrated with Oracle Enterprise Manager Ops Center. The compute nodes are configured to use Sideband Management, which allows the ILOM's Service Processor Port and Management LAN port to share the same network connection.

ZFS Storage Appliance Management

The ZFS storage management application is available as both a browser-based user interface (BUI) and a CLI. The management application is used to manage the Logical Unit Number (LUN) and shared files systems accessed by applications and middleware hosted on compute nodes. It is also used for creating, managing, and monitoring shares along with securing them at both the user and infrastructure levels. Figure 4-3 shows the BUI application and CLI scripting environment in Exalogic for ZFS storage.

The BUI is the GUI tool for administration of the appliance. It provides an intuitive environment for administration tasks and analyzing performance data. The CLI is designed to mirror the capabilities of the BUI, while also providing a powerful scripting environment for performing repetitive tasks. The ZFS management software is hosted on Oracle Solaris operating system, and direct access to this underlying operating system is not recommended. For some advanced administration scenarios, such as performing diagnostics on ZFS pools (zpool), you can log into the operating system shell prompt from the CLI. For more details refer to Sun ZFS Storage Appliance Documentation.

InfiniBand Management

The InfiniBand network can be managed through the CLI or GUI in the Sun QDR Gateway Switch. The CLI is used to define and manage IB-based virtual LANs (vLANs), partitions, virtual network interface cards (vNICs), subnet managers, and routing tables. The Exalogic machine has multiple switches, each of which can be accessed from the management LAN by using SSH sessions on port 22 or from the USB or serial connections on the switch. The CLI can be used for the following tasks:

- **Verify the switch's health**   Some of the useful commands are **showunhealthy** and **env_test**.

- **Verify the IB network health**   Some of the useful commands are **ibnetdiscover**, **ibdiagnet**, **ibcheckerrors**, and **listlinkup**.

- **Enable the subnet manager (SM) on the network**   Only one master subnet manager can exist in the InfiniBand network. When more than one of these engineered systems are connected, the master subnet manager is manually set up on a specific switch. The detailed instructions are defined in "Exalogic Owner's Guide." Some of the useful commands for this are **enablesm**, **setsmpriority**, **disablesm**, **sminfo**, and **getmaster**.

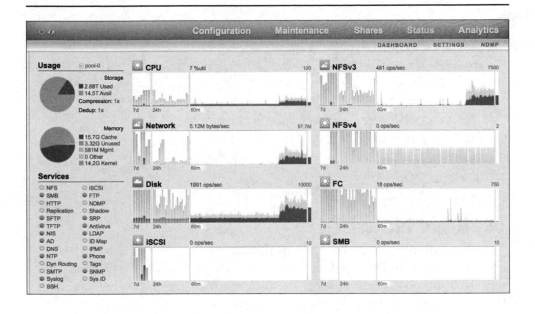

```
caji:maintenance system setup net> devices show
Devices:

      DEVICE UP        MAC                        SPEED
        nge0 true      0:14:4f:8d:59:aa           1000 Mbit/s
        nge1 false     0:14:4f:8d:59:ab           0 Mbit/s
        nge2 false     0:14:4f:8d:59:ac           0 Mbit/s
        nge3 false     0:14:4f:8d:59:ad           0 Mbit/s

caji:maintenance system setup net> datalinks show
Datalinks:

   DATALINK CLASS            LINKS          LABEL
        nge0 device          nge0           Untitled Datalink

caji:maintenance system setup net> interfaces show
Interfaces:

   INTERFACE STATE    CLASS LINKS       ADDRS              LABEL
        nge0 up        ip   nge0        192.168.2.80/22    Untitled Interface

caji:maintenance system setup net> done
```

FIGURE 4-3.   *BUI and CLI applications*

TIP
If you are connecting multiple Exalogic machines to one or more Exadata Systems, only spine switches and Top of Rack (ToR) switches should run the SM, and you must configure the master SM to run only on the ToR switches. If you are connecting a single Exalogic to a single Exadata, ensure that the SM runs on all the switches and that the master runs on only one of the spine switches.

Exalogic Network

The Exalogic machine uses the InfiniBand network for all internal communication and Ethernet for external communication. When applications require IP-based communication, the Exalogic machine uses OFED Internet Protocol over InfiniBand (IPoIB) drivers that enable transmission of IP and Address Resolution Protocol (ARP) packets on InfiniBand networks. This facilitates hosting IP-based applications without requiring changes. IPoIB has significant advantages over traditional IP-based communication. IPoIB can use all the available 40Gb/s bandwidth. The OFED drivers also aggregate multiple incoming packets from a single stream into a larger buffer before sending it onto the network layer, thus minimizing the number of packets processed. Additionally, the OFED drivers handle significantly larger MTU (maximum transmission unit) sizes for IP communication. This makes network communication for larger data more efficient. There are multiple flavors of networks in Exalogic. Figure 4-4 shows various network configurations in typical Exalogic machines.

Every component in an Exalogic machine is connected to one or more types of network. Different types of network adapters and ports are available on these components. The compute node has four 1GbE ports, but only the NET0 port is configured to work as a management LAN link. The compute node has one dual port QDR InfiniBand host channel adapter (HCA) for its private network. There is also a 100Mbps connection for the ILOM interface, but this is not connected, because the ILOM is accessible with a sideband configuration on the management LAN.

The ZFS storage server heads each have four 1GbE interfaces preconnected and configured for active/passive clustering. It is recommended that this

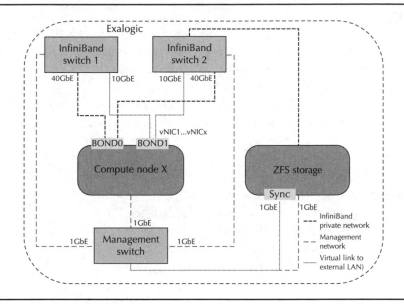

FIGURE 4-4. *Exalogic network topology*

configuration not be changed in any way. Each head has one dual port QDR HCA to link to the private InfiniBand network. The ILOM 10Base-T connections are not used because of the sideband configuration similar to the one used for compute nodes.

The Sun Network QDR InfiniBand Gateway Switch has eight 10GbE Ethernet ports. The number of ports used in an Exalogic deployment depends on your specific bandwidth requirements and on your LAN/VLAN connection requirements. A group of 16 compute nodes connects to two Sun Network QDR InfiniBand Gateway Switches in an active-passive bond. Each compute node is connected to two separate Sun Network QDR InfiniBand Gateway Switches for high availability. Note that each compute node requires a bond for each external network (physical network or vLAN).

The Exalogic machines can be connected to other systems in the data center on a high-speed Ethernet network through an external 10GbE connection. This network is commonly referred to as Ethernet over InfiniBand (EoIB) and will be used for routing external client traffic to the applications hosted on the Exalogic machine.

Management Network

The Exalogic machine is managed and monitored through a dedicated 1 GbE connection, commonly referred to as the management LAN. Your data center management software can be used to manage the Exalogic machines just as any other system in the data center through this management LAN. Oracle Enterprise Manager Grid Control and Oracle Enterprise Manager Ops Center are the recommended tools for this purpose.

TIP
If you rely on third-party management and monitoring tools such as Tivoli or HP OpenView, you can use the Oracle Enterprise Manager connectors for these products to integrate with Grid Control's management capability.

InfiniBand Private Network

This network connects the compute nodes and the Sun ZFS Storage 7320 appliance through the BOND0 interface on the dual port QDR HCA, which is a private InfiniBand network. The default IPoIB subnet is created automatically during the initial configuration of the Exalogic machine. This network is based on an InfiniBand partition allocated for the Exalogic machine; in most cases it is default partition.

NOTE
InfiniBand BOND0 interfaces are the default communication channel among Exalogic compute nodes and storage server heads. IP subnets and additional bonds can be added on top of this default bonded interface.

All the internal IP communication within the applications hosted with Exalogic will use this IPoIB network. This requires setting a default IP address and private host name for every compute node and storage head.

Normally, the Exalogic Configuration Utility is used to do this during the initial setup for the Exalogic machine. Detailed information on the Exalogic Configuration Utility is available in Chapter 5 and the "Exalogic Owner's Guide."

TIP
*The InfiniBand partition can be verified issuing the **smpartition list** command at the CLI on one of the InfiniBand switches.*

Client Access Network

This network connects the compute nodes to the application network through the BOND1 interface on the dual port QDR HCA. It provides client access to the compute nodes. Each Exalogic compute node has a single default access point to an external 10Gb Ethernet edge network via a Sun Network QDR InfiniBand Gateway Switch.

The logical network interface of each compute node for client network access is a bonded interface. BOND1 consists of two virtual network interface cards (Ethernet over InfiniBand vNICs). Each vNIC is mapped to a separate Sun Network QDR InfiniBand Gateway Switch for resilience, and each host EoIB vNIC is associated with a different HCA InfiniBand port (vNIC0 is associated with ib0, vNIC1 is associated with ib1), as shown in Figure 4-4.

Exalogic Architecture Considerations

In this section, we will explore the Exalogic architecture and its nonfunctional aspects such as reliability, availability, supportability, performance, scalability, multi-tenancy, recoverability, elasticity, and security.

Exalogic Deployment Views

Several deployment options for Exalogic are based on different scalability, security, and multi-tenancy requirements.

Exalogic with Database on Commodity Hardware

Consider a deployment in which a single Exalogic machine accesses a database running on a non-Exa* server in a data center. Typical requirements would include the following:

■ The applications hosted on Exalogic should be behind a demilitarized zone (DMZ).

■ The application and database servers must be separated by a firewall. Some businesses do not need this, because they would keep all applications and databases in same secure network.

■ There should be load balancing across applications and databases.

■ The consumer should be able to access the application without needing InfiniBand.

Figure 4-5 shows such a deployment for Exalogic connected to a commodity database server over a 10GbE network with a firewall

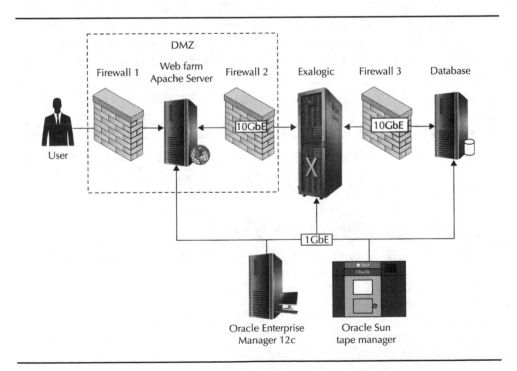

FIGURE 4-5. *Exalogic with database on commodity hardware*

separating the two tiers. The DMZ requirement is realized through a web farm of Apache servers that intercept the Internet-based requests. The Oracle Traffic Director is used to provide software load-balancing and firewall type capability within the Exalogic machine. The figure also shows Oracle Enterprise Manager 12c deployed on the management LAN to provide Exalogic and database monitoring. There is also a tape media server connected on the management LAN for database and application backup.

Exalogic with Exadata

The deployment of a single Exalogic together with Exadata in a data center will have requirements similar to those mentioned in the previous section. A key difference here is that they are more easily realized, have fewer components, and of course should exhibit superior end-to-end performance.

Figure 4-6 shows a deployment for Exalogic and Exadata connected over InfiniBand. The firewall requirement is realized through the InfiniBand

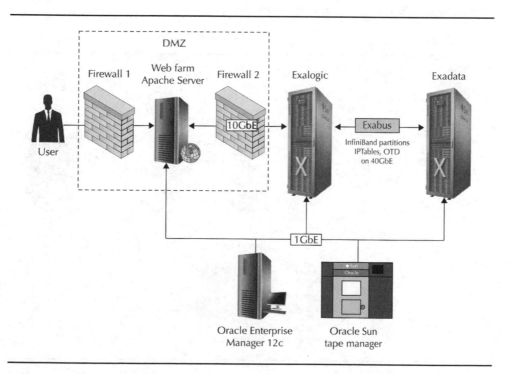

FIGURE 4-6. *Exalogic with Exadata*

partitions, entries in IPTables and Oracle Traffic Director. The InfiniBand partitions are described in more detail in the section "Multi-tenancy," later in the chapter. The InfiniBand partitions provide physical security of data on the network while removing the need to configure and maintain firewalls. Other requirements for DMZ, load-balancing, and backup are realized in the same manner discussed previously. The advantage of using Exadata with Exalogic, apart from the performance boost, is that it requires far less configuration and management overhead.

Multiple Exalogic with Exadata

The deployment of multiple Exalogic machines with Exadata in a data center is normally done to consolidate multiple applications and platforms. Therefore, multi-tenancy and application security will be key objectives of this solution.

In Figure 4-7, two Exalogic machines are connected to two Exadata machines over InfiniBand. Having more than one Exalogic machine helps provide an additional layer of high availability, as each machine has a separate internal ZFS storage appliance.

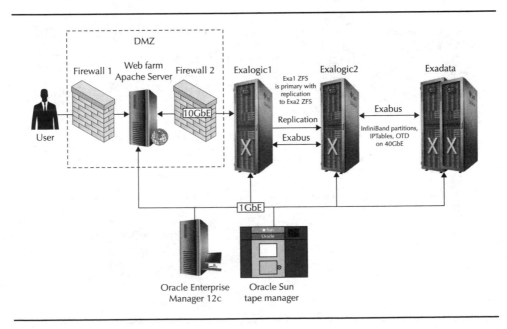

FIGURE 4-7.   *Exa-platform deployment*

Two design options are available to you in such a deployment:

- **Option 1** Use one of the ZFS storage appliance as primary storage and the other as an asynchronous-replication target, while hosting applications on both Exalogic machines.

- **Option 2** Use each ZFS storage appliance as local storage for the applications hosted within the respective Exalogic machine.

Option 1 allows the applications hosted on an Exalogic machine to work seamlessly with secondary ZFS storage in the event of the primary storage failure—although this is very unlikely, because each ZFS storage appliance has in-built redundancies for network, storage head, and disks. This option also allows whole-server migration of all the WebLogic servers to one Exalogic, in the event of a failure of another Exalogic machine.

Option 2 is a more "business as usual" scenario, in which each Exalogic machine hosts a set of applications either within its respective compute nodes or within a cluster across the Exalogic machines. In this option, both ZFS storage appliances host application data, while asynchronous replication is done to an external ZFS storage device.

In the next few sections, we will see how these deployment options can provide scalability, high availability, disaster recovery, and multi-tenancy.

Scalability

A full-rack configuration can scale into a multi-rack configuration using the InfiniBand fabric. You can potentially provide a cloud platform comprising hundreds of racks and tens of thousands of processors.

Figure 4-8 shows that a multi-rack deployment showing up to eight Exalogic and Exadata machines can be connected without additional external InfiniBand switches, because free ports are available for such a configuration within the internal InfiniBand switches in each of these machines. If more than eight machines are required, one or more external high-capacity data center InfiniBand switches are required to scale out further. The use of this shared InfiniBand fabric to connect the middleware and database tiers opens up many new possibilities, particularly for applications that are network bound, as they can leverage the 40Gb bandwidth at 1 micro-second of latency for highly scaled applications

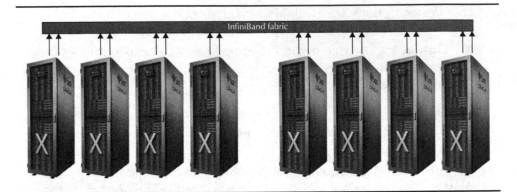

FIGURE 4-8. *Exalogic racks*

that would have much higher network latency in traditional non-Exalogic configurations.

WebLogic clusters can scale both horizontally and vertically on Exalogic. There is no degradation of system performance as the size of the deployment increases and as it spans multiple racks. For example, capacity can be doubled by simply doubling the number of Exalogic machines used (and associated WebLogic servers) without doubling network round-trip time. As capacity increases, response times stay constant.

Exalogic can be used as a resource pool and divided dynamically to allow WebLogic Cluster scale-out and scale-back. For example, consider an example in which you are running multiple WebLogic clusters and hosting different applications on Exalogic, such as online retail website and internal HR website. During peak load, you can expand the WebLogic cluster for the online retail website and scale back the internal HR website by reducing the number of WebLogic servers in its WebLogic cluster to create spare capacity.

WebLogic clusters can span a multi-rack configuration with ease as the InfiniBand network removes I/O contention from the cluster. Each Exalogic machine comes with 60TB of raw space, allowing the storage to scale in multi-rack deployments. This allows WebLogic clusters to use ZFS storage on one of the Exalogic machines as primary storage and use ZFS storage on other Exalogic nodes as secondary storage with asynchronous replication for backup in case of the unlikely event of a complete ZFS appliance failure.

The Exalogic Elastic Cloud software allows WebLogic Server's Active GridLink feature to use Sockets Direct Protocol (SDP) when connecting to Exadata. Active GridLink enables WebLogic server to communicate with Oracle RAC database deployment on Exadata in a scalable manner, with RAC-node load-aware load-balancing and quicker RAC-node failure detection and fail-over. DBAs can scale the Oracle RAC deployment by adding and removing database nodes to RAC without affecting the WebLogic Servers or requiring their reconfiguration. Specifically, these servers will automatically respond to the RAC events and increase or decrease the database connections, while ensuring minimum impact to ongoing transactions.

High Availability of Hardware and Software

Exalogic machines are engineered using Oracle hardware components that focus on dense compute clustering along with high performance networking. The Exalogic configuration of CPU/memory/networking/storage is based on a balanced system design that is generally applicable to mid-tier workloads and large-scale online transaction processing (OLTP) applications. The Exalogic machine also reduces compute node startup time because it uses no spinning disk drives and has only solid state drives (SSDs) in each compute node.

As shown in Figure 4-9, all components within an Exalogic machine use multiple physical InfiniBand (IB) ports and connections to multiple switches for high availability.

Each InfiniBand adapter has two ports and a single IP address, and it supports active/passive bonding. If the active port connection to one of the InfiniBand switches fails, connections transparently and automatically fail-over to the passive port. Exalogic machines have at least two network switches, and every component is connected to two of these switches to provide redundant network connections. If the physical connection to one of the switches has a problem, the connection transparently fails over to the physical connection on another switch. If a switch goes down, the remaining InfiniBand fabric works out alternative paths for nodes connected to the failed switch.

The compute nodes in Exalogic have redundant solid state drives (SSDs) with RAID 1 mirror configurations to ensure protection against disk (SSD) failure. The ZFS storage appliance also has built-in redundancies to protect against a storage head failure, by failing over to secondary storage head. It also has a RAID 1 configuration for all the hard disks and read/write caches

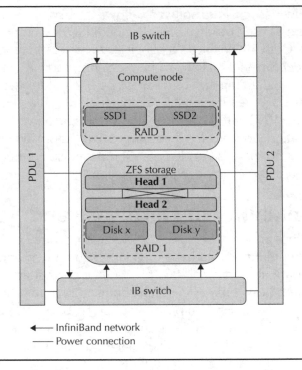

FIGURE 4-9. *Exalogic high availability in hardware*

to protect against disk faults. The Exalogic machine comes with multiple power distribution units (PDU). Each PDU is connected to all the components to provide a redundant power source.

WebLogic High Availability
In addition to the redundant hardware employed in Exalogic, WebLogic and Coherence provides an additional layer of redundancy and high availability at the software level. Exalogic machine leverages the clustering capability in WebLogic Server, which allows clustered WebLogic servers to work together and provide client access to applications in a highly available manner.

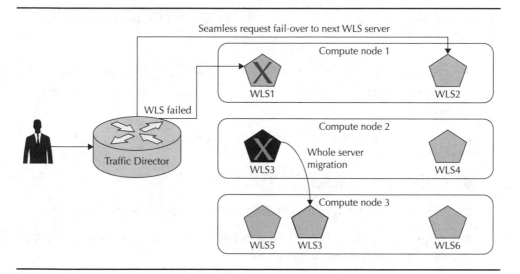

FIGURE 4-10. *Software high availability in Exalogic*

As shown in Figure 4-10, consider an application hosted on a WebLogic cluster that is formed of many WebLogic servers hosted on both the same and different compute nodes. If one of the servers fails, the application on the failed server will no longer be available, but another WebLogic server on the same compute node can continue to handle client request transparently. In an event of a hardware failure and loss of a compute node, WebLogic servers running on another compute node can transparently handle incoming requests of existing client sessions.

The applications hosted on WebLogic servers can also benefit from a server migration feature that allows a failed server on one of the compute nodes to be automatically migrated to another compute node. This feature is very useful if your application has singleton services such as JMS queues or timers that must be restored in the event of a failure. All of these clustering features ensure application continuity and availability.

Storage High Availability

To maximize Exalogic data availability, Sun ZFS storage appliances include a complete end-to-end architecture for data integrity, including redundancies at every level of the stack. Key features of the ZFS storage appliance include the following:

- Predictive self-healing and diagnosis of all hardware failures, such as CPUs, dynamic RAM (DRAM), I/O cards, disks, fans, and power supplies

- Two storage server heads in active-passive mode with automatic fail-over

- RAID 1 disk mirroring

- Multiple I/O paths between the controller and disk shelves

- A "phone home" service to report telemetry to Oracle support during all software and hardware issues

The storage disks on the Sun ZFS storage 7320 appliance are allocated to a single storage pool. The storage pool is assigned to one of the server heads, also referred to as storage controllers. The appliance is clustered with two server heads in an active/passive configuration through the use of CLUSTRON hardware.

The CLUSTRON hardware is specially designed to facilitate recovery from server head failure. It consists of three low-speed links with cross-wired cables connected between server nodes to provide a dedicated private network for their heartbeat. Clustered heads never communicate using external services or administration network interfaces, and the interconnects form a secure private network. Messages fall into two general categories: regular heartbeats used to detect the failure of a remote head and higher-level traffic associated with the resource manager and the cluster management subsystem. Heartbeats are sent, and expected, on all three links; they are transmitted continuously at fixed intervals and are never acknowledged or retransmitted, as all heartbeats are identical and contain no unique information. Failure to receive any message is considered link failure after 200ms (serial links) or 500ms (Ethernet links). If all three links have failed, the peer is assumed to have failed and takeover arbitration will be performed. In the event of a fail-over to the passive server head, it will take over the IP address of the active server head and resume normal service transparently to the compute nodes. The compute nodes access the Network Area Storage (NAS) using the Network File System (NFS) v3 or v4 protocol over the private InfiniBand network.

In a ZFS cluster, the compute nodes have two paths (or sets of paths for multiple protocols) to each storage share being accessed: one path to the storage head that has imported the storage associated with the share and the other path to the passive storage head. The first path is active, and the second is standby; in the event of a takeover during the failure of the active storage head, the active paths become unavailable and the standby paths become active. Disk I/O continues after this transition.

TIP
After the storage head fail-over event is resolved, it is important to fail back to the original state through the ZFS management web interface. You will need to ensure that the read/ write caches are available to both storage heads. You can add a read/write cache from the shell prompt. Please refer to the ZFS storage appliance manual for detailed steps.

Backup and Recovery

A backup and recovery strategy defines how your organization will handle the loss of data or a system and adequately recover it to a certain prior point in time. Different types of backup and recovery strategies are employed by businesses, such as full system backup, incremental backup, snapshots, point-in-time backup, and real-time backup.

Exalogic is intended to host all of its applications and associated configuration files on the ZFS storage appliance. In most cases, only the operating system base image should be hosted on the local SSDs. This approach helps to centralize the location of all critical data and configuration files and allows the selection of backup strategy that best suits the business. The ZFS appliance supports different backup mechanisms. You can capture snapshots of projects (collections of related file shares) at a specific point in time and also configure real-time backup onto a secondary storage unit.

Full System Backup

ZFS storage can be configured to perform a full system backup on a periodic basis to ensure a complete backup is available of all binaries, configuration files, and system files. This strategy is employed if the Exalogic machine is connected to a remote ZFS storage appliance in a different data center to a tape media server, or to a non-ZFS disk backup.

This strategy provides the following benefits:

■ It provides a complete backup of the system.

■ It ensures complete coverage of all the files.

■ It is nonintrusive to the application.

It is important to use another backup strategy in combination with full system backups, because a full system backup does not provide point-in-time recovery and may not contain the latest data backup. Figure 4-11 provides a deployment view of different combinations of backup options for ZFS storage in Exalogic.

Remote disk backups to an external ZFS storage appliance are recommended for single-rack Exalogic deployment. This provides the following benefits:

■ Protects against total storage appliance loss

■ Can be incorporated into a disaster recovery strategy (see the section "Disaster Recovery Terminology" later in this chapter)

■ Uses the built-in capabilities of the storage appliance

Alternatively, the data backup can be made to a non-ZFS storage appliance, but it will rely on other utilities and technologies that are either dependent on a remote disk backup system or on operating system utilities to write to a network mounted share. This is not a recommended solution for green-field deployments, but many customers already have an existing backup system, and these systems can be used as part of the backup strategy.

Depending on the backup strategy and data retention policy of the organization, a tape media server could be used for taking full system backups to archive large amounts of data for long periods.

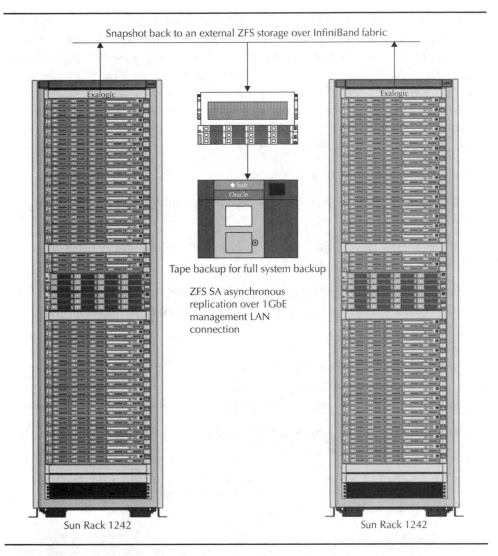

Snapshot back to an external ZFS storage over InfiniBand fabric

Tape backup for full system backup

ZFS SA asynchronous
replication over 1GbE
management LAN
connection

Sun Rack 1242

Sun Rack 1242

FIGURE 4-11. *Supported options for Exalogic backup*

TIP
*Employ a tape media server if your data
retention policies mandate that large amounts
of data (anything that runs in terabytes) be
stored for more than six months.*

Figure 4-12 shows an Exalogic machine connected to tape backup for a full backup solution. The tape media manager catalogs and manages the physical tape media, as well as acting as the interface between the Exalogic machine and the tape library. A media manager can back up to physical or virtual tape libraries.

Oracle Secure Backup can be used for tape-based backups. Backing up to tape can be used in conjunction with other backup methods to provide a tiered approach. The following benefits can be realized by using tape-based backups:

- Many different backup versions can be maintained for indefinite periods.

- Backups can be duplicated and held at more than one off-site location.

- Backups can be made to a physical tape library or to disk using a virtual tape library. This allows for using a combination of tape and disks for storing backups.

And here are some of the drawbacks:

- Backups can be slower depending on the environment.

- Restores can be slower if the backup to be restored is located in an offsite tape library.

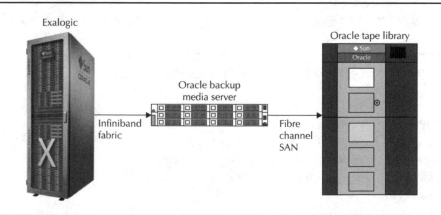

FIGURE 4-12.   *Tape backup for Exalogic*

These strategies are typically used for backing up the data that is stored on the ZFS storage. Since the operating system–related files reside on the local disks in the compute node, these should be backed up using traditional tools such as tar, dump, or rsync.

Snapshots Backup

Snapshots are a convenient and efficient way to capture system state at particular points in time, such as before or after a configuration or application change. As Exalogic machines employ RAID 1 configuration for disks on the ZFS device, snapshots can be taken and stored on the ZFS appliance itself without creating a single point of failure. If external backup is required, the ZFS appliance will need to be connected to an external ZFS storage appliance for real-time or incremental backups through the InfiniBand fabric. This secondary appliance can be in turn connected to a tape drive device to make a periodic full backup of the system.

ZFS storage uses a copy-on-write transactional model. A snapshot is an internal record of which data blocks are current at a moment in time. As ZFS writes new data, the blocks in a snapshot containing the old data are retained instead of discarded. Taking a snapshot is fast because it retains only the block locations currently in use; it does not need to make a copy of the data blocks. Following are the benefits of snapshots:

- Fast backup and restore

- Space efficient, since the storage footprint is only the amount of changed data

- Provides a consistent backup at a given point in time

- Can be made available on disk to allow the restoration of individual files or to compare current and prior file versions

- Can be used as part of a DR strategy

- Can be backed up to tape

- Once replicated to a remote ZFS appliance, can be mounted on a host that has access to the remote server and at the same time it can be backed up to tape

It is important to note that although snapshots are a very quick and easy ways of doing backups, they cannot provide 100 percent protection against a storage appliance failure or data corruption. Instead, snapshots are ideal for protecting against data loss or corruption due to accidental erasure or overlay.

Figure 4-13 shows different configurations for backup and recovery solutions based on different requirements. The figure shows Exalogic machines deployed across two data centers for disaster recovery. It also shows local data backup to external ZFS storage on the active site and utilizes snapshot and full system backup strategies. The remote tape media server is used to take physical tape backups over the management network.

TIP
The restore mechanism should be periodically tested by restoring the snapshot, incremental backup, or full backup on test or preproduction.

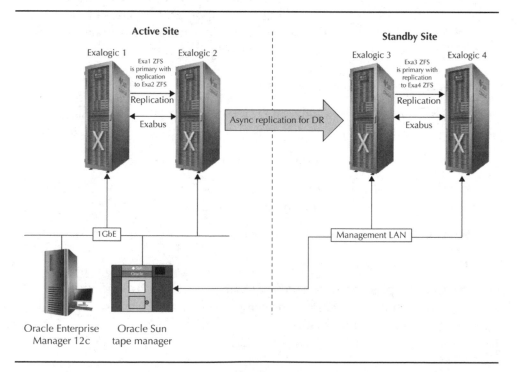

FIGURE 4-13. *Backup and recovery topologies*

The ZFS appliance uses the Network Data Management Protocol (NDMP) for backing up and restoring data. Using NDMP, the application data can be backed up both to locally attached tape devices and remote systems. Locally attached tape devices can also be exposed for backing up and restoring remote systems. These backup options can be implemented over the unused 1GbE ports on the storage heads.

Let us apply the backup strategies discussed earlier in this section to a WebLogic server deployment on Exalogic. Based on the Enterprise Deployment Guide, one of the recommendations is to install multiple WebLogic product binaries to separate middleware home directories for different compute nodes, as shown in Figure 4-14. It should be also noted that in some cases sharing middleware home directories across multiple compute nodes is a better option, as it allows for simpler patching process by limiting the number of middleware homes.

The WebLogic domain configuration files, data stores, and transaction logs (TLogs) for every WebLogic server should be managed in different shares, as shown in Figure 4-14. This facilitates whole server migration between compute nodes. All the shares are targeted for snapshot-type backup with a periodic full system backup to tape media. The JMS stores, TLogs stores, and domain configuration files are configured for asynchronous replication across the data center to the DR site's Exalogic ZFS storage.

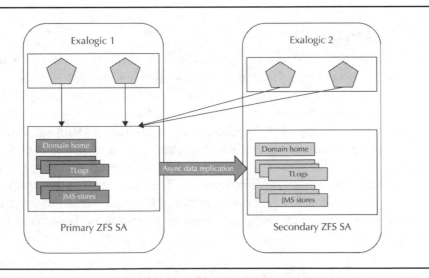

FIGURE 4-14.   *Backup strategy for middleware on Exalogic*

Now let's consider another example. Suppose you have multiple Exalogic machines connected together, and a WebLogic cluster spans these Exalogic machines. In this case, it is recommended that you select one of the Exalogic ZFS storage appliances as the primary target to host the domain and server configurations and select another ZFS storage appliance as the secondary. As shown in Figure 4-14, the domain configuration files, TLogs, and JMS store files are configured to be asynchronously replicated to the secondary target, while the WebLogic servers running on both Exalogic machines use the primary ZFS storage as their file store. Such a configuration offers maximum availability and protects the WebLogic cluster against ZFS storage appliance failure. Keep in mind, however, that this is not a DR strategy, because these systems are deployed within the same data center.

TIP
After a failure of the primary ZFS storage appliance, use the Distributed Command Line Interface (DCLI) tools to remount the NFS shares from the secondary ZFS storage appliance from another Exalogic machine on all the affected compute nodes. An alternative method is to use DNS-based IP mapping to a virtual hostname of the ZFS storage appliance.

Multi-Tenancy

The definition of multi-tenancy varies based on who you ask. For the purpose of this book, we define *multi-tenancy* as the ability to deploy, co-locate, or co-host multiple applications within the same Exalogic machine, where different deployments may have different security and resource requirements and/or distinct sets of end users. The ability of Exalogic to support different multi-tenancy deployments enables cost savings and economies of scale achieved by consolidating resources into a cloud platform. Exalogic enables co-hosting of different applications that might have a variety of requirements onto a single standardized platform, while at the same time ensuring data separation and addressing security concerns. Here are the benefits of Exalogic multi-tenancy:

- Single platform hosts multiple applications

- Reduced management overhead compared to managing different dedicated platforms for each application

■ Physical data separation for co-hosted applications on Exalogic

■ Elasticity and agility, providing on-demand resource allocation in order to accommodate peaks and valleys in application requirements without requiring additional hardware.

■ Reduced cost of ownership and operations through a single consolidated platform

Multi-tenancy can be achieved through a number of different features in Exalogic, some of which are mutually exclusive and others which must be implemented together:

■ InfiniBand partitions

■ InfiniBand Virtual Lanes

■ Ethernet virtual LANs

■ IP subnets

■ ZFS storage appliance data security

■ Solaris zones

■ Oracle VM-based virtualization

Oracle Solaris Zones and Oracle VM (for x86)–based virtual guests are mutually exclusive, whereas in both virtualized and nonvirtualized deployments, you can use InfiniBand partitions, InfiniBand Virtual Lanes, ZFS storage data security, and Ethernet virtual LAN features together in same Exalogic machine

InfiniBand Partitions
InfiniBand partitions are a unique feature of InfiniBand networking in Exalogic machines. To ensure that data is sent only to permitted physical locations, InfiniBand partitions group a set of nodes within the fabric that are allowed to communicate. Other compute nodes not part of this group can't see or send packets to these nodes. The embedded subnet manager on

the InfiniBand switch manages partitions on a per-port basis. Each port may be included in one or more partitions. This partitioning configuration is also automatically transferred to the alternate switch during subnet manager fail-over.

The Exalogic machine includes a single InfiniBand partition at the rack level. All Exalogic compute nodes and the storage appliance are full members of this default InfiniBand partition. The Exalogic network hardware allows you to configure multiple partitions to restrict traffic between specific InfiniBand connections.

InfiniBand partitioning enables the following:

- Secure isolation of a subset of compute nodes by enforcing physical data security policies

- Increased physical security of data passing through Exalogic's internal InfiniBand fabric

- Create multiple subnetworks on a large cloud network to support multi-tenant deployment

- Support IP vLANs by mapping them to InfiniBand partitions

InfiniBand partitions are defined to isolate communication between specific nodes on the InfiniBand network. It is possible for nodes to be assigned to multiple InfiniBand partitions, but this should be done with caution because it could lead to a very complex network design and possibly even be counter-productive.

There are two types of partition memberships, as shown in Figure 4-15:

- **Full membership**   This type of member can communicate with all other partition members, including other full members and limited members within its partition.

- **Limited-membership**   This type of member cannot communicate with other limited-membership partition members within its partition. However, a limited partition member can communicate with a full member within its partition.

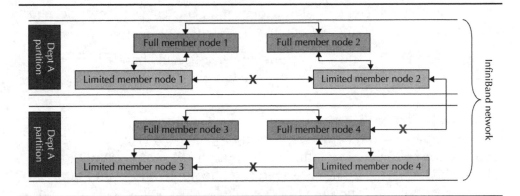

FIGURE 4-15. *InfiniBand partitions with types of members*

InfiniBand network data packets carry a partition key that defines an InfiniBand partition. In Exalogic, the default partition key is called Default. Every time a compute node receives a data packet, it checks the validity of the partition key based on the subnet manager's configuration. If the compute node is not in the partition defined by the partition key, the packets are discarded. This behavior enforces the physical security of the data flowing through the InfiniBand network.

InfiniBand Virtual Lanes

InfiniBand offers link layer Virtual Lanes (VLs) to support multiple logical channels on the same physical link. The host channel adapter (HCA) can divide (multiplex) each link into a set of Virtual Lanes. Using Virtual Lanes, an InfiniBand link can share bandwidth between various compute nodes simultaneously. In a multi-tenant environment, all applications will compete for fabric resources such as physical links and queues. To manage such interference and congestion, the Exabus implements Quality of Service (QoS) through InfiniBand Virtual Lanes as described here:

- **Flow control**   This service allows for members in the Virtual Lanes to trust that the packets will reach the target nodes without requiring the confirmation packets, through better and efficient means of data flow in the fabric.

- **Congestion management**   This service makes use of advance routing logic to bypass hot spots in the network and reduce congestions.

- **Latency** The service allows for assuring a latency to a specific Virtual Lane for point-to-point connection in the fabric.

- **Bandwidth** This service guarantees a specific bandwidth SLA to the Virtual Lane used for the connection.

Ethernet Virtual LANs

The Exalogic network hardware also supports virtual LANs (vLANs) to achieve a result similar to InfiniBand partitions. It should be noted that although vLANs can be used to segregate the applications into different virtual networks, they do not enforce same level of physical security on the data packets in the network as InfiniBand partitions do. The benefits of using vLANs include logical division of workload, enforcing security isolation, and splitting traffic across several manageable broadcast domains. The vLANs allow traffic separation from the 10GbE switch to the compute nodes. By design, Ethernet traffic on one vLAN cannot be seen by any host on a different vLAN. To enable communication between two vLANs, you should use an external router.

To understand the use of vLAN, consider an example in which you want to co-host development, test, and production environments on the same Exalogic machine. You will have to dedicate some of the external 10GbE connections from the gateway switch for production, testing, and development environments by creating vLANs on them and associating them with different subnet IP ranges. This will allow you to run applications in different lifecycle stages that listen on their respective vLANs for their clients.

IP Subnets

Finally, access to the network can be limited by using multiple subnet masks when configuring compute node network interfaces. However, these subnet masks are enforced at the OS level only and not by the network hardware.

ZFS Storage Appliance-Based Data Security

The ZFS storage appliances lets administrators isolate virtual or external hard drives (logical unit numbers, or LUNs) or NFS-based shares onto specific compute node or target groups, allowing resource demarcation at the file system level. However, it is important to note that although ZFS appliances can provide a storage solution as a Storage Area Network (SAN) or Network Attached Storage (NAS), for Exalogic purposes the best practice recommendation is to use the ZFS appliance as a NAS device with the file system mounted as NFS (version 4) shares across the compute nodes.

The ZFS storage can secure the LUNs or NFS shares by limiting the IP address range of compute nodes as targets or by restricting access to specific user accounts. This avoids exposure of the LUNs or NFS shares to unwanted or conflicting initiators. The following table shows the configuration parameters that can be used to limit access to the NFS shares for Exalogic compute nodes.

Configuration Property	Description
Prevent clients from mounting subdirectories	If this option is selected, clients will be prevented from directly mounting subdirectories. They will be forced to mount the root of the share.
Anonymous user mapping	Unless the root option is in effect for a particular client, the root user on that client is treated as an unknown user, and all attempts by that user to access the share's files will be treated as attempts by a user with specified UID. The file's access bits and access control lists (ACLs) will then be evaluated normally.
Security mode	Read-only or read-write.
Security exception type	Hostname: A single client whose IP address resolves to the specified fully-qualified name. Netgroup: A netgroup containing fully-qualified names to which a client's IP address resolves. Network: All clients whose IP addresses are within the specified IP subnet.

You can limit access to NFS shares by using both standard UNIX file permissions and IP- or DNS-based client exceptions. When a client attempts access, the access will be granted according to the first exception in the list that matches the client (or, if no such exception exists, according to the global share mode).

Figure 4-16 shows an example of two applications, Order2Cash and HRMS, that are hosted on the Exalogic machine. All the configuration and deployed files for these applications are hosted on the internal ZFS storage appliance within the Exalogic machine.

As Order2Cash is an external-facing application and HRMS is an internal staffing application, they have different security and resource requirements. The ZFS storage appliance security configuration is used to keep the respective files of these applications in different projects and shares. Access to these files is restricted to the specific compute nodes that host these applications, as shown in the figure. Shares related to Order2Cash can be mounted only on compute node 1 by the system user O2CUser. The HRMS-related shares are restricted to access by compute node 2 and these shares can be mounted only by the system user HRMSUser.

TIP
Configure network area shares using NFSv4 for application files and middleware so the compute nodes can easily access these files in an event of a failure.

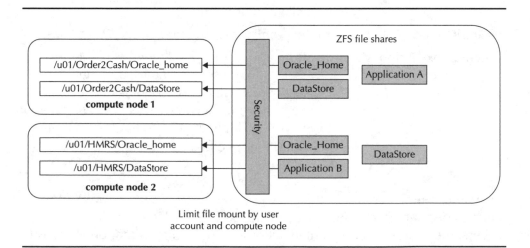

Limit file mount by user
account and compute node

FIGURE 4-16. *Securing NFS shares for multi-tenancy*

Oracle Virtual Machine (OVM) Virtualization

Virtualization is widely used as a means to achieve hardware and software consolidation. It can also help in providing elasticity in the data center that can expand and contract based on emerging business demands. Other advantages of virtualization include the following:

- Quicker IT service delivery with accelerated platform provisioning

- Improved operational efficiency, ensuring compliance and reducing risk (especially when used with Oracle Enterprise Manager cloud control to manage OVM deployments)

- Reduced costs and increased energy efficiency with less hardware through platform consolidation

- Reduced cost of ownership though balanced deployment of applications with varying resource needs and peak load requirements on a single infrastructure

- Improved disaster recovery and high availability through replication and migration of application environments, resulting in better business continuity

Virtualization is mainly adopted in two scenarios. The first is autonomic computing, in which the IT environment will be able to manage itself based on perceived activity. For example, as the demand increases, the virtual environment can spawn more application instances on the available capacity. Another scenario is utility computing, in which multiple users transparently share the same infrastructure without interfering with one another, while each user pays only for the exact computing resources they use.

There are many types of virtualization technologies, including the following:

- **Hardware virtualization** The guest OS does not have complete access to the hardware, and instead requires a software to imitate aspects of the hardware underneath it—in particular, details of memory mapping, I/O, interrupt handling, and processor state. Full virtualization can incur worse I/O performance than native (also known as bare-metal) installations of operating systems. Many current systems using this form of virtualization have hardware support (such as Intel's VT-x or AMD's AMD-V used in x86/64 platforms) to reduce this category of overhead. VMware is an example of full virtualization.

■ **Paravirtualization** Paravirtualization is a form of virtualization, in which the virtual machine monitor (also called the hypervisor) emulates only part of the hardware and provides a special API requiring modification to the guest OS. The modified guest OS kernel knows that it is running on a paravirtualized environment rather than bare metal, and asks the hypervisor kernel to perform I/O and hardware control functions. This can be less expensive than the method used in hardware virtualization and lets the hypervisor enforce security and fair resource sharing. Performance is generally very close to running bare-metal, nonvirtualized operating systems. The most popular representative of this approach is Xen, though it also supports hardware virtualization on the servers that provide the VT-x or AMD-V extensions, which permits operation of guest operating systems with unmodified kernels.

■ **Operating system–level virtualization** The guest OS acts as an isolated execution environment without the need for any hardware virtualization. All guests use the kernel of the hosting OS. (No per-guest kernel modification or variation is possible.) The most prominent advantage of this approach is performance, as it avoids the substantial performance challenges faced by other forms of virtualization. Solaris Containers are the best-known example of this type of virtualization.

Oracle VM Server for x86 is based on Xen virtualization. A thin software layer known as the Xen hypervisor is inserted between the server's hardware and the operating system. This provides an abstraction layer that allows each physical server to run one or more virtual servers, effectively decoupling the operating system and its applications from the underlying physical server.

Exalogic supports virtualization based on Oracle Solaris Containers and OVM virtualization. Virtualization technology enables engineered systems such as Exalogic to provide multi-tenant deployments in which the following requirements can be met:

■ On-demand resource allocation

■ Physical separation of applications and data

■ Resource pooling across multiple Exalogic machines

- Optimized use of hardware resources

- Rapid deployment and reduced total cost of ownership

- Snapshot-based point in time backup

OVM Server for x86 provides a very efficient paravirtualization technology, especially compared to some competitors in the market that rely on binary translation. OVM enables you to deploy operating systems and application software within a supported virtualization environment. An Exalogic deployment with OVM is shown in Figure 4-17.

Following are the components of OVM:

- **Oracle VM Server for x86**   A self-contained virtualization environment (aka hypervisor) designed to provide a lightweight, secure, server-based platform for running virtual machines. OVM Server is based upon an updated version of the underlying Xen hypervisor technology and includes the OVM Agent. In Exalogic, you can have one OVM Server per compute node, each running multiple guest VM instances.

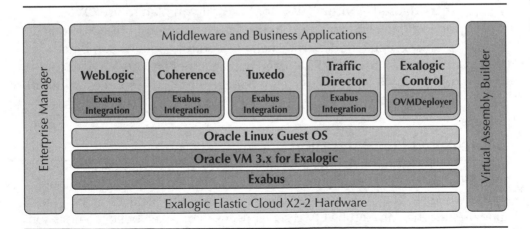

FIGURE 4-17.   *Exalogic deployment with OVM*

- **Oracle VM Agent** Installed once with each OVM Server. It communicates with OVM Manager for management of guest virtual machines and the OVM Server itself. It also includes a Web Services API to access and manage OVM Server, server pools, and resources from third-party tools.

- **Oracle VM Guest OS** This is the virtual instance of an operating system running on top of OVM Server. OVM instances could also be configured to use different subnets (vLANs) or InfiniBand partitions on the Exalogic machine. On Exalogic the only supported guest OS is a variant of Oracle Enterprise Linux 5.6 with additional InfiniBand and Single Root I/O Virtualization (SR-IOV) capabilities. The general purpose OS versions are not supported as guest OS on Exalogic.

- **Oracle VM Manager** Provides a browser-based user interface to manage OVM servers. It manages the virtual machine lifecycle, including creating the virtual machines from installation media, a virtual machine template or assembly template, deleting the virtual machines, powering them off, uploading them, and live migration. The VM Manager manages resources, including server pools that can host virtual machines, ISO files, virtual machine templates, sharable hard disks, Exalogic networking and Exalogic ZFS shares that are used as virtual disks for OVM. If you plan to use OVM on Exalogic, you will need to use Exalogic Control hosted on one of the compute nodes. The Exalogic Control contains combined capabilities of both ZFS storage management and OVM Manager to provide a single interface to manage all OVM resources within Exalogic.

Oracle VM Live Migration*

The OVM Server has live migration that enables an active guest OS virtual machine instance to be migrated to another OVM Server (that is, compute node) while the guest OS instance continues to run. This feature is important, and useful, when an existing OVM server needs to be taken out of commission for maintenance purposes, or to balance workloads across servers.

Guest OS instances are deployed across the compute nodes and have the ability to migrate on another compute node in the event of a hardware component failure, as shown in Figure 4-18.

---

*At the time of writing this book, "live migration" was not supported on Exalogic.

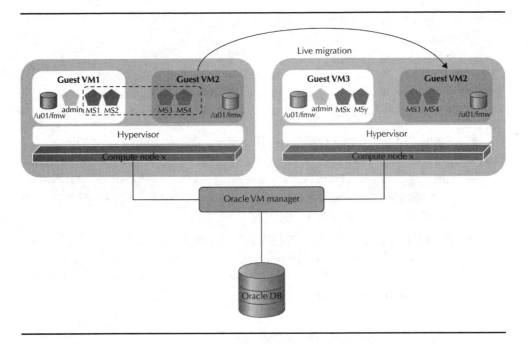

FIGURE 4-18.   *OVM-based migration and restart in Exalogic*

You can migrate only one virtual machine at a time. It is important to note that cross-server pool live migration is not allowed; for example, if you have defined two OVM server pools; you cannot do live migration of guest virtual machines from one OVM server pool to another. As a result, if you are planning to use multiple Exalogic machines, it is best to create a single server pool of OVM servers across these Exalogic machines. You can migrate virtual machines only from one OVM server to another within the same server pool. To migrate a virtual machine, use the OVM Manager or Exalogic control console:

1. From the OVM Manager console, select the Home view, and then select the virtual machine in the Server Pools folder.

2. Right-click the virtual machine and select Migrate from the context menu.

3. Select the Oracle VM Server to which you want to migrate your virtual machine and click OK.

Live Migration offers the following benefits:

■ **Ease of maintenance** You, as an administrator, can minimize downtime by using the OVM Server Live Migration feature. If you must shut down some equipment, use this feature to preserve running applications by moving them to a different compute node server.

■ **Optimize hardware resource utilization** You can use Live Migration to move an active guest OS VM to a compute node with more available physical memory, more CPU capacity, or a better I/O subsystem. This change improves application performance by permitting resource balancing across compute nodes.

■ **Greater availability of applications** You can maximize application availability during the migration because there is no need to shut down the application while the migration is in process. The applications can continue to process new requests during the live migration.

Oracle VM for Solaris (Container)

An Exalogic machine supports Oracle Enterprise Linux and Oracle Solaris operating systems. If you choose to use Oracle Solaris as the operating system running on all compute nodes, virtualization based multi-tenancy can be achieved through the use of Oracle Solaris Containers.

Containers use virtualization and allow you to maintain the one-application-per-server deployment model as shown in Figure 4-19, while sharing hardware resources.

Following are the key features of Solaris Containers:

■ Oracle Solaris operating system built-in virtualization for administrative flexibility

■ Efficient native-performance virtualization with very low overhead compared to hardware-based virtualization

■ Granular resource management and allocation

■ Robust isolation to run multiple applications on a single system safely and securely

■ Rapid scalability to meet growing demand

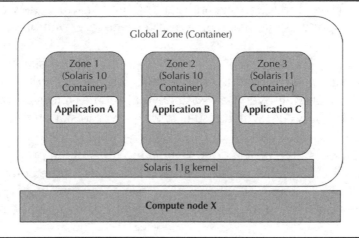

FIGURE 4-19. *Solaris containers for multi-tenancy*

Oracle Solaris Containers isolate software applications and services using flexible, software-defined boundaries. This lets multiple private execution environments run side-by-side within a single instance of the Oracle Solaris operating system running on a compute node of an Exalogic machine. Like other virtualization technologies, each Container behaves as if it's running on its own system, making consolidation simple, safe, and secure. The Solaris Container technology also allows running legacy versions of Oracle Solaris 10 as Containers on a single instance of Oracle Solaris 11.

Disaster Recovery Terminology

Disaster recovery refers to a site's ability to safeguard against natural disasters or unplanned outages at a production site, by having a recovery strategy for failing over applications and data to a geographically separate standby site.

Disaster recovery is a familiar concept these days, but it is important to set a common understanding on the terminology used for disaster recovery, especially with respect to how Oracle's Maximum Availability Architecture (MAA) addresses it. This will also ensure that you can map the concepts used in Oracle's terminology with those used in your organization. For example, in some organizations, *site switchback* is referred to as *failback*.

Topology   The production site and standby site hardware, network, and software components that make up a disaster recovery solution.

Site fail-over   The process of making the current standby site the new production site after the production site becomes unexpectedly unavailable. An example of site fail-over is a disaster event, such as a loss of power supply to a primary site, which results in a fail-over to standby site.

Site switchover   The process of reversing the roles of the production site and standby site. Switchovers are planned operations on the current production site. During a switchover, the current standby site becomes the new production site and the current production site becomes the new standby.

Site switchback   The process of reversing the roles of the new production site (former standby) and new standby site (former production). Switchback is applicable after a previous switchover.

Site instantiation   The process of creating a topology at the standby site and synchronizing the standby site with the primary sites so that the primary and standby sites are consistent.

Site synchronization   The process of applying changes made to the production site at the standby site. For example, when a new application is deployed at the production site, you should perform synchronization so that the same application will be deployed at the standby site.

Recovery point objective (RPO)   The maximum age of the data from which you want the ability to restore in the event of a disaster. For example, if your RPO is six hours, you will want to be able to restore the systems back to the state that they were in as of no longer than six hours ago.

Recovery time objective (RTO)   Time needed to recover from a disaster. This is usually determined by how long your organization can afford to be without its critical running IT systems.

MAA with Exalogic and Exadata

The Maximum Availability Architecture (MAA) is Oracle's blueprint and best practices for implementing Oracle's High Availability (HA) and Disaster Recovery (DR) technologies. It is based on proven Oracle HA technologies and recommendations. The goal of the MAA is to minimize the complexity when designing optimal HA architecture. It does so by providing configuration recommendations and tuning tips to optimize IT architecture and Oracle features. Figure 4-20 shows a typical MAA configuration for Exalogic and Exadata deployment. For more details, refer to the MAA guide for Exalogic and Exadata.

This platform architecture facilitates data protection for product binaries, product configuration data, and business-critical database contents. The remote replication feature of Exalogic's ZFS storage appliance is used to protect the middleware product binaries, configurations, and metadata files. Oracle Data Guard is used to synchronize all of the Oracle Exadata database changes

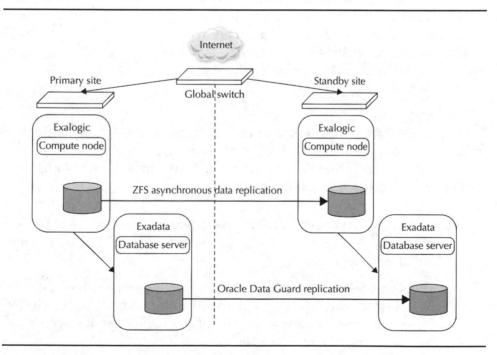

FIGURE 4-20. *Exadata and Exalogic MAA*

between the two sites. This database contains the system data used by Oracle Fusion Middleware Repositories as well as the customer's business data.

Users access the primary site during normal operations. During disaster recovery conditions, the users access the standby site. This switchover is generally seamless from the user's perspective, since the entire infrastructure along with the mount points and host names are configured identically for both the primary and standby sites.

Once the primary site is restored, the application data and files system are synchronized with the standby site to ensure that the primary site has the latest copy of the data and transactions. This is achieved using Exalogic's ZFS storage replication mechanism and the Oracle Data Guard mechanism, but in the reverse direction. The site switchback process is initiated to restore the primary site as actively serving the user access, and the standby site is restored as the passive site.

TIP
It is recommended that all application data as well as transactional data be kept in the database so site switchover and switchback result in a consistent transactional state. The latest versions of WebLogic include a feature to host TLogs in a database. This feature should be used where possible.

Implementing the MAA is one of the key requirements for any Exalogic deployment to maximize availability and reliability. When Exalogic is used to host Oracle Fusion Middleware specifically, an additional set of high availability features are available to use:

- **WebLogic Server process death detection and restart**   WebLogic Node Manager monitors WebLogic Server process state and restarts failed servers.

- **WebLogic Server clustering**   WebLogic clustering enables a group of servers to work as a unit and allow users to interact with a cluster rather than specific servers, providing an ongoing service even if a server belonging to the cluster fails.

- **WebLogic Server migration** WebLogic Server automatically migrates to another compute node if the original host compute node fails.

- **WebLogic rolling upgrades and rolling configuration changes** WebLogic protects the deployment from unplanned downtime and also minimizes planned downtime.

As discussed earlier, Exalogic deployments provide protection from unforeseen disasters and natural calamities. One protection solution involves setting up a standby site at a location geographically different from the production site. The standby site may have equal or fewer services and resources compared to the production site, and it may be sized to host only the most business-critical applications and databases. The Oracle MAA describes several different multi-site deployment options:

- **Symmetric sites** The production site and standby site are identical in all respects.

- **Partial symmetric sites** The production site and standby site are identical in topology but not hardware. For example, you may use an Exalogic full rack in the production site and a half rack in the standby site.

- **Asymmetric sites** The standby site has fewer host systems, application instances, and database instances than the production site. For example, you may use a RAC database in production and a non-RAC database in standby.

TIP
Many organizations implement symmetric sites for MMA but use the standby site for preproduction and load testing during normal operations. This is most effectively achieved through the use of virtualization technology.

In all of the preceding configurations, the application data, metadata, configuration data, and security data are replicated to the standby site in near real-time through asynchronous replication technology. The standby site is normally in a standby mode; it is activated when the production site is not available. This deployment model is sometimes referred to as an active/standby model. This model is normally adopted when the two sites are connected over a WAN and network latency does not allow clustering across the two sites.

Storage Appliance Data Replication

The ZFS appliance in Exalogic is used to store all the data for the application and Oracle Fusion Middleware. The data is replicated from the primary to the standby site, with data blocks asynchronously streamed to the remote storage appliance. Source data is modified at the granularity of a ZFS transaction; therefore, the data is always consistent. Modified data is replicated to the target site, which ensures the target site data is also consistent.

To help you understand the storage appliance–based data replication, it is important that we define the terminology; the next section provides the definition of terminology used in discussion data replication.

Storage Considerations and Terminology

Let's review the terminology and storage concepts for the Sun ZFS Storage 7320 appliance. This appliance is a part of every Exalogic machine.

Storage pool   The storage pool is created over a set of physical disks. File systems are then created over the storage pool. The storage pool is configured with RAID 1.

Projects   All file systems and LUNs are grouped into projects. A project can be considered a consistency group. A project defines a common administrative control point for managing shares. All shares within a project have common settings, and quotas can be enforced at the project level in addition to the share level. Projects can also be used solely for grouping logically related shares together, so that their common attributes (such as accumulated space) can be accessed from a single point. It is important to note that storage replication is normally configured at the project level.

Shares   Shares are file systems or LUNs that are exported over supported data protocols to the compute nodes. Exported file systems can be accessed over Common Internet File System (CIFS), Network File System (NFS),

HTTP/WebDAV, and File Transfer Protocol (FTP). LUNs export block-based volumes and can be accessed over iSCSI. The project/share is a unique identifier for a share within a pool. Oracle recommends that compute nodes from an Exalogic machine access the shares over NFS. The shares are mounted using NFS over IPoIB (IP over InfiniBand). Both NFSv3 and NFSv4 are supported in Exalogic. It is important for you to understand that NFSv3 is stateless in nature and NFSv4 is a stateful protocol. As a result, NFSv4 is better for performance, but it will take longer to recover from a storage head failure in a ZFS storage appliance.

TIP

Multiple projects can contain shares with the same name, but a single project cannot contain shares with the same name. It is best practice to name the shares based on the application name and/or compute node.

FMW Storage

It is recommended that each FMW installation that you require on Exalogic be associated with its own storage project. Product binaries within a FMW installation will then map to shares. Configuration files, such as WebLogic Server domains, should be maintained in projects and shares separate from those used for FMW installations.

TIP

Define a unique project for each business unit in which to place domains and similar configurations related to that business unit.

Figure 4-21 shows an example of an Oracle Fusion Middleware file structure configured on the ZFS storage appliance. Using this type of structure results in the ability to configure the system at a central location, making backup easy.

You can create multiple WebLogic domains and servers from one single binary installation. This allows the installation of binaries in a single location on shared storage and the reuse of this installation by the servers in different

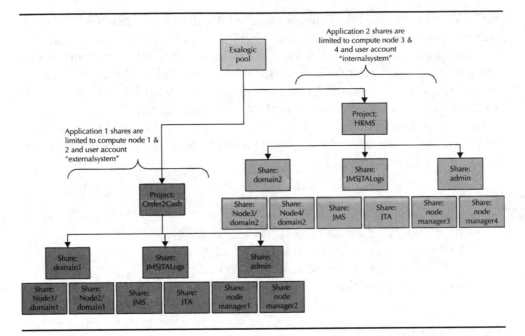

FIGURE 4-21. *Example share structure on ZFS*

compute nodes. However, for maximum availability, it is recommended that you also use redundant binary installations. This will allow for rolling upgrades and patches. (Refer to Exalogic owner's guide for more details on rolling upgrades and patches.)

It is recommended that the domain directory used by the administration server is separated from the domain directory used by managed servers. This allows a symmetric configuration for the domain directories used by the managed servers and isolates the fail-over of the administration server. The domain directory for the administration server must reside in a shared storage to allow fail-over to another node with the same configuration.

The administration server directory should not be tied to a specific compute node. It is possible to use a shared domain directory for all managed servers in different nodes or use one domain directory per node. Sharing domain directories for managed servers facilitates the scale-out procedures, but this approach can also limit whole server migration to other Exalogic machines, especially if you consider a multiple Exalogic deployment topology, in which each Exalogic machine uses its internal ZFS storage appliance as primary. In this scenario, the shares' domain directories for managed servers will limit the domain to be confined only to one of the Exalogic machines. In this case, having a domain directory per managed server provides the flexibility to mount a managed server–specific share on another Exalogic machine without potentially affecting other servers in the domain.

The WebLogic JMS file stores, JTA transaction logs, and server logs need to be placed on a shared storage to ensure that they are available for recovery in case of a server failure or migration. The latest version of WebLogic Server includes a new feature that allows TLogs to be written to the database. This feature greatly improves the disaster recoverability of applications as transactional information. JMS persistence stores and application data are all stored at the same place and replicated to the standby site together. This will provide the required transactional consistency across data and transactions during a disaster recovery.

Replication

The ZFS storage appliance can be configured with data replication in synchronous and asynchronous modes. The advantage with asynchronous mode is that it can replicate data over a long distance, with only a small lag for data write actions, as the storage heads are not required to wait for remote storage acknowledgement. Exalogic DR strategies are typically based on asynchronous replication mode so that the standby site can be physically located as far away as needed.

Replication can be set up at a project level or at the share level. In project-level replication, all the shares (file systems and LUNs) in the project are replicated. An implicit, consistent snapshot is performed for the share or all the shares in a project, and the data from the snapshot is streamed to the target site. The target's receipt of the replication is called a package. After a successful receipt of the package at the target, another implicit snapshot is performed at the source, and this time only the incremental data between the two snapshots is replicated. The write ordering and consistency is preserved across the shares in the project. One source can be replicated to one or more targets. Likewise, a target system can receive packages from multiple sources. The data can be optionally encrypted using Secure Sockets Layer (SSL) and then transmitted. Replication can be configured to use a dedicated private network or a public network. Replication is also supported between different releases of the ZFS appliance.

Replication can occur in scheduled, on-demand, and continuous modes of replication. The following sections explore each of these modes.

Scheduled Replication In this mode, the user defines a schedule for automatic replication. After a schedule is established, replication occurs at the defined interval. The interval can be every half hour, hour, day, week, or month. This mode is preferred in situations where replication during off-peak time is preferred or where backup must occur at specific times.

TIP
In Exalogic the binaries and other static configuration files such as domain configurations can be replicated using scheduled replication mode. This approach is based on the principle that this data does not change as much on a periodic basis.

On-Demand Replication In this mode, also called manual mode, replication occurs only when the user requests it explicitly. This is the default behavior when scheduled mode is chosen but no schedule is defined. This mode can be used, for example, when applying a certain patch to the system and the same information must immediately be replicated to the standby site.

Continuous Replication In this mode, the replication process happens continuously without any user intervention. As soon as the package successfully arrives at the target, the subsequent replication process automatically begins. This mode is preferred in cases where the target and source sites must always be synchronized. In Exalogic deployments, this mode is generally used for replication of WebLogic TLogs and JMS stores, which are business-critical to recovery in the event of a disaster.

In all of these modes, the underlying architecture is similar and the replication occurs asynchronously. For most types of data in Exalogic, scheduled replication is recommended. The following table lists the shares in a typical Exalogic deployment and indicates the suggested replication mode.

Project Name	Share Name	Replication Level	Replication Mode	Information
Middleware_1 (contain binaries and patches for middleware)	mw_home1	Project	Scheduled	Daily at 23:00
	soa_home1	Project	Scheduled	Daily at 23:00
	coherence_ home1	Project	Scheduled	Daily at 23:00
Configuration (contain domain_ homes, logs, persistence for applications)	domains	Share	Scheduled	Daily at 23:00
	admin	Share	Scheduled	Daily at 23:00
	logs	Share	Scheduled	Daily at 23:00
	jms_jta	Share	Continuous	
OS_x (contains OS level files for logs and dumps)	logs	Project	On-demand	
	dumps	Project	On-demand	

Storage Replication Channel

A storage replication channel is a network channel that is dedicated specifically to replication traffic between the Sun ZFS Storage appliances at the production site and the standby site. The Sun ZFS Storage appliance within Exalogic has four 1GbE ports (igb0, igb1, igb2, and igb3). The first two ports (igb0 and igb1) are used by the Sun ZFS Storage appliance internally for direct communication between the two storage heads. A replication channel can be created by connecting the unused ports (igb2 and igb3) to the corporate network in the datacenter and then creating a bonded interface using IP multipathing (IPMP). The use of a bonded interface protects the replication process from hardware faults within the network ports or from physical connection faults in the network. This bonded interface is dedicated for replication traffic and provides high availability for the storage replication channel.

Hostnames and Aliases

In a disaster recovery topology, the production site host names must be resolvable to the IP addresses of the corresponding peer systems at the standby site. This can be achieved by creating host name aliases in the /etc/host file. For example, edit the /etc/hosts file on compute node 1 at the production site and add the host name aliases for the apphosts, the client access network VIPs, and the private InfiniBand VIPs. The host names mapping can also be managed through the DNS configuration at the standby site.

Oracle Data Guard

Oracle Data Guard is another part of Oracle's disaster recovery solution prescribed by the MAA that protects mission-critical databases residing on the Exadata Database System. Data Guard is also used to maintain availability should any outage unexpectedly impact the production database and to minimize downtime during planned maintenance. Data Guard provides a comprehensive set of services that create, maintain, manage, and monitor one or more standby databases. It enables production Oracle databases to survive disasters and data corruptions. Data Guard maintains these standby databases as copies of the production database. Therefore, if the production database becomes unavailable because of a planned or an unplanned outage, Data Guard can switch any standby database to the production role, minimizing the downtime associated with the outage. Data Guard can be used with traditional backup, restoration, and cluster techniques to provide a high level of data protection and data availability.

As shown in Figure 4-22, Oracle Data Guard comes in two configurations: Data Guard and Active Data Guard. The Data Guard configuration asynchronously replicates the database redo log files to the standby site. This allows the standby site to be switched to the production instantaneously in an event of a disaster. The other configuration is Active Data Guard, which is used for replicating data to a secondary database within the same site, while

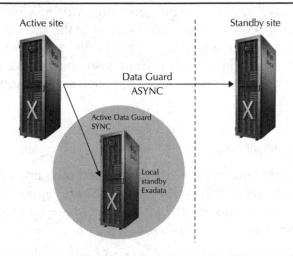

FIGURE 4-22. *Oracle Data Guard configurations*

also allowing other applications to read data from this secondary database. It is very useful for situations in which you want to run warehouse reports from the OLTP database but without affecting the actual production database.

MAA Best Practices

Some best practices should be considered while designing the MAA for the Exalogic platform. Some of these important considerations are listed here:

- Use the Sun ZFS Storage Appliance to replicate all non-database content and to ensure a small RTO and RPO for the Oracle Fusion Middleware environment.

- Store applications and their related middleware infrastructure within a project and replicate the project.

- Use the Scheduled mode of replication for a typical Oracle FMW DR deployment.

- Use the Continuous mode of replication if the standby site is required to be up to date irrespective of the rate of change at the primary site.

- Follow the disaster recovery procedure during switchover and fail-overs to ensure correct role reversal of the standby and primary sites. For example, after the switchover, the tape media and external ZFS storage should take backups from the new active site. This will enable much faster sync-back to the old primary during switchbacks and failbacks.

- Snapshots and clones can be used at the target site to create backup, test, and development environments.

- When configuring high availability within the same data center, consider setting SSL to off. Removing the encryption algorithm enables greater throughput between the sites when data transmission is across secure physical networks.

- It is recommended that you do not perform a rollback operation for any single share at either the primary or standby site, since this type of rollback invalidates the replication and a fresh replication will need to be initiated.

- Although arbitrary numbers of storage pools are supported, creating multiple pools with the same redundancy characteristics is not advised. Doing so will result in poor performance, suboptimal allocation of resources, artificial partitioning of storage, and additional administrative complexity. Configuring multiple pools on the same host is recommended only when drastically different redundancy or performance characteristics are desired; for example, a mirrored pool and a RAID-Z pool. With the ability to control access to log and cache devices on a per-share basis, the recommended mode of operation is a single pool.

- Use Virtual Hostnames for WebLogic Server listen-addresses to ensure that the domain configuration functions without additional network changes at the standby site. This recommendation is specific to an active/standby DR strategy. If you use floating virtual IP addresses instead of virtual DNS names or host names, you could end up having IP conflicts across the two sites. Or, even worse, you might have to change your WebLogic configuration as part of the switchover. For further details, refer to "Enterprise Deployment Guide" for Oracle Fusion Middleware.

Summary

In this chapter, we have discussed how to address various architectural aspects for successfully deploying Exalogic, including high availability, scalability, multi-tenancy, disaster recovery, and backup/recovery. The Exalogic machine comes with various configuration options to allow organizations to put together a very flexible and scalable solution. Exalogic and Exadata systems can be connected through the InfiniBand fabric to provide unparalleled transaction processing power in the data center. Exalogic lays the foundation for a cloud-based deployment across multiple sites to ensure resilience and to maximize availability.

This chapter showed you how to design your architecture on Exalogic and Exadata so that it addresses high availability, networking, virtualization, multi-tenancy, and other important non-functional requirements.

PART
II

Administration and Deployment for Oracle Exalogic Elastic Cloud

CHAPTER
5

Deploying Exalogic

t this point you should have a firm grasp of Oracle's vision for Exalogic, including its overall hardware and software architecture. You, too, may share this vision, and perhaps you've even purchased one or more Exalogic machines. But now it's time for the vision to meet reality. Does your data center meet all of the technical requirements and recommendations for Exalogic? What kinds of tasks are involved in deploying an Exalogic machine and making it ready to host applications? This chapter takes you through this deployment process step by step, from requirements analysis, to hardware installation, to network and storage configuration.

Oracle's Exalogic Installation Services

This guide is intended to familiarize you with the process of installing and configuring a new Exalogic rack. Using the combination of this book and the online documentation, a typical data center system administrator will be able to get Exalogic up and running. However, there are a significant number of initial configuration steps to perform and therefore significant opportunity for error. You've just spent a lot of money on this hardware, and you should strongly consider leaving these initial setup tasks to the experts at Oracle.

Oracle's Advanced Customer Support Services (ACS) group is responsible for accelerating customer deployments. Their job is to understand the IT requirements of your specific data center environment and to then initialize one or more Exalogic machines to exist optimally in this environment. Optionally, Oracle ACS can also design and implement an ongoing maintenance plan that's tailored to your needs. Consider utilizing Oracle ACS to reduce the potential risks associated with the adoption of a new infrastructure and to help accelerate the return on your new investment.

Facility Requirements

You'll need to perform many steps even before an Exalogic machine is delivered to your data center. Exalogic requires specific environmental considerations, such as available floor space, appropriate ventilation, temperature, and power. Exalogic also needs to be compatible with the existing network infrastructure in your data center. Although this book does include many of these specifications, you should always consult the latest online documentation and view the latest requirements. Refer to the "Exalogic Machine Owner's Guide."

Checklists

The "Exalogic Machine Owner's Guide" in the online documentation also includes an appendix named "Site Checklists," which is an invaluable reference when you're preparing for an Exalogic installation. As the name suggests, this appendix is an exhaustive list of questions pertaining to your data center environment. Use these checklists to ensure that you haven't accidentally overlooked some requirement.

Following are some examples of the types of questions that you can expect to encounter in the "Site Checklists" appendix:

- If more than one rack will be installed, was the cable upgrade kit ordered?

- Are all Exalogic machine racks adjacent to each other?

- Does the floor layout meet the equipment maintenance access requirements?

- Does the raised floor satisfy the weight requirements for the new hardware?

- Will the new hardware location require any non-standard cable lengths?

- Will the equipment be positioned so the exhaust air of one rack does not enter the air intake of another rack?

- Have you confirmed that all route incline angles are within the permitted range?

- Are enough power outlets provided within 2 meters of each rack?

Size and Weight

Remember that all Exalogic machines use the same type of rack hardware and therefore have the same space requirements. Following are the physical dimensions of a single rack:

- **Height** 1998 mm (78.66 inches)
- **Width** 600 mm (23.62 inches)
- **Depth** 1200 mm (47.24 inches)

The depth measurement includes the rack door handles, but these can be removed if required. Also keep in mind that these measurements do not include the packaging material in which the rack is shipped. For example, the height of the shipped rack is 2159 mm (85 inches), or 7 inches taller than the hardware itself. Therefore, the receiving area must be large enough to support this size. Whenever possible, Oracle recommends that the rack remain in its shipping container until it arrives at the actual installation site. But on the other hand, make sure that this site has enough space for you to remove and dispose of the packaging material.

A common mistake is to give all of your attention to the final installation site and ignore the access route from the loading dock to this location. Do all hallways and elevators support these dimensions? Similarly, will the rack need to be transported up or down any ramps? Exalogic is rated only for a maximum incline of six degrees.

The weight of a rack varies depending on the selected configuration and also whether or not the shipping container is included. Here are the specifications for the hardware only:

- **Eighth Rack** 399.133 kg (880 lbs)
- **Quarter Rack** 491.240 kg (1083 lbs)
- **Half Rack** 679.481 kg (1498 lbs)
- **Full Rack** 966.605 kg (2131 lbs)

If using a pallet jack to transport the container, the access route must also be able to support 1134 kg (2500 lbs) or more (hardware + shipping container + jack). Oracle recommends that the flooring at the installation site have a maximum allowable load of at least 1004.71 kg (2215 lbs). This value allows you to update to a full rack later if desired.

Another often-overlooked facility requirement is the space around the install location. To initialize and later upgrade and maintain the rack, Oracle recommends a setback of at least 914 mm (36 inches) in the front, rear, and top of each rack.

Temperature and Ventilation

By keeping Exalogic in its optimal temperature and humidity range, you greatly increase the longevity of all hardware components and minimize downtime due to component failures. Higher temperatures and humidity have been shown to cause corrosion and decrease overall performance. Very dry conditions (low humidity), on the other hand, can increase the likelihood of hardware issues due to static discharge in the air. An optimal Exalogic deployment site has the following traits:

- **Ambient temperature**   21–23 degrees Celsius (70–74 Fahrenheit)

- **Humidity**   45–50 percent, non-condensing

Exalogic can actually function properly in a much wider range of temperatures and humidity, as shown in the online documentation, but these values also provide a safety net should the data center cooling system fail.

Proper spacing around the machines facilitates future maintenance and also ensures proper airflow and cooling of the internal components. Fans within each node and switch direct cool air into the front of the rack, and the heated air leaves the rear of the rack. As mentioned earlier, Oracle recommends a setback of 914 mm (36 inches), particularly in the front and rear. But this also implies a minimum ceiling height of 2300 mm (90 inches). Heated air will rise, after all. In addition, unless you have purchased a full rack configuration, some portions of the rack will be empty. Be sure that these areas are covered with filler panels so that air continues to flow properly.

Cooled air is generally supplied to the data center via the floor using some form of vented tile. In the case of Exalogic, these floor tiles should ideally be located in front of the rack, as shown in Figure 5-1.

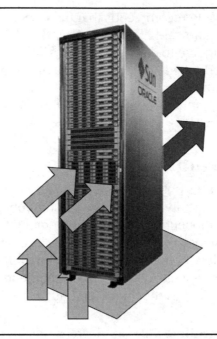

FIGURE 5-1. *Proper air flow for an Exalogic machine*

Power

The floor of your data center not only supplies cooled air but also typically provides the machine with electrical access. Remember that each Exalogic rack includes two power distribution units (PDUs), and these are found near the bottom of the rack. Depending on the selected Exalogic configuration, you can choose from either high or low voltage PDUs, from 15 kVA, 22 kVA, or 24 kVA PDUs, and also from either 1-phase or 3-phase PDUs. Consult your facilities manager to make sure that you select a type of PDU that is compatible with your building. All of the PDU options support a fairly wide range of power voltages and frequencies, but an important consideration is the distance to the power receptacle. The PDU cords are only 4 m (13.12 feet) long, and half of that is routed within the rack itself. Power receptacles are generally either located in the ceiling above the installation site or below the floor.

Network

You should conduct a detailed assessment of your network requirements as early as possible when planning an Exalogic deployment. Exalogic uses very modern networking technology, which may not be compatible with older data center equipment.

Each Exalogic rack includes two or more Quad Data Rate (QDR) InfiniBand (IB) Gateway Switches to bridge the internal Exalogic network to your existing client network. These switches include special gateway ports with quad small form-factor pluggable (QSFP) transceivers, so that cables (purchased separately) can be used to link Exalogic to a 10Gb Ethernet switch. The IB Gateway Switches do not support 1Gb Ethernet. Each switch provides up to eight 10GbE physical connections. Therefore, a full rack has 32 available links.

Although Oracle offers a selection of fiber-optic or copper cables that are compatible with the gateway ports on the Exalogic switches, customers are responsible for providing the necessary transceivers (SFP+, QSFP, or XFP) to link these cables to their existing 10Gb Ethernet network hardware. Cables are available in standard lengths up to 50 meters (copper up to 5m). Larger cables can be obtained from other vendors. At a minimum, each gateway switch in a rack should have one connection to your external 10Gb Ethernet switch. However, to meet bandwidth requirements, Oracle recommends at least two connections per gateway switch. Figure 5-2 depicts the cabling requirements for a full-rack Exalogic configuration.

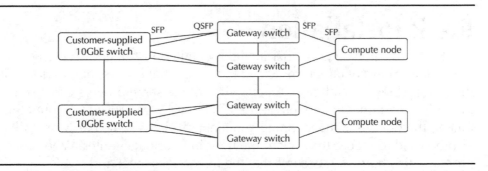

FIGURE 5-2. *Connecting your client network to an Exalogic full rack*

NOTE
If your external network supports only 1Gb Ethernet, you will require an additional intermediary switch that supports both 10Gb and 1Gb connections. Oracle offers a selection of switches that meet this requirement, or you can obtain this hardware from a third party.

The Exalogic management switch (Cisco Catalyst 4948) utilizes traditional 1Gb Ethernet connections. Oracle does not support using this management switch to route client or other external traffic into Exalogic. Instead its intended purpose is to do the following:

■ Provide administrative access to the host OS on the compute nodes (via Secure Shell [SSH] or other monitoring and management tools that you might be running in the wider data center management network).

■ Provide access to Exalogic-hosted administrative tools such as Integrated Lights Out Manager (ILOM) and those on the storage appliance.

■ Enable communication with other management and monitoring software such as Oracle Enterprise Manager.

Rack Installation

The Exalogic shipping container includes detailed instructions on removing the rack from its container, moving it to the installation site, and performing the physical rack installation. An overview of the same process can also be found in the online documentation. Special hardware is used to mount the rack to the bottom of the shipping container, and this same hardware will also be used to secure the rack to the floor in your data center. When used properly, this hardware ensures that the machine is level and stable.

After securing the rack, you must connect all of the PDU cables to your AC power source. Access the PDUs through the rear panel. Also be sure that all PDU circuit breakers are in the off position before plugging them into the available receptacles.

Although not strictly required at this point in the process, you can now use the procured 10Gb cables to connect the gateway switches to your data center client network, and also use the supplied 1Gb cables to connect the management switch to your management network. The online documentation includes reference tables and diagrams that depict all of the internal network connections within the rack itself, including those from the following:

■ Compute nodes to gateway switches

■ Compute nodes to management switches

■ Storage nodes to gateway switches

■ Storage nodes to management switches

■ PDUs to management switches

The following is an excerpt from the cabling table for a full rack's management network. Notice the uplink to the external management LAN.

From Rack Slot	Type of Equipment	From Port	To Cisco Switch Port	Part Description
N/A	External LAN	NET	1	10 ft. Blue Cat 5
N/A	PDU	NET	3	1M Grey Cat 5
U42	Compute Node	NET0	4	10 ft. Blue Cat 5

Multi-Rack Installation

When multiple Exalogic (and/or Exadata) racks are installed together, you will likely want them all to participate in the same private network. For example, this approach enables a WebLogic installation running on Exalogic to communicate with an Oracle Database running on Exadata over the InfiniBand fabric. For smaller rack configurations (eighth and quarter racks), this task may be as simple as interconnecting the InfiniBand Gateway Switches in each rack. But for larger configurations, there will not be enough available ports in the gateway switches, so you must also utilize the InfiniBand spine switches in each rack.

For convenience, each Exalogic machine is bundled with a spare cable kit containing several 5-meter InfiniBand cables. In fact, there are enough cables in these kits so that you can readily connect two full rack configurations to one another. Of course this assumes that the two racks are located in very close proximity to one another. Also note that in addition to cables, this same kit includes several spare hard disks and solid state disks for the compute nodes and the storage appliance.

A separate area of the online documentation, the "Multirack Cabling Guide," documents the process of linking together various combinations of Exalogic machines. This type of cabling work is somewhat of an art form and generally requires a specialized skill set (along with a very close attention to detail). Although the documentation is very thorough, you might consider employing Oracle ACS for these additional networking tasks.

Powering It On

After you have connected all of the power and network cables and then checked your work, you are ready to power on the machine for the first time. Switch on all of the PDU circuit breakers in the rear of the rack. During the next 60 seconds or so, the service processors on the compute nodes and storage nodes will boot and the nodes will be placed in standby mode. You can verify this by the blinking power LED found on the front of each node, as shown in Figure 5-3. At this point, power is not yet supplied to the remainder of the nodes' components, such as the CPUs.

Unlike the nodes, the network switches do not have external power buttons. The act of supplying power to the rack (via the breakers) automatically powers on the switches. So before continuing any further, you should quickly verify that power has been supplied to all of the InfiniBand Gateway Switches

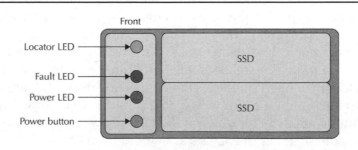

FIGURE 5-3. *LED panel on an Exalogic compute node*

(and the spine switch for multi-rack installations) as well as to the Cisco management switch. In fact, it's a good idea to wait a few minutes to allow them to complete their startup operations.

Next locate the power buttons on the nodes. They are found near the standby LEDs. Power on the nodes in the following order:

1. Power on the two storage nodes.

2. Wait a few minutes for the storage appliance to boot.

3. Power on all of the compute nodes.

When a node has been powered on, the power LED will turn a solid green. Although not a common occurrence, if you ever need to power down an entire rack, perform these steps in reverse order (compute nodes, storage nodes, PDUs). Nodes can be powered off by pressing the same power button or by remotely accessing the node's ILOM interface (via SSH or a web browser).

Connecting a Laptop to Exalogic

To initialize the network settings of the compute nodes or to install a different operating system on the compute nodes (Solaris, for example), you need to access the rack's management network. However, the management switch's default configuration is unlikely to be compatible with your data center's network configuration. Therefore, until the management switch is properly configured, you will need to connect a laptop directly to the switch to perform work on the compute nodes. You have two connectivity options:

- Connect your laptop's Ethernet port to one of the available Ethernet ports on the management switch.

- Connect your laptop's serial or USB port to the DB9 serial port on the management switch. A USB/DB9 serial cable is included with your Exalogic installation kit.

Later, this chapter will describe the default factory network settings of all of the Exalogic components. Until these network settings have been properly configured and integrated into your existing networks, you will need to use these default IP addresses. To get started, assign your laptop a static IP address on the default 192.168.1.*x* management subnet (192.168.1.150, for example).

Default Security Settings

All devices in Exalogic include a default root user account, including the compute node's base operating system and ILOM, the storage appliance, and the switches. At the factory, the password for all of these root accounts is typically set to "welcome1". As part of the initial setup of your new machine, be sure to modify these root credentials. You'll also probably want to create additional non-root users to support the administration of different types of middleware and application environments.

Selecting an Operating System

Recall that currently you can select from one of three operating system images for Exalogic compute nodes:

- Oracle Linux
- Oracle Solaris
- Oracle VM Server (hypervisor used to run Oracle Linux guest VMs)

At the factory, compute nodes are preloaded with the Exalogic Linux base image. This Linux image is an enhanced version of the standard Linux installation. In fact, all of these OS options have been specifically configured for and tuned against Exalogic's hardware and network environment. They also include InfiniBand-capable drivers and other Exalogic-specific configuration and diagnostic tools.

If you wish to re-image the compute nodes with either Solaris or OVM Server, you must download the corresponding Exalogic base image and follow the installation steps found in the Exalogic online documentation. Keep in mind that Oracle supports only homogenous OS deployments, meaning that all compute nodes within the same rack must have identical base OS images. All of these platforms support some form of distributed and automated installation, so you need not go through a completely manual process to update each compute node.

For Solaris-based Exalogic installations, you must also download to your laptop Oracle VM VirtualBox as well as a special Oracle VM appliance that you run in VirtualBox. This appliance runs Oracle's Solaris Automated Installer (AI) software for Exalogic. To trigger each Solaris installation, the compute nodes are rebooted in Preboot Execution Environment (PXE) mode and directed to the AI VM running on your laptop. The compute nodes make use of the storage appliance and NFS to access the Solaris installation files during the automated installation process.

Network Configuration

After your Exalogic machine has been successfully powered on, the next major task is to update the network settings on the nodes and switches so that Exalogic can interface with your management and client access networks. Many steps are required to complete this task, but scripts are available to help automate most of them. At a high level, you must do the following:

1. Use the Exalogic Configuration Utility to update all compute nodes and the storage appliance.

2. Update the settings for the Cisco management switch.

3. Create virtual network interface cards (vNICs) on the Sun gateway switches.

4. Configure virtual LANs (vLANs) on the Sun gateway switches if needed.

Keep in mind that if you have purchased an installation service package from Oracle ACS, all of these steps will be performed for you. Even if that's the case, it's still important that you familiarize yourself with Exalogic's internal networking implementation. As you will see in the following sections, it's certainly not as trivial as plugging in a few cables.

NOTE
Deploying Exalogic may seem like a very detailed process, but keep in mind that all of these same tasks would also be necessary on a non-engineered system to provide adequate performance and redundancy. However, with Exalogic, Oracle has already engineered and thoroughly tested these settings.

Whoever is responsible for this work will require several inputs from you regarding your existing network infrastructure, including the following:

■ Management IP address ranges and subnet masks

■ Location of your Domain Name Service (DNS)

■ Location of your Network Time Protocol (NTP) server

The Exalogic online documentation includes a set of tables called network configuration worksheets. The worksheets inventory all of the information that you will need as you configure the Exalogic networks.

Default Factory Settings

Another valuable asset in the online documentation is a list of the default network settings that are preconfigured on a newly installed rack. First, the compute nodes, storage nodes, gateway switches, and PDUs are all set up to use a default management network. This network is often referred to as the ILOM network, because it can be used to access the service processors on the compute nodes and storage nodes. But it's also used to access the management interfaces of the switches and PDUs as well. The default ILOM network is configured as follows:

■ **Starting IP address**   192.168.1.101

■ **Subnet mask**   255.255.252.0

Next, recall that the compute node service processors are configured for "sideband" management, meaning that both the host OS and ILOM are bound to this same management network. This configuration allows the OS as well as custom applications running on a compute node to be remotely monitored and administered. This network is often referred to as either NET0 (the name of the physical Ethernet port) or ETH0 (the name of the corresponding interface on the Linux host OS). It is part of the same subnet as the ILOM network but uses a different range of addresses:

- **IP address range**   192.168.1.1-100

- **Subnet mask**   255.255.252.0

Finally, the compute and storage nodes are also configured to use a default private InfiniBand network, via the gateway switches. This network is intended for internal communication between different applications on the compute nodes, and also for compute nodes to access the storage appliance. It is usually referred to as BOND0, which is the default name of this network interface on Linux. For a single-rack installation, this network is non-routable and will not be linked to another external network. Therefore, the default configuration is often sufficient:

- **Starting IP address**   192.168.10.1

- **Subnet mask**   255.255.255.0

TIP
To accommodate future multi-rack installations, consider changing the default private network IP addresses to ensure that each Exalogic and Exadata component in the private IB network has a unique IP address and shares the same subnet. For example, if you know that this new Exalogic machine will be connected to an existing Exadata machine, consider changing the start IP address to 192.168.10.51.

Note that a newly installed Exalogic machine has no default network interfaces on the compute nodes for the client access network. As you will see later, these external network interfaces must be explicitly created on the gateway switches (vNICs) and also explicitly bonded on the compute nodes (BOND1).

Although these factory settings are described in the documentation, this same information is also available in another location. If you access one of the compute nodes, locate and view the text file /etc/exalogic.conf. It also lists all of the default IP addresses and host names for the compute nodes and storage nodes.

Exalogic Configuration Utility

Individually updating the network parameters on each compute node and storage node would be very tedious, time consuming, and error prone. Instead, Oracle provides the Exalogic Configuration Utility (ECU), which is a set of tools that are freely available for download. To use ECU, you must download it to a laptop and connect this laptop to your newly installed rack, as described earlier.

NOTE
ECU is certified to update only a rack that is currently configured with all of its factory settings. Oracle does not support using this tool to reconfigure a rack that has already been modified.

ECU consists of two main components: a spreadsheet document and a collection of shell scripts. Open and edit the input document using the OpenOffice application (http://www.openoffice.org). The spreadsheet relies on several custom macros, so you will also need to enable macros in OpenOffice. This document prompts you to enter values for all of the previously mentioned network parameters. These values will override any default factory settings. Enter the following types of information:

- Rack configuration type (eighth, quarter, half, or full)

- IP addresses of DNS and NTP servers

- Local region and time zone

- Starting IP addresses, subnet masks, and gateway addresses for the compute nodes' ILOM, NET0, BOND0, and BOND1 networks

- Starting IP addresses, subnet masks, and gateway addresses for the storage nodes' ILOM, NET0, and BOND0 networks

- IP addresses for the switches' and PDUs' management interfaces (ILOM network)

The spreadsheet also allows you to customize the host names assigned to each generated network interface, if desired. You can supply a combination of machine name, name prefixes, and name suffixes. The machine name is used to begin each host name. Consider the following example:

- Machine name = "exl10"

- Compute node prefix = "cn"

- Private network suffix = "-priv"

Given these settings, ECU would set the first compute node's management host name to "exl10cn01" and its private host name to the value "exl10cn01-priv".

The document includes a Save button that generates a text file named exalogic_deploy.conf. You must upload this file along with the ECU scripts to one of the compute nodes, and at the location /opt/exalogic/one-command ("One Command" is the former name of ECU). For the purpose of using ECU, this chosen compute node is referred to as the "master" node. You are then ready to run the ExalogicOC.sh script on this master node. The ECU script takes a single parameter—the step number to perform. For example, here's how to perform step one:

```
./ExalogicOC.sh -s 1
```

At the time this was written, there were 32 steps to execute. Each step generates a separate log file for troubleshooting purposes. At a high level, ECU does the following:

- Checks that all hardware can be reached on the management network

- Distributes the ECU script files to all compute nodes

- Checks that the versions of the firmware and OS are supported

- Checks that IB network cabling was done correctly and that there are no connectivity issues

- Updates the ILOM and OS network settings on all compute nodes and storage nodes

- Updates the management network settings on the InfiniBand Gateway Switches

- Checks that all hardware can be reached using the updated settings

- Updates the NTP settings on all compute nodes and storage nodes

Chapters 3 and 4 introduced the concept of active-passive bonding on the InfiniBand network. Recall that each compute node has two physical IB ports for high availability. On Linux, ECU creates a bonded interface that spans these two ports and assigns it a single IP address. On Solaris, ECU creates an IP multipath (IPMP) group to achieve the same effect. Specifically, ECU creates two of these bonded interfaces on each compute node: BOND0 for the private network and BOND1 for the client network. Figure 5-4 illustrates these tasks.

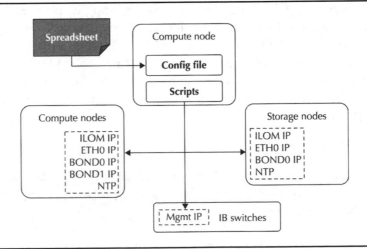

FIGURE 5-4. *Exalogic Configuration Utility tasks*

The ECU is certainly a major time-saver, but it does not automate all of the required setup tasks. It does initialize the IB Gateway Switches, but it does not initialize the Cisco management switch nor the IB spine switch. Nor does it perform the complete setup of the 10Gb client access network. And although ECU updates the storage appliance's network configuration, it does not perform other necessary changes to the default storage projects. The remainder of this chapter concentrates on these other manual tasks.

Management Switch

The management switch being the only non-Oracle hardware component in Exalogic, it's assumed that customers will refer to Cisco's online documentation for a complete walkthrough of its available features and setup procedures. As a result, this section describes only the basic configuration steps. In some cases, these steps alone may be sufficient in meeting your requirements.

To integrate the Cisco switch in Exalogic with your management network, connect a laptop to the switch's serial port. The default serial port settings are 9600 baud, 8 bits, no parity, 1 stop bit, and no handshake. After logging into a terminal session, provide the switch with an IP address, subnet mask, and gateway that's compatible with your existing management LAN. You can also specify the host name. Here's an example:

```
enable
configure terminal
interface vlan 1
ip address 10.100.1.50 255.255.255.0
end
no ip routing
ip default-gateway 10.100.1.1
hostname exl10ethsw01
end
write memory
```

Next, you need to set the location of your DNS and NTP servers, just as you did earlier when using the ECU. Here's an example:

```
configure terminal
ip domain-name example.com
ip name-server 10.100.1.5
clock timezone EST -5
ntp server 10.100.1.6
end
write memory
```

Finally, apply all of the changes you made:

```
copy running-config startup-config
exit
```

vNICs on Gateway Switches

Each gateway switch in a rack must be configured with at least one vNIC for each compute node that wants to communicate with an external 10Gb Ethernet network (Ethernet over InfiniBand). The vNIC maps one of the 10Gb connections to a MAC address on a compute node. This MAC address does not map to a real physical port on the compute node, however. Although this vNIC approach adds some initial complexity, you also gain a great deal of flexibility. As your middleware topology changes within Exalogic, you can reroute external traffic without touching a network cable. For high availability, Oracle recommends that you create two of these vNICs for a single compute node, and on different gateway switches.

First, you must prepare a list of virtual MAC addresses to use for your vNICs. Each MAC address must be unique. Then you must gather some information about the links between the compute node and the gateway switches. Each physical link in the IB network has a numeric link ID, or LID. Similarly, each physical port has a globally unique ID, or GUID. Figure 5-5 shows the relationships between MACs, LIDs, and GUIDs.

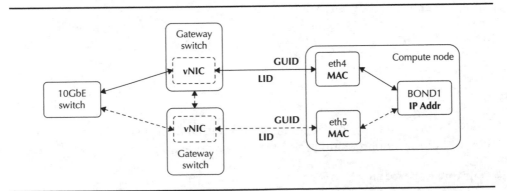

FIGURE 5-5. *VNICs on the IB gateway switches*

Access the compute node, and as the root user, run the following script:

```
iblinkinfo.pl -R | grep <compute_node_hostname>
```

The output includes the LID of each switch to which the specified node is connected. Now run the following utility:

```
ibstat
```

This tool outputs the GUID for each of the two compute node's IB ports. It also displays the LID associated with each GUID. But how do you know which switch corresponds to this LID? Run the following to view the host name associated with each switch LID:

```
ibswitches
```

You now can connect to a specific switch using its host name and create a vNIC for a specific GUID on a compute node. But you need one final piece of data: the name of the 10Gb Ethernet connection on the switch for which you want to create the vNIC. Access the switch using SSH. The default username is root. After logging in, run this command to view the name and status of each of the eight gateway ports:

```
listlinkup | grep Bridge
```

If you did not cable the gateway ports yourself, you may need to seek advice from your network administrator as to which 10Gb port ("connector") to use. Finally, you are ready to create a vNIC; the syntax is as follows:

```
createvnic <connector> -guid <compute_node_guid> -mac <mac_address> -pkey default
```

A typical invocation would resemble the following:

```
createvnic 0A-ETH-1  guid 00:21:28:d0:a2:c0:a0  mac a2:c0:a0:a8.1.1  pkey default
```

Now SSH to the other gateway switch that is connected to your compute node and repeat this command. However, this time use the GUID for the node's second IB port, and also specify a different MAC address.

NOTE
*On Linux the **ibstat** command lists the GUIDs for each IB port. On Solaris this same information can be obtained using the **dladm** command. The rest of the steps are identical on both platforms.*

Remember that these **createvnic** commands were run on the IB switches and not on the compute nodes. You do not need to explicitly create a new network interface on the compute node for these vNICs—they are automatically detected by the host OS (they appear as physical Ethernet NICs to the host). However, just as with the BOND0 interface, you must now define a new bonded network interface (or IPMP group) on the compute node that exposes these two vNICs as a single interface to applications (and a single IP address). Oracle refers to this bonded interface as BOND1.

The following BOND1 example uses Linux. Create a configuration file for each of the new network interfaces (/etc/sysconfig/network-scripts/ifcfg-eth4, for example). Do not specify an IP address; instead, indicate that it is a slave interface and provide the name of the bonded (master) interface:

```
DEVICE=eth4
HWADDR=a2:c0:a0:a8.1.1
MASTER=bond1
SLAVE=yes
```

Ensure that the MAC address in this file matches the one used to create the vNIC on the switch. Now create the configuration file /etc/sysconfig/network-scripts/ifcfg-bond1 and assign an available IP address from your client network:

```
DEVICE=bond1
IPADDR=10.11.12.13
NETMASK=255.255.255.0
```

Congratulations! You have connected one compute node to your client network. Repeat this process for all other compute nodes that require connectivity to your client network. If you have multiple external 10Gb networks connected to the gateway switches, it may also be necessary to repeat this entire process on the same compute node. Another scenario in which this may become necessary is the use of vLANs, which is discussed next. In either case, the compute node would be configured with multiple EoIB bonded interfaces (BOND1 and BOND2, for example).

vLANs on Gateway Switches

Many IT organizations employ the use of virtual local area networks, or vLANs, in their Ethernet networks. vLANs allow you to divide a single IP subnet into logical groups that are assigned different numeric vLAN IDs.

Members of the same vLAN can communicate with one another but not with other vLANs. For example, you might want to isolate development traffic from production traffic, or separate traffic for different business units. vLAN IDs are assigned to the individual physical connections on an Ethernet switch, which then enforce these vLAN boundaries.

If your client access network utilizes vLANs, then you must do some additional configuration on the Exalogic IB Gateway Switches in order for them to participate in the vLANs. One or more vLANs can be assigned to a physical 10Gb Ethernet connection on a gateway switch. Access the switch via SSH and then use the **createvlan** command, which uses this syntax:

```
createvlan <connector> -vlan <vlan_id> -pkey default
```

This example tags the 0A-ETH-1 gateway port with the vLAN ID 100:

```
createvlan 0A-ETH-1 -vlan 100 -pkey default
```

You can also assign vLANs to particular vNICs that are associated with a gateway port. This gives you the ability to have different compute nodes be members of different vLANs, while still sharing the same physical uplink to your client network. Simply specify the vLAN ID when creating the vNIC:

```
createvnic 0A-ETH-1 -guid 00:21:28:d0:a2:c0:a0 -mac a2:c0:a0:a8.1.1 -vlan 100
-pkey default
```

Multi-Rack Configuration

Earlier you learned that when installing multiple racks, the IB spine switches are used to link the racks together. As a result, the racks may communicate with each other over the same high-speed InfiniBand network. After you complete the task of cabling the spine and gateway switches together, you must also do some additional configuration tasks on the switches so that they can properly interact with one another.

All IB switches support a software process called the Subnet Manager. The Subnet Manager is responsible for discovering the topology of the IB fabric, for calculating the different routes in the network, and for distributing this information to other switches in the network. If multiple Subnet Managers are running within the same network, one is elected as the master and the remaining ones are placed on standby. Therefore if the master switch fails, another Subnet Manager is automatically promoted to be the new master.

This nomination process is determined using numeric priorities that are assigned to each switch.

In environments with a single Exalogic machine, the spine switch is not connected and therefore the Subnet Manager runs on one of the gateway switches, and each gateway switch can have the same priority. For a multi-rack environment, however, the Subnet Manager should run on the spine switches and also be assigned a higher priority. SSH into each spine switch and run the following commands:

```
disablesm
setsmpriority 8
enablesm
```

Next, access each gateway switch and disable the Subnet Manager:

```
disablesm
```

Storage Configuration

The Exalogic storage appliance is the primary storage device for your compute nodes. Use it to store product installations, server configurations, and applications. Although the storage appliance supports a variety of protocols, Oracle recommends that compute nodes access the storage appliance through NFS remote file systems. You can create these shared file systems and control access to them by using the appliance's browser user interface (BUI) or its SSH command line interface.

Default Factory Settings

The ECU is responsible for updating the network settings for the storage appliance based on your supplied inputs. At this stage the storage nodes should be accessible via the private and management networks. To access the BUI (shown in Figure 5-6), direct your browser to the management IP or host name of one of the storage nodes, and specify port 215. Here's an example:

```
http://exl10sn01:215
```

By default, the storage appliance has a single storage pool named exalogic. It includes all of the disks in the storage array, although only 18 of them are active at a time and the remaining two are treated as hot spares.

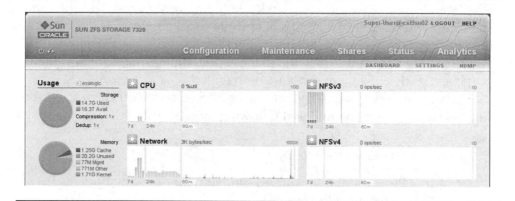

FIGURE 5-6. *ZFS storage appliance home page and top-level menu*

The 18 data disks utilize a mirrored configuration, meaning that disks are allocated in pairs (one active and one backup). Oracle does not support any modifications to the storage pool for an Exalogic configuration.

You may recall from earlier chapters that shared file systems on the storage appliance are organized into logical projects. Unless a property is explicitly overridden for a share, it inherits the settings from its parent project. For example, if a project is flagged as read-only, then by default all of the shares within that project are also read-only. A share can be a member of only a single project. At the factory, several projects and shares are predefined within the appliance, as shown here:

Project	Share
Default	*none*
Common	general
	images
	patches
NODE_1, NODE_2, . . . NODE_n n = 30 for a full rack	general
	dumps

At the factory, the only share that is populated with any files is common/ images. It contains a copy of the base Linux image for Exalogic, should you ever need to reimage a compute node. As the names suggest, the common shares are intended for data that's accessible to all compute nodes, while the NODE_*x* shares are intended for data that is specific to a single node. Future Exalogic revisions may utilize these predefined shares for specific purposes, so deleting them is not recommended.

Each of these projects is configured for NFS access. You can view these settings by accessing the BUI and following these steps:

1. Click Shares on the top menu.

2. Click Projects from the Shares submenu (or open the Projects Panel on the left side of the screen).

3. Mouse over the name of a project and click the Edit icon (a pencil).

4. Click Protocols.

Figure 5-7 shows some of the available protocol settings for a project. You can control access to shares in several ways, depending on the protocols in use. For NFS, you can configure NFS exceptions, which limit access based on client IP address or host name. In the case of

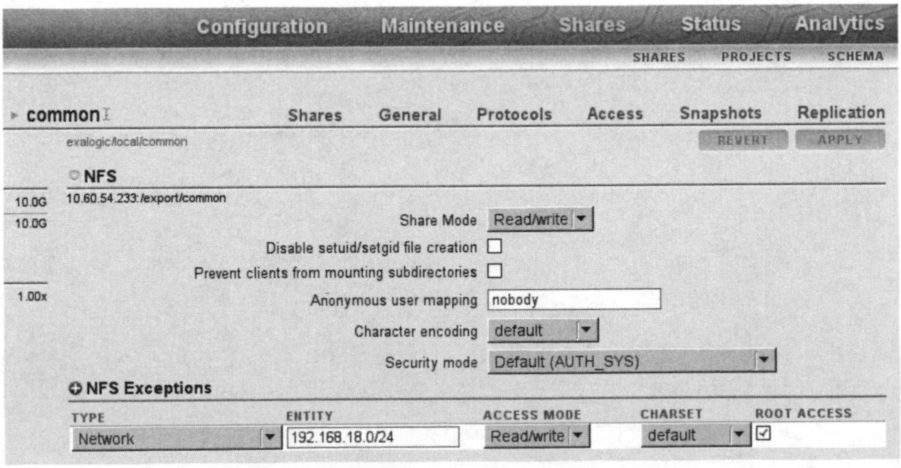

FIGURE 5-7. *Editing the protocols for a project on the ZFS storage appliance*

Exalogic, compute nodes are the only storage clients and they access the appliance via the private IB network. You can either specify individual addresses within this subnet or alternatively use CIDR notation to identify multiple addresses. For example, the value 192.168.10.0/24 identifies all addresses in the range 192.168.10.0–192.168.10.255 (the equivalent of a 255.255.255.0 subnet mask).

If you previously used the ECU to modify the compute nodes' default IP addresses on the private (BOND0) network, you will need to modify these NFS exceptions. Otherwise, the compute nodes will be denied access to these shares. If you prefer to work from the command line, you can also make these changes by logging into the appliance over SSH. The following commands modify an existing project:

```
shares
select NODE_1
set sharenfs="sec=sys,rw,root=192.168.18.0/24"
commit
quit
```

Creating Custom Projects and Shares

Although you can certainly make use of these default shares for your middleware storage needs, you can also create your own custom project hierarchy. Refer to Chapter 4 for Oracle's suggested storage organization for Fusion Middleware deployments. To create a new project, follow these steps:

1. Click Shares on the top menu.

2. Click Projects from the Shares submenu.

3. Click the Add icon (plus sign).

4. Type a name for the new project and click Apply.

5. Click General.

6. Enter a base Mountpoint path for the project. Oracle recommends the format /export/<project_name>. Edit other settings as desired and click Apply.

7. Click Protocols.

8. Edit the NFS settings as desired, including NFS exceptions.

You can then add one or more new shares to this project:

1. After selecting a project, click its Shares tab.

2. Ensure that Filesystems is selected (not LUNs) and click the Add icon (plus sign).

3. Name the new share. Confirm that the Inherit Mountpoint checkbox is selected and click Apply.

4. If desired, override any default properties in the parent project under General or Protocols.

By default, the mountpoint for a share is the concatenation of the parent project's mountpoint and the name of the share: /export/*<project_name>*/*<share_name>*. Once again, these same tasks can also be accomplished from the command line interface. Here's an example:

```
shares
project Dept_HR
set mountpoint="/export/Dept_HR"
commit
select Dept_HR
filesystem domains
commit
quit
```

Mounting File Systems

On each compute node that requires access to a shared file system, you will need to update the OS file system table and then mount the file system using NFS. But first, create a local directory to which the share will be mounted—for example, /u01/domains. Next, add an entry to the file system table. On Linux, edit the file /etc/fstab and add the following line:

```
<storage_host>:<mountpoint> /u01/domains nfs4
rw,bg,hard,nointr,rsize=131072,wsize=131072
```

Here, *<storage_host>* is the host name of the storage appliance on the private network. By default it is el01sn-priv. *<mountpoint>* is the share mountpoint that you configured on the storage appliance.

On Solaris, edit /etc/vfstab and add the equivalent settings:

```
<storage_host>:<mountpoint> /u01/domains nfs yes
rw,bg,hard,nointr,rsize=131072,wsize=131072,vers=4
```

To perform the actual NFS mount on either platform, use the **mount** command:

```
mount -a
```

Fusion Middleware Installation

At this stage, your Exalogic machine has been officially initialized and is ready to begin hosting applications, including those built on Oracle Fusion Middleware. Due to the shared storage architecture of Exalogic, you can use one compute node to install a piece of software once, and then access this same installation from other compute nodes. Of course, you may still be required to install the same software multiple times if different nodes require different versions of it.

Earlier chapters included specific best practices regarding the installation and configuration of FMW on Exalogic. You can also refer to the "Enterprise Deployment Guide" in the Exalogic online documentation. The "Enterprise Deployment Guide" currently focuses on the core FMW infrastructure such as WebLogic Server, Web Tier, and Coherence. But similar deployment guides are available in the online documentation of other FMW and application products, such as Service-Oriented Architecture (SOA), Web Center, Identity Management, and Fusion Apps.

Although the exact installation steps will vary from product to product, most FMW products employ a similar installation process and have a common look and feel. In addition, FMW installers tend to support graphical, command line, and silent modes. To perform a graphical installation, you will need to access the compute node by using some desktop sharing software such as NX or VNC.

Here some other general guidelines regarding FMW installations on Exalogic:

- Download a Linux or Solaris 64-bit installer.

- Place the installer on shared storage (via a compute node).

- Do not install as root ("oracle" is the recommended username).

- Set your middleware home directory to some location on a mounted NFS share.

The following example demonstrates the installation of WebLogic Server in graphical mode. WLS installers are available for specific platforms, and each includes a platform-specific, 64-bit copy of the Java Developer Kit (JDK). If instead you download the WLS "generic" installer, you will need to install the prerequisite JDK separately. Note that a WLS installation also includes a copy of Coherence by default.

First, launch the installer:

```
./wls1036_linux64.bin
```

Next, enter a root Middleware Home directory in which you want to place WLS. Refer to Figure 5-8.

By default, all components of WebLogic Server and Coherence are installed, except for the Java code examples. Consider the Custom option if you are creating an installation for development purposes. Refer to Figure 5-9.

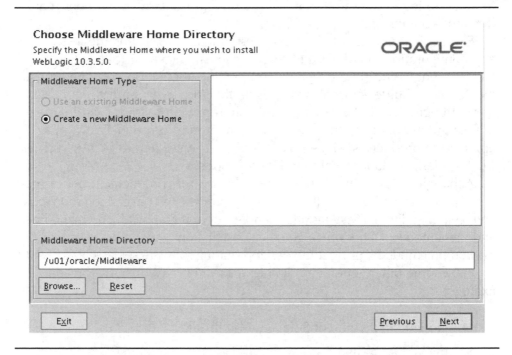

FIGURE 5-8. *Selecting a Middleware Home during the WebLogic Server installer*

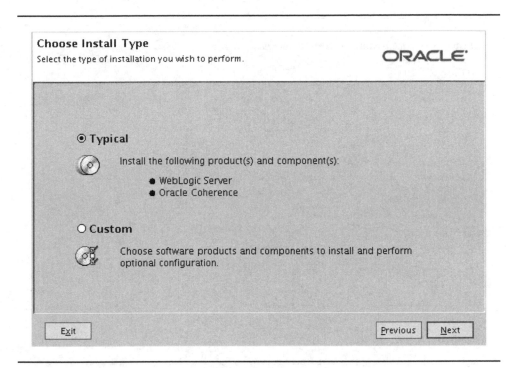

FIGURE 5-9. *Selecting an installation type for WebLogic Server*

Next, you may modify the default root directory names used for WLS
and Coherence if desired, as shown in Figure 5-10.

The installation will then begin. For most Fusion Middleware
deployments, one of your next tasks will likely be running the Fusion
Middleware Configuration Wizard tool, which is included in your
WLS installation. Remember that this Configuration Wizard is used to
initialize a new WebLogic domain configuration that will support one
or more products. Refer to Chapter 3 for more about domains, servers,
clusters, node managers, and so on. You can launch the wizard from
the common/bin folder of your root WLS installation directory:

```
./config.sh
```

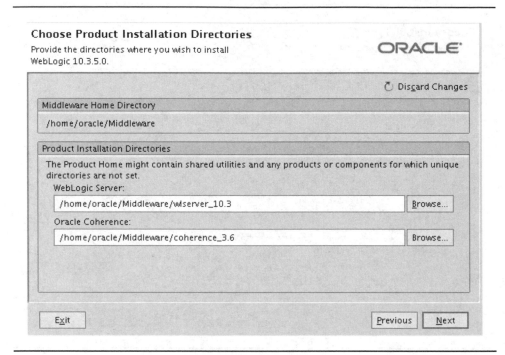

FIGURE 5-10. *Selecting destination folder names during the WebLogic Server installer*

Summary

Deploying Exalogic involves a significant amount of planning. Your data center facility must meet Exalogic's space, weight, power, cooling, and network requirements. Fortunately, the online documentation includes various checklists and worksheets to help you evaluate these requirements and prepare for the machine's arrival. Upon arrival, the rack must be physically installed in the data center and cabled together. Then you can power on the machine for the first time and connect a laptop to the factory-configured management network.

The primary reason for accessing the machine in this way is to run the Exalogic Configuration Utility. Input your network specifications into a supplied spreadsheet, and this tool will then update the corresponding network settings on each node to match these specifications. Some additional network configuration tasks must be performed manually, however, including the setup of the management switch and the client access network. The latter task involves the creation of vNICs and vLANs on the gateway switches as well as the corresponding network interfaces and bonds on the compute nodes. After the network setup is complete, you're ready to configure the storage appliance. Define projects, shared file systems, and access rights to meet the storage requirements of your middleware applications.

Additional deployment steps are required if multiple racks are installed together. The proper cabling needs to be performed using the spine switches, and the IB subnet manager on the switches may require additional configuration. Given the relative complexity of an entire Exalogic installation process, you might choose to take advantage of the Installation Service offered by Oracle ACS, particularly if your organization is new to these technologies.

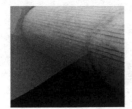

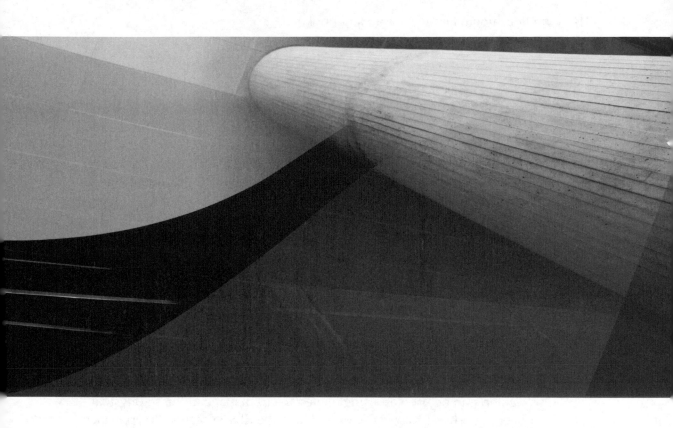

CHAPTER
6

Exalogic
Administration

 ow that you understand how to deploy an Exalogic system in your data center, it is important that you also understand how to administer the Exalogic system. Several tools are available for managing and monitoring the Exalogic system. This chapter describes these tools and Oracle Enterprise Manager to show how they form part of routine operational and administrative tasks.

In addition to reading the advice in this chapter, the administrator should refer to the "Exalogic Machine Owner's Guide." If the administrator chooses to use Oracle Enterprise Manager for application and data center management, he or she should also refer to Oracle Enterprise Manager help guides.

Managing and Monitoring Exalogic

The Exalogic machine has a number of physical components that have embedded management control features, called Integrated Lights Out Management (ILOM). The Oracle Enterprise Manager Operations Center (Ops Center) can be used as a single interface to manage all these physical components, such as Exalogic compute nodes, the ZFS Storage 7320 appliance, and the Network QDR InfiniBand Switches.

Using Oracle Enterprise Manager

Oracle Enterprise Manager is typically installed on other hardware in the data center, connecting to the Exalogic machine over the management LAN to perform the management and monitoring tasks. Oracle Enterprise Manager has the following important features that provide benefits beyond the basic capabilities of the individual ILOM interfaces:

- Integrated Management Tool, a single tool for the entire stack, from application level down to hardware components (also known as "application to disk")

- Software provisioning and imaging that also covers firmware, operating systems, middleware, and applications

- Monitoring and end-to-end diagnostics with hardware alarms, service levels, and root cause analysis

- Configuration management, including change tracking and automation

- Lifecycle management for both hardware and software

- Patch automation and patch compliance checking

- Remote management and telemetry

- Management of InfiniBand fabric and Ethernet networks

- Complete topological view of hardware assets

- Energy utilization and impact analysis

- Oracle support site integration with the ability to raise instant service requests to Oracle Support

Oracle Enterprise Manager provides capabilities to manage and monitor both hardware and software. It is divided into two tools: Cloud Control and Ops Center. The Cloud Control tool is focused on application and software management such as management of operating system, Fusion Middleware, database, and Fusion Applications, whereas Ops Center is focused on data center management such as discovery and management of physical assets. Enterprise Manager also integrates with Oracle Support, making it a complete engineered system management tool. Figure 6-1 shows the complete ecosystem of Oracle Enterprise Manger.

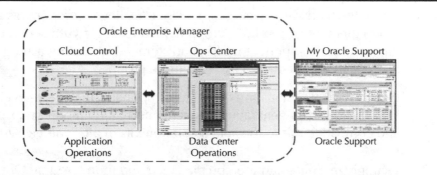

FIGURE 6-1. *Oracle Enterprise Manager ecosystem*

Oracle Enterprise Manager allows administrators to track dependencies in Exalogic's hardware and software topology. It also provides health checks and continuous validation of Exalogic optimizations against configuration best practices. Integration with Oracle Support enables it to alert the administrator with patch bundle recommendations. In the next few sections, we will focus on the use of the Ops Center tool to administer Exalogic.

Discovering Exalogic Components Using Ops Center

To use Ops Center for managing the Exalogic machine, some specific steps should be performed:

1. Install Oracle Enterprise Manager Ops Center on dedicated hardware in the data center.

2. Ensure that Ops Center can connect to the same management LAN as Exalogic.

3. Log in to the web console of Ops Center.

4. Discover the hardware components of Exalogic based on the IP address through the custom discovery page in the asset discovery section.

5. Enter one or more IP addresses of all the components within the Exalogic system to scan. These can be entered as a comma-separated list, an IP address range specified by (starting address)–(end address), or a subnet specified by (network address).

6. Verify the hardware assets discovered as Exalogic components and group them into a top-level group named Exalogic with subgroups for switches, component nodes, and storage by creating asset groups and assigning discovered assets to these groups.

7. Perform a final verification of all the components in the top-level Exalogic group by generating a system information report on Exalogic and comparing this to the actual components in the Exalogic system.

The Exalogic machine can then be managed and monitored by Oracle Enterprise Manager Ops Center and visualized in the Ops Center console as a set of components under the Exalogic group.

Management Users and Roles

Oracle Enterprise Manager Ops Center can be configured with users from the local operating system or from an external Lightweight Directory Access Protocol (LDAP) provider. Each user can be given a different role that grants or denies access to the different capabilities of Oracle Enterprise Manager. You can view the existing users from the Users tab of the user administration section in the Ops Center console. You can view the roles of existing users from the Roles tab of the Administration section.

A user with the "Enterprise Controller Admin" role is known as an Oracle Enterprise Manager Ops Center *super user.* The super user can perform any action within Oracle Enterprise Manager Ops Center, including updating the Ops Center software itself and modifying or removing other users and roles. A user with the "All Assets Admin" role can perform any action, such as discovery, OS provisioning, or firmware provisioning for any asset. However, such a user cannot modify or remove other users, update the Ops Center software, or perform actions that directly affect the Oracle Enterprise Manager Ops Center infrastructure.

Assets managed by the Ops Center can be configured to generate notifications when user-defined criteria are met. For example, a compute node could be set to generate a notification if its temperature climbs too high. Notification profiles let you specify how these notifications should be sent to each user and under what circumstances. Notifications can be sent by e-mail, by pager, or on the Ops Center console. Different severities of notifications, or notifications for different assets, can be sent through different methods. For example, you could create a notification profile that would send low-priority notifications to your e-mail and high-priority notifications to the Short Message Service (SMS).

Monitoring Exalogic

Ops Center has specific functions for day-to-day administration of Exalogic, ranging from hardware fault monitoring, to OS performance monitoring, patch automation, configuration, and compliance reporting. These functions can be performed by the administrator through the web-based console interface. Figure 6-2 shows an Exalogic machine being managed in the Ops Center console.

The console in the figure shows Exalogic's hardware components, including the compute nodes on the left panel and a graphical representation

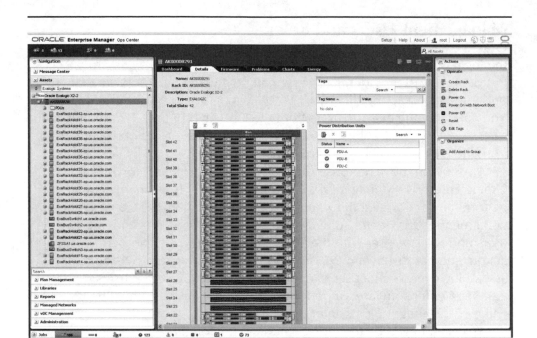

FIGURE 6-2. *Ops Center console web interface*

of the Exalogic system in the center panel. The Exalogic view is similar to what you would physically see when looking at the front of an Exalogic system on the data center floor, including the different LED alerts. The right panel shows administrative actions such as power on and power off. To review a specific component in detail, you can select the component from the left panel, which will then show a summary page for the selected component.

In addition, Oracle Enterprise Manager provides automated configuration management. It confirms that Exalogic Elastic Cloud configurations are valid, using policies on OS parameter and other compute node configuration. It can detect configuration drifts from Oracle-defined standards and alerts the administrators.

Monitoring Hardware Components

Each Exalogic hardware component can be viewed and monitored through the Ops Center console by navigating through asset groups and subgroups sections of the console. The Details view tab shows information on elements such as CPU, memory, network adapter, disk, power supply, and fan tray (fan) for compute nodes, and details of the Network File System (NFS) shares on the storage device. Figure 6-3 shows an Exalogic compute node viewed in the Ops Center console.

This information can be very useful for the administrator in identifying the type of subcomponents in the node, the firmware version, the status, health indicators, and the temperature. Each of the hardware components in Exalogic has sensors that monitor aspects of the hardware such as these:

- CPU temperature

- Ambient temperature

- Fan speed in revolutions per minute

- Voltages

- LEDs

- Hardware faults

These sensors are read by the Ops Center to capture and display the health state of the hardware components. The power consumption sensors for

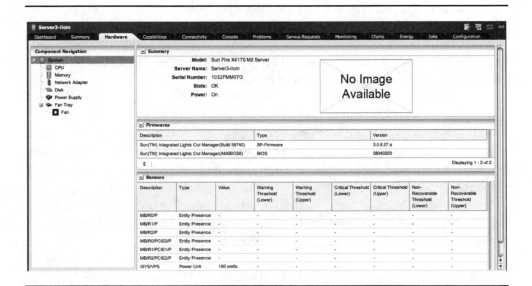

FIGURE 6-3. *Compute node screen in the Ops Center console*

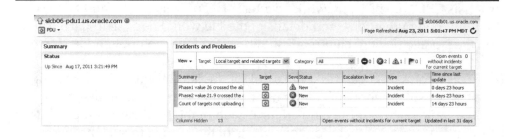

FIGURE 6-4. *PDU Summary page*

hardware components and power output sensors for the power distribution units (PDUs) are used to calculate power utilization and efficiency charts for the Exalogic machine. Figure 6-4 shows the PDU Summary page.

The PDU monitoring feature measures the power consumption used by Exalogic components and issues early warnings of impending power threshold violations. It also monitors the electric current being used by equipment connected in the Exalogic rack. This is very useful, for example, for producing reports to validate targets that need to be met in green energy initiatives in the data center.

Monitoring Software Components

The Cloud Control can be used to manage and monitor Oracle Solaris and Oracle Linux operating systems, middleware, and applications as managed assets. Figure 6-5 shows the Oracle Enterprise Manager Cloud Control summary page on software assets being managed.

The Cloud Control allows administrators to deploy applications, provision middleware infrastructure, and perform operational tasks such as starting and stopping applications. It can also be used to define and monitor Key Performance Indicators (KPIs) and Service Level Agreement (SLA)–based alerts. It monitors the status, activity, and usage of these software assets through an agent embedded within the operating system on compute nodes. One of the most useful features of Cloud Control is the automated health check on software running on Exalogic systems, which includes the following capabilities:

- Verify Exalogic network configuration

- Verify whether the central ZFS storage is correctly mounted from each compute node

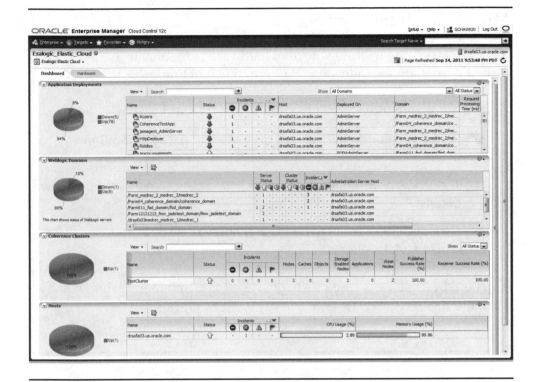

FIGURE 6-5. *Cloud Control summary page*

- Verify middleware configuration

- Verify that the Internet Protocol over InfiniBand (IPoIB) network is correctly utilized for mid-tier communication

- Test that the Exalogic software optimizations are enabled in the hosted WebLogic domains

- Check the InfiniBand throughput within Coherence clusters

Cloud Control provides default thresholds to trigger alerts in its monitoring profiles; for example, to test whether the CPU utilization threshold of 80 percent is being exceeded. You can adjust the thresholds to meet your data center and IT guidelines. You can set different thresholds for each software asset for notification and corrective actions. Cloud Control also shows historical data such as CPU, memory, I/O, and power to generate graphical reports for trend analysis and forecasting.

Monitoring InfiniBand Fabric

The InfiniBand fabric in Exalogic can be monitored from the Ops Center, which relies on the ILOM interface of hardware components in the Exalogic system to provide the following administrative functions:

- Automatic discovery of InfiniBand network and switches

- Real-time monitoring, alerts, and historical data of InfiniBand network

- Topology view of the entire network showing switch- and port-level details

- Configuration metrics to detect and notify configuration changes/best practice violations

The Ops Center Console's view of an Exalogic InfiniBand fabric is shown in Figure 6-6.

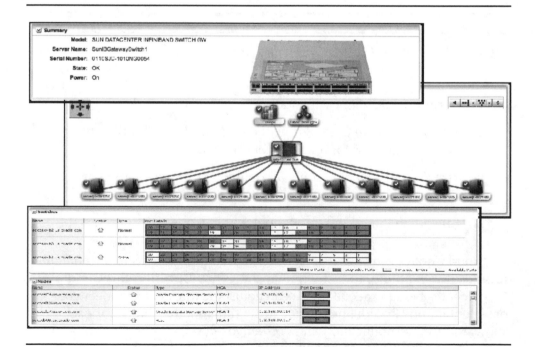

FIGURE 6-6. *Monitor InfiniBand fabric in the Ops Center*

Figure 6-6 shows the live links in the fabric across the different components, compute nodes, switches, and shared storage within the Exalogic system. In addition to Ops Center, many command-line tools can be used to monitor and perform diagnostics on the InfiniBand fabric from any Exalogic component:

- **ibswitches**   Use this command to identify the QDR InfiniBand Gateway Switches in the InfiniBand fabric within the Exalogic machine. The output displays the globally unique ID (GUID) for the devices connected to InfiniBand network across various subnets, name, and local identifier for the devices connected on InfiniBand network with a specific subnet (LID).

- **ibhosts**   Use this command to display identity information about the host channel adapters (HCAs) in the InfiniBand fabric for a subnet. The output displays the GUID and name for each HCA.

- **ibnetdiscover**   Use this command to understand the routing rules that are configured within your InfiniBand fabric. The output displays the node-to-node connectivity.

- **ibtracert source_lid destination_lid**   Use this command to show the route trace between two nodes by displaying the GUIDs, ports, and LIDs of the nodes in the InfiniBand fabric.

- **Ibportstate lid port**   Use this command to show the link status of a node in the InfiniBand fabric.

- **perfquery lid port**   Use this command to ascertain the health of a node in the fabric. Pass the LID of the node in the fabric, and port number to which the node is connected on the switch as arguments to the command. Note that if a port value of 255 is specified for a switch node, the counters are the total for all switch ports.

- **ibdatacounts lid port**   Use this command to list the data counters for a node in the fabric—that is, received data and packets.

- **ibdiagnet -v -r**   Use this command to perform overall health testing on the InfiniBand fabric.

- **osmtest** Use this command to take a snapshot (inventory file) of the fabric and later compare that file to the present conditions. The inventory file contains a list of all the devices connected with their LIDs and health status.

- **ibdiagnet -c 100 -P all=1** Use this command to find which InfiniBand network links are experiencing packet drops.

Troubleshooting and Problem Management

The Exalogic system is a very sophisticated engineered system, designed to keep things from going wrong. Even when they do go wrong, redundancies are built into the system to continue its functions, while raising alerts in management and monitoring tools such as ILOM and Ops Center. These alerts can also be configured to be sent to the administrators using Short Message Service (SMS) or e-mail.

Typically, an administrator uses management tools such as Oracle Enterprise Manager Ops Center to review alerts and take remedial actions.

Problem Management in Ops Center

Problem management in Oracle Enterprise Manager Ops Center comprises several elements that are designed to work together to simplify diagnosis. The elements include monitoring rules, suggested actions, and tools to automate problem identification and resolution.

The monitoring system is connected with a problem management and notification system. It includes a predefined standard set of rules and attributes, many of which can be modified to meet your monitoring requirements. In addition, you can add custom monitoring attributes and alert conditions.

Problem management provides a number of features to enable the administrator to perform the following tasks:

- View unresolved problems
- View problem details
- Assign a problem

■ Acknowledge problems

■ Add an annotation for recommended actions or fixes

■ Display an annotation on recommended actions or fixes

■ Use maintenance mode to disable assets from generating problems temporarily, while replacing failed hardware components

■ Take action on a problem based on suggested actions—for example, run a predefined executing script to reboot the server

■ Mark a problem repaired

■ Close a problem

The administrator can also use a service request function to raise a service request with Oracle Support, directly from the Ops Center console. Oracle Enterprise Manager also offers another feature, Oracle Auto Service Request (ASR), which provides automated support case generation, when common hardware component faults occur. ASR is designed to enable faster problem resolution by eliminating the need for a human administrator to initiate contact with Oracle Support Services, reducing both the number of phone calls needed and time consumed to resolve the problem. It also simplifies support operations by automatically capturing and sending electronic diagnostic data.

NOTE
To use ASR feature within Exalogic, you will need to install the ASR Manager on a standalone system external to Ops Center and make sure it is activated to communicate with Exalogic compute nodes on their ILOM interfaces.

Troubleshooting Switches

Although Oracle Enterprise Manager Ops Center provides extensive capabilities to perform diagnostics on problems that might occur in an Exalogic system, in some situations, administrators will have to look under the hood of the system to investigate the problem. The InfiniBand fabric and networking switches of Exalogic are one such area for which administrators may occasionally want to log into the console interface, review logs, and use command-line tools.

On the InfiniBand leaf switches, the following log files are available to troubleshoot network or device related issues:

- /var/log/messages

- /var/log/opensm.log

- /var/log/opensm-subnet.lst

Additional utilities can also be used to collect data for troubleshooting and review the network health on these switches:

- **/usr/local/bin/version**

- **/usr/local/bin/env_test**

- **/usr/local/bin/listlinkup**

- **/usr/bin/ibdiagnet -skip dup_guids -pm**

- **/usr/sbin/ibcheckerrors -v**

In addition to the preceding tools and log files, the Gateway InfiniBand switch provides other tools to help diagnose issues that could occur with respect to the eight 10GbE ports bridged (not switched) into the IB (InfiniBand) fabric. This topology of the 10GbE connectivity to the data center's client network can be verified through following tools:

Command	Description
ibdiagnet -ls 10 -lw 4x	Verifies all data links to the 10GbE network from InfiniBand. **-ls** is link speed; **10** is 10 Gbps, the raw link speed of QDR on a lane. **-lw** is link width; **4x** is the link used. The command output will state whether links in the IB subnet are not operating at the full 4x QDR speed. The possible cause of this could be a cable not correctly fitted in the connector.

Command	Description
lbhosts	Lists the names of HCAs, the IB switches and the gateway names for those.
lbswitches	Lists the names of IB switches.
lbnodes	Shows all IB devices in the IB subnet (compute nodes, storage nodes and switches).
lbnetdiscover	Shows the IB devices and switches in the IB subnet and the connections between the IB devices.
showunhealthy	Shows a list of switch components that appear to have a problem.
showvnics	Shows the virtual NIC resources on the gateway.
showvlans	Shows the virtual LAN resources.
generatetopology	Generates an IB subnet topology file that describes the IB subnet in a readable format.
matchtopology	Matches the current IB subnet topology with a topology file that is provided as input to the command.
showtopology	Shows the current IB subnet topology to the user in the command-line console as a list of IB devices.

In general, the best course of action to perform diagnostics of EoIB connectivity is to check the topology and compare it with your last-known generated topology, as this will identify any unknown physical change to the EoIB configuration. Another useful tool worth particular attention is **ibdiagnet**, which verifies whether the full quad speed is available on the Ethernet bridge to the IB fabric.

NOTE
*It is a best practice to take a periodic snapshot of the InfiniBand topology using the **generatetopology** command and store it on central ZFS storage for future diagnostics.*

Exalogic General Administrative Tools

Some administrative tasks aren't frequently required for Exalogic systems. These tasks are required for the initial one-off rack set-up, factory restores, repurposing of systems or ad hoc administrative changes to configuration. Exalogic includes a number of very specialized tools that ensure the correct installation and configuration of the Exalogic system and can quickly and easily diagnose critical system-level issues:

- **Exalogic Configuration Utility** A desktop tool used to configure the Exalogic system management and data center service network interfaces and internal subnets.

- **Exalogic Distributed Command Line Interface** A command-line tool used to execute commands on some or all of the Exalogic nodes simultaneously from a single console.

- **Exalogic Topology Verifier** A command-line tool that verifies the InfiniBand topology of the Exalogic system, ensuring that the correct topology is applied for each given system configuration: eighth rack; quarter rack, half rack, or full rack.

- **Exalogic InfiniCheck** A command-line tool that verifies the correct operation of every InfiniBand device and port on the fabric, ensuring that all ports and connectors are functioning correctly.

- **Exalogic Hardware & Firmware Profiler** A command-line tool that verifies that all of the hardware devices and firmware versions connected to the Exalogic system fabric are verified and supported, with the correct and compatible device firmware versions.

- **Exalogic Software Profiler** A command-line tool that verifies that all of the Linux or Solaris software packages installed on any of the system's compute nodes are of the correct version and do not jeopardize the Exalogic system's performance, security, or stability.

■ **Exalogic Boot Manager** A command-line tool that allows system operators to easily re-image individual Exalogic compute nodes, via external Preboot Execution Environment (PXE) servers or network-mounted disk images.

Exalogic Distributed Command Line Interface

The Exalogic base operating system image includes a tool called Distributed Command Line Interface (DCLI) that can be used to run a set of commands on all or a subset of the compute nodes in parallel. This saves a lot of time and helps avoid errors that would otherwise often occur when running the same command multiple times on each individual compute node, especially when you consider that a full-rack Exalogic system consists of 30 compute nodes.

Each Exalogic compute node has the exalogic.tools package installed by default, which contains the DCLI tool in addition to other useful Exalogic command-line utilities. All these commands can be found in the /opt/exalogic.tools directory. The DCLI tool specifically is located at /opt/exalogic.tools/tools/dcli.

DCLI is a Python script that essentially determines the list of compute nodes in the Exalogic machine on which the specified individual commands should be executed. Under the covers, the batch of commands run on each compute node is executed using Secure Shell (SSH). The SSH is a network-based protocol for secure data exchange and command execution on a remote server over an insecure network.

DCLI captures the output from the command executions on each compute node and prints that information in the shell from which the DCLI command is executed. The output from each individual compute node is prefixed by that particular compute node's name so that it is easy for the administrator to see if something unexpected occurred on one of the compute nodes when running DCLI.

DCLI requires a text file input that contains the list of all the target compute nodes on which commands will be executed. For example, following is a snippet of such a file (called nodelist), with entries in the first three lines, and a comment on the fourth line to exclude the fourth compute node from being issued remote commands:

```
el01cn01
el01cn02
el01cn03
#el01cn04
```

Here is an example of the output that you can see when running the DCLI command:

```
# /opt/exalogic.tools/tools/dcli -t -g nodeslist /bin/date
Example output:
Target nodes: ['el01cn01', 'el01cn02', 'el01cn03',....]
el01cn01: Sat Jan 21 21:11:42 UTC 2012
el01cn02: Sat Jan 21 21:11:42 UTC 2012
el01cn03: Sat Jan 21 21:11:42 UTC 2012
....
```

In this example, the **-t** option tells DCLI first to print out names of all target compute nodes that have been targeted, and the **-g** option provides the name of the file that contains the list of nodes to operate on (in this case, nodelist in the current directory).

When the command is executed for the first time, you will be prompted for the password for each compute node that DCLI connects to using SSH. To use DCLI without being prompted for a password for each compute node, first set up SSH Trust between the master compute node and all the other compute nodes.

Exalogic Configuration Utility

The Exalogic Configuration Utility (ECU) is the main tool used to commission a brand new Exalogic rack in a specific data center. The utility comprises a spreadsheet and a set of shell scripts that are used to configure the Exalogic rack's network settings to complement the host data center's network configuration. It is also important that you understand this utility if you need to perform a factory reset of an Exalogic system. When the ECU's shell scripts are run, they perform the following operations:

- Identify any hardware issues (problems that could have occurred during transit of the rack from the factory)

- Configure IP addresses and host name and other networking elements (such as DNS) on all components in the rack

- Configure the date and time of all the rack's components, synchronized to a single Network Time Protocol (NTP) source

Exalogic Configuration Utility/OneCommand Spreadsheet

The Configuration Utility, a spreadsheet named MWM_Configurator.xls, contains macros that process configuration data and produce configuration scripts. During the initial Exalogic hardware setup phase, you will need to fill out a minimum set of information:

- Domain name

- Country

- Time zone

- At least one of each required IP address (Eth0, NET0, NET1, ILOM)

- At least one of each optional IP address (BOND0, BOND1)

- At least one NTP server IP address

- At least one name server (DNS) IP address

- At least one search domain

- A default gateway IP address

You will need to choose one of the compute nodes as master node and move configuration files and OneCommand scripts to a master node. The Exalogic Configuration Utility must be used from this master node. For detailed information on using the configuration utility, refer to the Exalogic owner's guide.

Perform a General Health Check on Exalogic

Several other general purpose tools are available on Exalogic compute nodes to perform general health checks on the system. These are generally used when the administrator wants to identify software and hardware profiles, device firmware versions, and network status from the command line. Following are some of the tools that can be used:

- **/opt/exalogic.tools/tools/CheckHWnFWProfile**

- **/opt/exalogic.tools/tools/CheckSWProfile**

- **/usr/sbin/ibchecknet**

- /usr/sbin/iblinkinfo

- /usr/sbin/ibnetdiscover

- /usr/bin/ibdiagnet –rs

- /usr/sbin/ibcheckerrors

- /opt/exalogic.tools/tools/check_ibports

- /opt/exalogic.tools/tools/verify-topology [-t halfrack | fullrack | quarterrack | eighthrack]

- /opt/exalogic.tools/tools/infinicheck –H host1,host2,...

- /opt/exalogic.tools/tools/ibping_test

Of course, many of the functions for these commands can be achieved by using Oracle Enterprise Manager Ops Center or the ILOM interface for a component. The ILOM interface can be accessed through a browser over the management LAN.

Reimaging Exalogic Compute Nodes with Oracle Linux

You can reimage Exalogic compute nodes with the original Oracle Linux base image. Note that Oracle Linux is preinstalled on Exalogic compute nodes. But there could be situations where the compute nodes are required to be reimaged. The administrators should refer to the Exalogic owner's guide to reimage the compute node with Solaris.

NOTE
Exalogic-specific operating system base images are available on Oracle software delivery cloud, and only these image files should be used for reimaging compute nodes. A generic version of Oracle Linux should not be installed, because this won't include all the modifications, drivers, and extra tools that the Exalogic-specific Linux base image includes.

Reimaging compute nodes to Oracle Linux may become necessary in repurposing compute node scenarios or when you reinstall a hardware component in the Exalogic machine due to hardware failure. The reimaging process uses the PXE, an environment to boot compute nodes from the network interface independently of the installed operating system on the local disks. The Exalogic base image templates are available on the ZFS Storage 7320 appliance at the /export/common/images path, or the latest version of the base image templates can be downloaded from the Oracle Software Delivery Cloud (aka e-delivery).

TIP
It is best practice to use the latest version of the Exalogic-specific base operating system image downloaded from e-delivery.

The reimaging process consists of the following steps:

1. Connect to the ILOM interface in a web browser by entering **http:// <IP address of the compute node to be re-imaged>**.

2. Log in as an administrator. If you are setting up Oracle ILOM for the first time, use the default root account and *welcome1* password to log in. After you log in, the home page of Oracle ILOM is displayed.

NOTE
It is highly recommended that you create new user accounts for each Oracle ILOM user and the administrator after you set up ILOM.

3. Click the Remote Control tab.

4. Under Launch Redirection, click Launch Remote Console. The remote console for compute node is displayed in a separate window.

5. In the ILOM web interface, click the Host Control tab.

6. Under Host Control, select PXE as the Next Boot Device from the drop-down list, and click Save.

7. Click the Remote Power Control tab.

8. Under Server Power Control, select Power Cycle from the drop-down list, and click Save. This action reboots the compute node.

9. Switch to the remote console for the compute node. After the compute node reboots, the PXE menu with the list of available Exalogic base options is displayed.

10. Type the name of the Exalogic base image option that you want to install on the compute node. Press ENTER. This action starts reimaging the compute node. Wait approximately 10–15 minutes for the reimaging to occur, and then you will be prompted to configure the compute node. The following prompt is displayed: "Enter the Exalogic rack type (integer value) this node belongs to [1=quarter, 2=half, and 3=full]"

11. Enter the rack type (integer value), as applicable. The compute node reboots again and completes the configuration for the reimaging process.

TIP
To begin with, image one compute node at a time and assess the performance and speed. The performance depends on several parameters, such as the laptop's Ethernet interface and processor speed. If you are satisfied with the performance and speed, try to image two compute nodes simultaneously and assess the performance. You can image more compute nodes simultaneously, based on the performance.

12. Log in to the compute node as a root user with the *changeme* password to verify that the operating system installed.

TIP
It is highly recommended that you change the root password and also create new user accounts on the compute node. You can repeat these steps for every compute node in the Exalogic system, if required.

Summary

Exalogic brings all the elements of IT solutions such as networking, hardware, and operating system together into one system and provides a sophisticated management and monitoring solution to ease the burden of administration.

Exalogic is manageable using a variety of tools, as you have seen in this chapter. Irrespective of the specific tools used, managing Exalogic is substantially less complex and error-prone than managing traditional systems built from individually sourced components, because Exalogic is explicitly designed to be administered and maintained as a single, integrated system.

The Oracle Enterprise Manager provides a single place for administrators to manage all aspects of the Exalogic systems, from applications to disks.

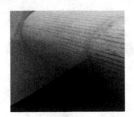

CHAPTER
7

Building Private
Cloud Applications

n previous chapters, you have learned how to deploy Exalogic in your data center and architect a scalable cloud infrastructure using Exalogic and Exadata. In this chapter, you'll learn how to build and deploy applications on Exalogic-based clouds and make use of the Exalogic cloud software–based optimizations in your application.

This chapter is organized into three main topics:

■ Building applications on Exalogic, focusing on using Platform as a Service (PaaS)–type cloud deployments

■ Building applications for Exalogic, to take advantage of Exalogic-based optimizations

■ Special use cases that can benefit most from the Exalogic platform

Building Applications on Exalogic

Many organizations procure Exalogic as a platform to implement a private cloud with a view to support IT needs in a cost-effective, scalable, and highly agile environment. Such a platform can support the entire software development lifecycle (SDLC) from development and testing, to deployment of applications to production environments. One of the advantages of using a cloud infrastructure is that you can develop and test the application on a target platform that is very similar to the production environment. A private cloud approach also provides the ability to reuse infrastructure services for different projects and allocate spare capacity to scale-out and scale-back production environments as required.

Many organizations over the years have tried and failed to self-engineer such shared infrastructure–based deployments. Let us explore what an organization needs to do to implement a self-engineered private cloud, based on commodity components for its IT systems:

1. The IT organization will need to go through a vendor selection process to select hardware suppliers (servers, network appliances, storage, and so on), hosting partner (if not hosting internally), and software vendors (core technology, commercial off-the-shelf [COTS] applications, management, and monitoring).

2. The organization puts together an engineering team to define private cloud design and architecture, including networks and hardware.

3. Extensive work begins, assembling and engineering a private cloud system. The effort for building such a private cloud would run into many man years and millions of dollars, because it requires both hardware assemblies and software development to support cloud management.

4. The next phase is provisioning a Platform as a Service (PaaS) to provide self-management capabilities for the projects; this is very difficult to do except for software vendors, who build these capabilities into their products. As a result, the process of patching and maintenance could be very involved on a custom-built cloud infrastructure.

By selecting an Exalogic system as the foundations of a private cloud, organizations can reduce all the aforementioned effort required to build and maintain a private cloud. Oracle has spent many years of effort engineering private cloud building blocks, in the form of Exalogic and Exadata.

In the next section, you will see an example of a private cloud–based deployment on Exalogic. It will also highlight the software delivery process that can be followed on a private cloud, providing the benefits expected from a shared infrastructure.

Why Private Cloud?

Let's consider an example of a gaming company named DizzyGames, which is based on a composite of multiple customer's requirements and experiences with Exalogic. Today, most of its systems are managed by third-party hosting partners on a heterogeneous platform with dedicated servers for each online game and supporting backend systems.

DizzyGames is not able to deliver the expected quality of service that its web site customers expect, including support for the growing demand from its online gaming customers. The cost of extending its current platform is regarded as very high, as it will not only include the cost of procuring new hardware but also paying the hosting provider's high expansion costs. DizzyGames has also realized that not all the systems have peak loads at the same time. If the hosting provider offered shared infrastructure, metered on usage, it could instead balance its resource requirements (and costs) across the different systems' peak overloads to a much lower average throughout the whole year.

Lately, the CIO at DizzyGames has recognized that by creating its own private cloud, DizzyGames will have better control of its application and its ability to scale on a standardized platform with minimal cost of change. DizzyGames will have the ability to balance spare capacity across different applications. By building a private cloud, DizzyGames will reduce capital expenditures through shared infrastructure and reduce operational expenditures through cloud-based platform management and enabling self-service for users. As a result, DizzyGames has decided to buy two Exalogic quarter-rack systems to build its private cloud.

DizzyGames' Private Cloud Requirements

The IT organization at DizzyGames has identified the following requirements for its private cloud implementation:

- It should be able to deploy development and test environments, on-demand, for new games, at minimal additional cost and effort.

- It must ensure that spare capacity in the data center for disaster recovery and preventive fail-over is always provided.

- Development and test environments must be similar to production environments.

- Its private cloud should span two data centers that are 50 miles apart in Woking and London (UK) for disaster recovery purposes; these will be used as active and passive data centers respectively.

- Under normal circumstances, the Woking data center mostly hosts the production systems in the cloud.

- The London data center primarily hosts nonproduction environments, including target disaster recovery environments.

- The London data center will host internal systems such as human resource management systems and order and billing systems.

- The two data centers will be connected by 1GbE network to facilitate disaster recovery and backup recovery.

The organization plans to use an Exalogic-based deployment to host production and nonproduction environments in a private cloud that spans the two data centers. Figure 7-1 shows such a deployment of Exalogic systems across the two data centers to form the private cloud.

Figure 7-1 shows that Woking data center hosts the production environments for all the online games that are rehosted on standardized Exalogic-based platforms. The London data center hosts the nonproduction environments such as development and test environments for the online games on the Exalogic platform. The London data center also acts as the disaster recovery environment for the online games hosted in the Woking data center, by having standby Oracle virtual machine images of the instances in Woking data center. This is achieved by implementing the disaster recovery mechanism described in Chapter 4 through the use of ZFS-based file replication of application files.

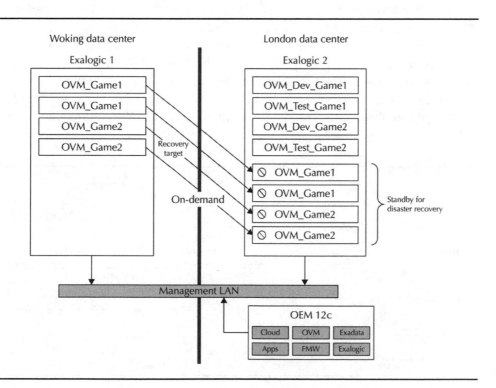

FIGURE 7-1. *DizzyGames Exalogic deployment*

Introduction to Oracle VM

Before we go further with the private cloud deployment on Exalogic, let's take a look at the Oracle Virtual Machine (OVM) technology (Figure 7-2); it is a core component of the Exalogic-based cloud. OVM is a server virtualization technology that lets multiple guest virtual machines run efficiently on a single host machine, with features for provisioning guest instances with preconfigured applications from OVM templates. It allows administrators to create and manage a large pool of resources comprising CPU, memory, disks, file storage, networking, and applications, as virtual machines, providing an agile and scalable platform. The OVM technology allows multiple operating system instances to run on a single host machine.

The OVM ecosystem consists of components, which work together to provide the virtualization platform leveraged in Exalogic-based clouds. OVM Manager provides the interface in which distributed virtual machine management tasks are performed, such as defining virtual machines and assigning resources to them. The OVM Manager interface is embedded in the Oracle Enterprise Manager Cloud Control to provide an integrated management console for the whole IT infrastructure in a data center. OVM Server is the Oracle hypervisor that hosts multiple virtual machines on the same physical server. Bare-metal machines can be enabled for virtualization, by provisioning the OVM Server hypervisor software directly on the physical machine, ready for hosting guest virtual machines. *Virtual*

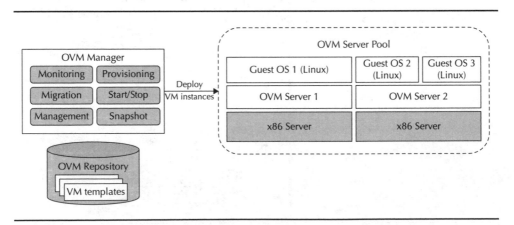

FIGURE 7-2. *Oracle VM ecosystem*

server is a target type in Enterprise Manager that represents these OVM targets.

A *server pool* is a logical grouping of one or more OVM servers that share common storage. A server can belong only to one server pool at a time. Guest virtual machines and resources are also associated with server pools.

When an OVM server pool is created, the user is asked to provide the details of the *master server* for that pool. The master server controls load-balancing of the OVM provisioning requests, which is based on the load on each physical server.

A *guest virtual machine* is the container running on top of a host server, and it runs a complete OS instance. Multiple guest virtual machines can run on a single virtual server. Guest virtual machines can be created from OVM assemblies or templates. They provide preinstalled and preconfigured software images to deploy a fully configured software stack.

A *zone* is a collection of virtual server pools. It is a logical entity used to organize the guest virtual machines. Zones have metrics that show the aggregate utilization. This should not be confused with Solaris zones, a lightweight, low-overhead virtualization capability in the Solaris OS that can also be used with Exalogic.

Characteristics of Private Cloud

One of the principles of a private cloud is that the actual physical location of the online games application within a data center is not important. Exalogic cloud software makes it easy to move application services transparently within the cloud, without disruption to users.

As the underlying infrastructure of DizzyGames' London data center is based on Exalogic and OVM, Exalogic Control enables the rapid creation of OVM-based virtual instances for development and test purposes. These virtual instances can be started on any Exalogic compute node running the OVM server, using the centralized Exalogic Control console. The use of OVM technology allows the application platform environment to be location and hardware independent; these virtual environments can be hosted and moved anywhere within the private cloud. This will also enable DizzyGames to reuse its legacy hardware along with Exalogic to provide additional cloud capacity, by adding more OVM servers running on non-Exalogic hardware, as required. These additional resources can be used for noncritical applications that do not need the performance optimizations provided by an Exalogic system. It should be noted that non-Exalogic OVM servers cannot be in same OVM server pool as the one containing Exalogic OVM servers.

A private cloud deployment on Exalogic has all the typical characteristics of a cloud-based implementation, providing the following key benefits to DizzyGames:

- **On-demand self-service**   This allows project teams to deploy new platform instances on the cloud to host new and existing applications and games, without going through a lengthy IT provisioning process.

- **Resource pooling**   IT infrastructure resources are brought into a common, shared cloud-based pool for allocating to applications that need them the most, at any one time, leveling off the peak spikes in usage that would otherwise occur.

- **Rapid elasticity**   Additional Oracle VM instances can be added and removed as needed to scale up or scale down. Also, additional capacity can be allocated to the private cloud at runtime without any downtime.

- **Measured service**   The Oracle Enterprise Manager Cloud Control software allows metering based on measuring the actual usage of resources such as CPU, memory, disk space, and I/O by the projects. This allows for business units to pay for only what they use. This ensures that DizzyGames can more accurately account for profitability of each game by comparing operations costs and the revenue it generates.

How to Provision a Private Cloud

Deployment of Exalogic in the data centers is just the first step in setting up the private cloud for DizzyGames. The Exalogic machine will be set up by Oracle to factory setting with preconfigured storage, networking, and compute node–based operating systems.

The process of building a private cloud starts after the Exalogic machines are deployed in the data centers. This is a role typically owned by an IT administrator. Four major steps are involved in this task, as shown in Figure 7-3. Some of the steps may be optional depending on business requirements.

1. Create and establish Infrastructure as a Service (IaaS) capability.

2. Create and establish Platform as a Service (PaaS) capability.

3. Create and establish Software as a Service (SaaS) capability.

4. Deploy cloud management capability and establish associated policies.

Infrastructure as a Service

IaaS is built by deploying Exalogic and Exadata systems in the data center along with the Oracle Enterprise Manager Cloud Control. This delivers a standardized cloud infrastructure that can be used to provision any environment to host applications for DizzyGames through a self-service cloud management console, as shown in Figure 7-4, to create application environments as needed. It should be noted that Exalogic Control is pre-installed in every Exalogic as part of Exalogic deployment in the data center. The Exalogic Control provides services such as OVM management and monitoring, guest VM provisioning, network and storage management similar to Oracle Enterprise Manager Cloud Control, but within the context of Exalogic Machine.

The deployment of Exalogic will require some additional configuration to allow IaaS-based services. Most of these steps are performed through Oracle Enterprise Manager Cloud Control console or Exalogic Control as to ensure the IaaS services follow the policies required by DizzyGames. (Note that steps 1 to 4 may be provided as part of the factory setting, this depends on the version of Exalogic.)

1. Deploy Oracle VM Manager in the data center (preferably as part of Oracle Enterprise Manager deployment); alternatively, use Exalogic Control if pre-installed within Exalogic.

2. Install Oracle Virtual Server on each of the available compute nodes of the Exalogic. Refer to the Exalogic owner's guide for detailed steps.

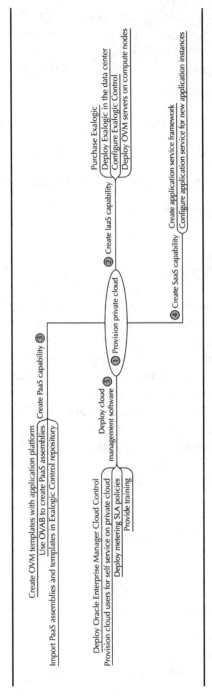

FIGURE 7-3. *Steps for provisioning a private cloud*

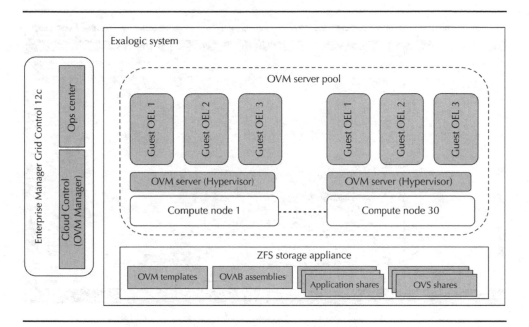

FIGURE 7-4. *IaaS deployment for DizzyGames*

   3. Discover all the physical hosts (compute nodes) in Oracle Enterprise
      Manager Cloud Control or Exalogic Control by discovering Oracle
      VM servers. Figure 7-5 shows an example of such discovery in a
      Cloud Control console.

   4. Register NFS storage as the software repository for the OVM servers
      on each of the compute nodes through the Oracle Enterprise
      Manager. This is preconfigured in Exalogic Control.

   5. Create additional network configuration required for different
      aspects of the private cloud. For example, in the Exalogic-based
      private cloud, you will need to create network configuration for
      Internet Protocol over InfiniBand (IPoIB), Ethernet over InfiniBand
      (EoIB), management LAN, and InfiniBand.

   6. Download OVM-based templates for base operating systems such as
      Oracle Enterprise Linux 5.5 or 5.6.

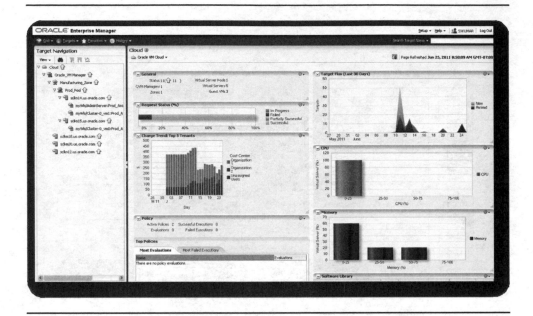

FIGURE 7-5. *Oracle Enterprise Manager Cloud Control discovery of OVM servers*

TIP
It is important that correct OVM templates are built for Exalogic with specific OS releases that support Exalogic and contain Exabus optimizations.

7. Import the OVM templates in the software repository of Oracle VM Manager. This is preconfigured in Exalogic Control.

8. Create a private cloud zone in the Oracle Enterprise Manager.

9. Create users/roles for cloud control with permissions to request new Oracle VM instances.

10. Create security, metering, and charging policies and apply them to the cloud zone.

After successfully deploying an IaaS-based private cloud, the IT organization can allow business users to start requesting and using the cloud-based infrastructure, through the Oracle Enterprise Manager Cloud Management Console, as shown in Figure 7-6.

Figure 7-6 shows that user John Smith is using IaaS-based services to run an environment consisting of five servers with 1GB of RAM each. Simply providing IaaS-based cloud services is not enough for many organizations, and it is certainly true that DizzyGames has greater requirements. Further enhancements are needed to the private cloud to deliver the required types of common platforms for hosting the games at DizzyGames.

Platform as a Service

PaaS is achieved by extending our Exalogic-based IaaS private cloud infrastructure with new services. While IaaS is generally limited to providing computing infrastructure in the form of virtual operating system instances that can be used to consume infrastructure capacity in the cloud, PaaS provides all the capabilities required to host and support the entire lifecycle of an application. PaaS services would generally involve a virtual instance

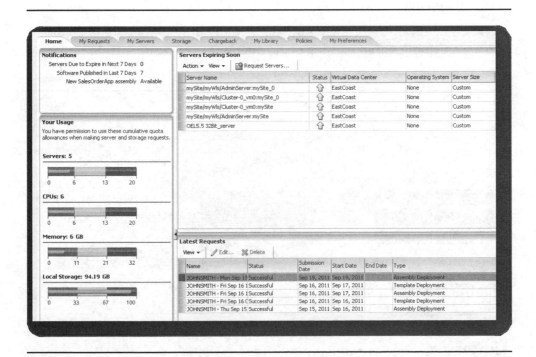

FIGURE 7-6. *Self-service screen for IaaS cloud on Exalogic*

of an application server (container) and required services such as security and a database.

Consider the example shown in Figure 7-7 to help you understand the difference between IaaS and PaaS. The left side deployment shows the cloud capability of IaaS, which allows users to deploy a virtual operating system on demand, while the right side PaaS deployment shows that users can deploy a virtual operating system along with prebuilt database or application server capabilities on demand. The PaaS allows projects to quickly deploy application platforms on the cloud, which can dramatically reduce the application build and deployment efforts. Using IaaS would require projects to spend more time building database and application server tiers.

To build a PaaS capability in a private cloud, a number of strategies can be employed by DizzyGames:

- Strategy 1: Build custom templates on OVM to match its platform requirements.

- Strategy 2: Download and use existing Oracle product OVM templates.

- Strategy 3: Use Oracle Virtual Assembly Builder (OVAB) to create assemblies from existing deployments.

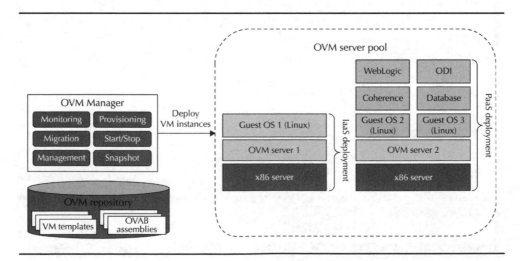

FIGURE 7-7. *IaaS versus PaaS*

All of these strategies are used in specific scenarios to achieve certain types of PaaS services. The first strategy is normally employed to create OVM-based templates if the platform requirement for the target applications is very specific and requires multiple Oracle products or non-Oracle products to support the applications. The second strategy is used for applications having simple infrastructure requirements based on distinct Oracle products. The third strategy is useful in situations in which existing deployments of applications can be cloned as assemblies to be deployed on the Oracle cloud.

The following steps can be taken to build custom templates:

1. Create OVM instances with an Exalogic-specific base image of OEL 5.5. or 5.6, matching the number of different templates required. For example, if the application requires an application server, a web server, a database, and MQ Broker instances, you can create four instances.

2. Install required products on each guest virtual machine and ensure that the products are configured as operating system- and network-agnostic as possible—for example, the product configuration should not use a host name, a physical IP address, and so on. This will allow the administrator to change configuration when deploying the product as PaaS instances.

3. Take a snapshot of the OVM instances and create the OVM templates. The administrator can use these templates to deploy PaaS virtual instances in the cloud.

4. Import these templates in the OVM Manager's software repository; this step makes the template accessible to Oracle Enterprise Manager Cloud Control or Exalogic Control for the purposes of deploying PaaS instances.

The second strategy is based on the availability of downloadable OVM templates on Oracle's *Software Delivery Cloud*, also known as Oracle e-delivery, for the specific versions of the Oracle products required by DizzyGames.

This is the best approach to provision a PaaS instance quickly, because no time is spent in building OVM-based templates. This is an innovative solution for faster application deployment with OVM templates. Oracle provides templates, and you can download and import preconfigured virtual machines containing preinstalled Oracle enterprise applications or other software to get up and running in hours rather than weeks. OVM images are normally supplied by Oracle on e-delivery for fast deployment of PaaS-based cloud environments. The limitation with this approach, however, is that it is limited to the OVM templates available for download, although Oracle aspires to provide downloadable OVM templates for all appropriate products.

The third strategy depends on OVAB; this is a game changer in terms of building a PaaS capability for the cloud. OVAB is a tool for virtualizing installed Oracle components, modifying those components, and then deploying them into a cloud environment. Using OVAB, you capture the configuration of existing software components in artifacts called *software appliances*. Appliances can then be grouped and their relationships defined into artifacts called *software assemblies*. An appliance represents a single software component and its local execution environment. An assembly is a collection of interrelated software appliances that are automatically configured to work together upon deployment. Assemblies are deployed onto a pool of hardware resources exposed through an OVM server pool with minimal user effort.

To understand the concept of assemblies, let's consider an example of a two-tier application deployed and configured on a single server, with one tier as WebLogic Server and the other tier as the Oracle database. You can use OVAB to create two software appliances for WebLogic and the Oracle database. These appliances will include all application-specific configuration including the .ear file, database schemas, Java Message Service (JMS) queues, and so on. You can create an assembly by wiring these appliances using Java Database Connectivity (JDBC). This assembly can be used to deploy as many instances of WebLogic and the database as required on the cloud along with your application and its required configuration with a click of a button.

Assemblies are a collection of appliances with defined interconnects, but they also provide a set of capabilities to be useful in a production environment, such as the following:

■ Allowing for the composition of many related appliances including dependencies on external systems

■ Externalizing configuration in the form of metadata that can be easily customized, for deployment of the same functionality to different runtimes

■ Optionally defining the start order of appliances to reflect interdependencies accurately

To summarize, the notion of creating prebuilt assemblies for deployment is extremely powerful and has a number of advantages that drive down operational costs and complexity, including the following:

■ Ability to replicate complex multi-tier environments easily in production while allowing for unique host-specific settings (such as host names)

■ Reduced risk of configuration errors when such multi-tier assemblies are moved between development, test, and production environments

■ Replicated environments facilitating a high level of standardization and consistency across application infrastructures, allowing for simple implementations of best practices

■ Accelerated deployment of new infrastructures and applications resulting in more commonality between development, test, and production environments

The OVAB enables you to construct complex assemblies containing a multi-tier application that may contain application-based configurations of each tier, including Oracle technologies such as WebLogic Server, Oracle Database, and Coherence, as shown in Figure 7-8.

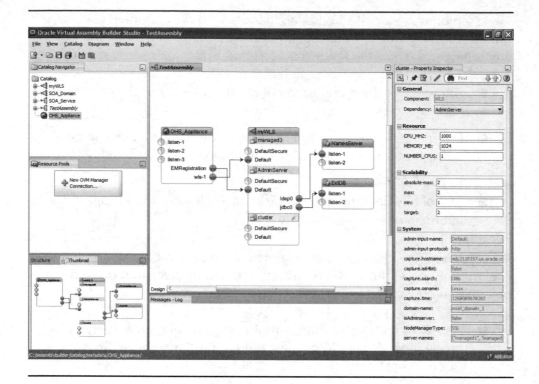

FIGURE 7-8. *OVAB Studio used to introspect an existing deployment*

Figure 7-8 shows that the OVAB Studio is used to introspect an existing reference deployment of a distributed application that has multiple tiers. The result of this produces a single OVAB assembly, capturing the essence of the multi-tier application, published to the Oracle Enterprise Manager software repository, as shown in Figure 7-9.

Oracle Enterprise Manager uses its Cloud Control functionality to deploy an assembly as a set of OVM instances to Exalogic compute nodes.

It is noteworthy that OVAB goes beyond OVM templates, where all aspects of an application are stored in a single file, and which can be deployed on an individual OVM instance. OVAB-based assemblies are multi-tier and can be deployed on multiple virtual machines. In other words, OVAB assembly is

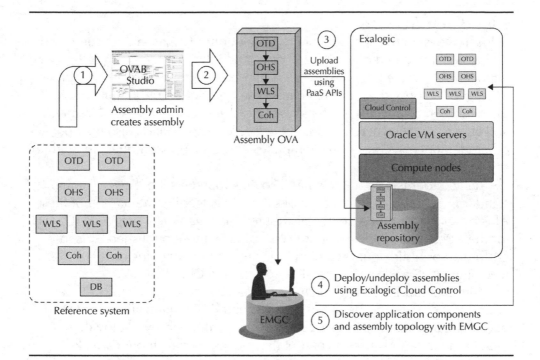

FIGURE 7-9.   *Lifecycle of using OVAB assemblies for PaaS on Exalogic*

a complete end-to-end assembly including startup sequences and scripts, configuration parameters and files, interconnects, and input/output parameters.

This lets you very quickly provision the application platforms for development, testing, preproduction, and production, using the same assembly, and thus ensuring consistency across all environments. OVAB-based assemblies enable PaaS services to scale out and scale back easily in terms of size and capacity, offering a better control of application capacity over time.

The next logical step for DizzyGames is to deploy cloud management services for end users to start deploying new environments for hosting new and existing games, based on self-service.

Cloud Self-Service

Self-service is a critical aspect of private cloud for DizzyGames. Some early adopters of the cloud have actually developed their own custom self-service application. Oracle provides an out-of-the-box solution: Oracle Enterprise Manager 12c provides a comprehensive self-service solution that enables the definition of policies, such as resource limits, charge-back, retirement, and quotas for different resources. The self-service application also incorporates other elements, such as OVM templates and OVAB assemblies, to enable self-service capability.

Related to this area, Oracle has also developed a set of APIs to define standards around cloud management. Oracle is leading ratification of these APIs by submitting them to the Distributed Management Task Force (DMTF) for the APIs to become a standard. You can use these published APIs to customize or build your own cloud-management capabilities while still leveraging IaaS and PaaS capabilities for Oracle Cloud.

With a cloud-based approach, DizzyGames can empower developers, who may belong to a line of business or central IT organization, to start packaging applications targeted for cloud and more easily deploy them on the cloud for general use. As part of this process, a developer can take advantage of PaaS and shared components to assemble applications and deploy them through self-service. If their role entitles them to make that request, it is automatically provisioned. If not, the request gets routed to management and/or IT for workflow approval, just like a procurement process.

Because the cloud is a shared environment, DizzyGames must be able to enforce standards; otherwise, the environment can get out of hand and become difficult for the operations team to manage. This is achieved by defining Oracle Enterprise Manager policies to ensure that user and application environments do not extend beyond levels that could pose risks to the overall cloud deployment in terms of performance, availability, security, and compliance. Figure 7-10 shows Oracle Enterprise Manager (OEM) screens that can be used to define policies to protect the cloud implementation, including metering and charge-back.

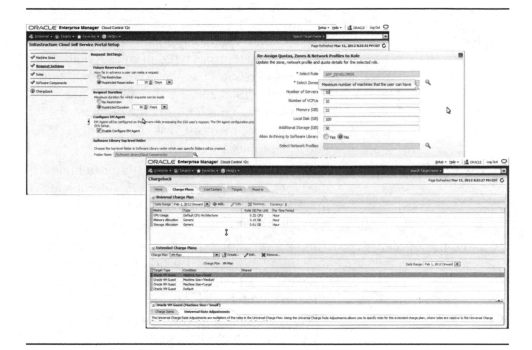

FIGURE 7-10. *Setting cloud-based policies*

Figure 7-10 shows how to define cloud-based policies that span across the parameters described in the following table:

Policy Category	Description
Machine Size	This allows the administrator to set up virtual machine sizes such as small, medium, and large with recommended resource allocations in terms of CPU, memory, disk space, and so on.
Request Settings	This defines how far in advance users can request an IaaS-based infrastructure and the maximum duration for which they can use it. This is useful for restricting time allocated to development and testing environments.

Policy Category	Description
Roles	This section is used to apply security-based restrictions in terms of types of roles required by the users to request IaaS-based infrastructure in a particular cloud zone. It also allows an administrator to put limits on the number of CPUs, servers, memory, disk space, and network profile.
Software Components	This section allows an administrator to limit the types of components and OVM templates that can be used to provision infrastructure in a specific cloud zone.
Charge-Back Policies	This section allows an administrator to define a charging model for the cloud zone that will have these policies applied. Examples of such charging models include: – Base Charge per server: rate per day – CPU use charge: rate per hour – Memory allocation: rate per GB per day – Storage allocation: rate per GB per month

Metering and Charge-Back

Oracle offers a comprehensive solution for addressing the billing and charge-back aspects of cloud computing. In Figure 7-10, you see Oracle Enterprise Manager and Oracle Billing and Revenue Management (Oracle BRM) in a combined solution that will cover needs of most customers—from simple charge-back to very flexible billing, for private as well as public clouds.

Oracle Enterprise Manager tracks resources within the cloud platform. It tracks how resources are utilized by applications, including extensive information about the hardware platform such as how much CPU, memory, disk, and network bandwidth is used. Oracle Enterprise Manager offers two capabilities depending on requirements. For most IT organizations, including that of DizzyGames, to perform simple charge-back based on CPU, disk, and network bandwidth usage, Oracle Enterprise Manager offers the capability to generate generic bills. For more flexible charging models, such as the case of service providers and telecommunications companies, Oracle Enterprise Manager passes usage data to Oracle BRM for more sophisticated billing processes.

In summary, you've learned how to use Exalogic to build a private cloud quickly via the fictional organization DizzyGames, which needed to fix scalability issues while keeping the cost to a minimum. Once DizzyGames has deployed its PaaS-based private cloud, different engineering teams working on various games can deploy standard-based assemblies containing Oracle WebLogic Server and Oracle Database to create development, test, and production environments on an Exalogic-based private cloud. DizzyGames can also control the scaling out and scaling back at a click of a button through the Cloud Control interface.

Building Applications for Exalogic

You've seen how DizzyGames uses the Exalogic-based private cloud to support the software development lifecycle (SDLC) for building applications and games. In this section, we will explore how developers at DizzyGames can build applications designed to take advantage of the performance optimizations offered by Exalogic.

Oracle Exalogic Elastic Cloud is designed to maximize performance and reliability for the applications deployed on it. The optimizations built into Exabus are the primary sources of application performance benefits, because they leverage Quad Data Rate (QDR) InfiniBand fabric in the Exalogic system. Exabus consists of hardware, software, and firmware distributed throughout the system. It involves every major system component by engineering them to work together in the most optimal way.

Although virtually all applications will demonstrate a significant performance improvement when moved to Exalogic, the applications that utilize Oracle's latest Fusion Middleware products and the Exalogic Elastic Cloud Software can achieve the maximum possible performance gains on an Exalogic system. This has prompted a change in the thinking of developers at DizzyGames, as they would like to leverage all of the available performance optimizations, not only to create faster games, but also to ensure that the hardware and software footprint required is significantly lower, yet scales to support more users. The key optimizations are discussed in the next section.

Exalogic Optimizations for Oracle Fusion Middleware

Several key optimizations in Exalogic for Fusion Middleware provide performance improvements to all the applications over commodity-based deployments. Exalogic-specific optimizations are engineered into the JRockit JVM and WebLogic Server to increase its throughput and scalability-related performance. This has been achieved through more closely engineering aspects of networking, thread management, and data management.

Parallel Muxer Optimization

Some optimizations can be leveraged in your application to provide high performance and throughput. These optimizations especially benefit I/O-bound or network-bound applications.

WebLogic Server uses software modules called *muxers* to read incoming requests on the server. Normally the muxers have dedicated socket-reading threads that multiplex over multiple protocols to read/write data onto the network. But because Exalogic system uses QDR InfiniBand, this approach is modified to leverage the extra bandwidth better and provide extremely low latency by employing multiple parallel muxers, as shown in Figure 7-11.

This enhancement provides a more efficient use of threads and allows greater utilization of the available bandwidth on the InfiniBand network for inter-JVM communication between WebLogic Servers. This optimization will greatly assist the redesign of highly distributed games at DizzyGames,

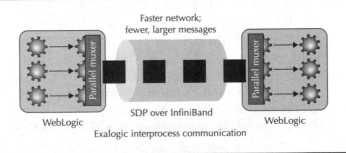

FIGURE 7-11. *Parallel muxer optimization on Exalogic*

as the rate of data exchange between different components of a distributed application can be far greater on Exalogic.

Using Hardware-Aware Thread Management

The DizzyGames application will benefit from optimized hardware-aware thread management to react better to sudden increases in load, especially during peak hours of afternoons and school breaks when there is an increase in load on online games.

As shown in the Figure 7-12, Thread Management makes adjustments, if necessary, every several seconds by incrementing the number of pooled threads by the number of (physical) hardware threads on the host machine. On non-Exalogic–based deployments, an increment of one thread is used

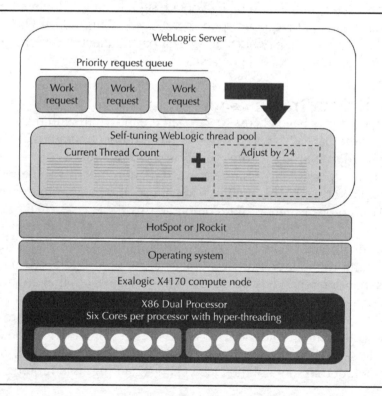

FIGURE 7-12. *Hardware-aware WebLogic thread management*

by default. For Exalogic, this increment becomes 24 (12 cores with 2 threads per core due to hyper-threading). This self-tuning strikes an optimum balance between workload and the number of threads available on the host machine.

Optimized Data Management

Other optimizations that will help DizzyGames developers reduce the CPU cycles in the application are modifications that reduce the number of incoming request and outgoing response copies. Traditionally, WebLogic Server has been engineered to use byte arrays to collect data responses. As a result, multiple array copies are created at different layers of the subsystems within WebLogic Server, as the data is passed from one layer to another. The optimizations ensure that the data buffers are shared between the WebLogic's subsystem layers, rather than being copied, significantly reducing the amount of objects created for request/response processing. This reduced heap usage also reduces the frequency of expensive garbage collections, increasing the overall responsiveness of online games.

Efficient Data Transmission

WebLogic Servers have access to very large bandwidth within Exalogic. This allows a large packet size to be used for communication among the different JVMs. Given that a single homogeneous IPoIB network is present inside Exalogic, it is possible to assume a much higher known ceiling value for network packet sizes. This optimization allows the maximum transmission unit (MTU) to be as high as 64K compared to 1.5K MTU size in traditional Ethernet.

As a result, WebLogic Servers can transmit large data very efficiently over the InfiniBand fabric. In addition, the use of a special I/O pattern ensures that different data objects (such as 4K size each) that are transmitted from JVM can be copied in system memory as a single chunk (for example, a single 64K size). The JVM is then able to make a single and more efficient network call to the InfiniBand user-space libraries provided by the operating system, to send the data over the network. Some very complex distributed data is included in some of the DizzyGames offerings that requires large data-driven interaction across a number of JVMs. This optimization will provide benefits to applications because the data transmission time is dramatically reduced, increasing the games' resilience and reducing response times.

These optimizations that transmit data among different JVMs make both clustered and multi-tiered applications quicker. All of the optimizations can be enabled on an Exalogic-deployed WebLogic Server using the following steps:

1. Log in to the Oracle WebLogic Server Administration Console.

2. Select Domain Name in the left navigation pane. The Settings for domain screen is displayed. Click the General tab.

3. In your domain home page, select Enable Exalogic Optimizations, and click Save.

4. Activate the changes.

5. Stop and start your domain.

These optimizations can also be enabled by setting the Java options described in following table:

Feature	Description
Scattered reads and gathered writes	Increased efficiency during I/O in environments with high network throughput **-Dweblogic.ScatteredReadsEnabled=true** **-Dweblogic.GatheredWritesEnabled=true**
Lazy deserialization	Increased efficiency with session replication **-Dweblogic.replication.enableLazyDeserialization=true**
Self-tuning thread pool optimization	Increased efficiency of the self-tuning thread pool by aligning it with Exalogic's processor architecture threading capabilities. Use the following MBean interface: **KernelMBean.addWorkManagerThreadsByCpuCount**

WebLogic Optimizations for Increased Session Replication

WebLogic Server traditionally uses a single network channel on a particular port to facilitate all the communications using muxer-based threads that multiplex across the socket to exchange data for different protocols. This can cause a bottleneck for web applications with large user session footprints, because replicating large HTTP session data across to secondary servers can take significant time.

Until this point, DizzyGames has stayed away from HTTP session replication, because it was too costly to the games' performance, as the HTTP session object for a game user is very large. WebLogic Server has been optimized to leverage higher bandwidth and MTU size on the InfiniBand network and can replicate data more efficiently; this reduces latency for HTTP request/response processing. These optimizations provide a significant boost to the online games, because they will, for the first time, have HTTP session resilience, ensuring that gamers do not lose their position in the game if a node failure occurs. The following are the specific optimizations:

- **Multiple replication channels**   Allows multiple network connections to be used between two WebLogic Servers to replicate session data. This reduces the time spent performing synchronous session replication.

- **Lazy deserialization of session objects**   Allows just-in-time deserialization of the session data on the secondary server during a failover scenario. This further reduces the CPU cycles and latency of the request/response, because the replicated session data usually will not be used on the secondary server.

- **Use SDP for session replication**   Using Sockets Direct Protocol (SDP) to transmit session data to the secondary server saves CPU cycles as it bypasses the kernel and network stack by directly copying data into the remote server's memory.

The session replication-based optimizations can be configured on a WebLogic Domain using the following steps:

1. Set up replication ports on each WebLogic Server in the cluster through console. Under Domain Structure, click Environment and Servers. The Summary of Servers page is displayed.

2. Click the server name from the list of servers. The settings for the selected server are displayed.

3. Click the Cluster tab.

4. In the Replication Ports field, enter a range of ports for configuring multiple replication channels. For example, replication channels for a server can listen on ports starting from 7005 to 7015. To specify this range of ports, enter **7005-7015**.

5. Create a custom network channel for each managed server in the cluster. In the left pane of the Console, expand Environment and select Servers.

6. In the Servers table, click server instance name.

7. Select Protocols, and then Channels.

8. Click New.

9. Enter **ReplicationChannel** as the name of the new network channel and select t3 as the protocol, and then click Next.

10. Enter the following information: **Listen address: 192.168.10.150, Listen port: 7005**. (Note: This is the floating IP assigned.)

11. Click Next, and in the Network Channel Properties page, select Enabled and Outbound Enabled.

12. Click Finish.

13. Expand the Advanced settings for the replication channel, and select Enable SDP Protocol.

14. Click Save.

15. After creating the network channel for each of the Managed Servers in your cluster, click Environment | Clusters. The Summary of Clusters page is displayed.

16. Click the cluster name.

17. Click the Replication tab.

18. In the Replication Channel field, ensure that ReplicationChannel is set as the name of the channel to be used for replication traffic.

19. In the Advanced section, select the Enable One Way RMI For Replication option.

20. Click Save.

This optimization makes it possible to have applications with large sessions work far more efficiently and at great speed on the Exalogic machine.

Active GridLink-Based Optimization for Exadata

The Active GridLink data source capability is a new way of connecting WebLogic to an Oracle Real Application Clusters (RAC) database cluster. With Active GridLink, WebLogic subscribes to the database's Fast Application Notification (FAN) events using Oracle Notification Services (ONS). Additional scenarios are feasible as a result of this new capability, such as the following:

- Informed runtime load-balancing decisions in WebLogic based on the current workload of each RAC node

- Improved performance by sending database calls to the node with the lowest current workload; the average latency of user request/response times is reduced

- Fast Connection Failover (FCF) to enable rapid database failure detection to reconfigure its connection pool automatically

- Single Client Access Name (SCAN) can be used, so that a simple Java Database Connectivity (JDBC) URL can be specified for the WebLogic connection pool, and so you don't have to change the URL each time a RAC node is added to or removed from the database cluster

The biggest optimization in Active GridLink for Exalogic is an option to communicate with Oracle RAC nodes in Exadata using SDP over InfiniBand (SDPoIB) rather than IPoIB; this dramatically reduces database transaction time. This is a major advantage for DizzyGames, because several games are strategy games that rely on heavy database interaction. This optimization will improve the response time for these games.

This enhancement avoids the use of the operating system's TCP/IP stack and the added latency that it would otherwise incur. When the option is enabled, WebLogic configures the Oracle Thin JDBC Driver with a URL and specific JDBC property to indicate to the JDBC Driver that SDP should be used for all JDBC communication with the database. SDP, rather than TCP/IP over InfiniBand, yields better response times, especially where the data payload is large, as is often the case for large JDBC result sets.

A WebLogic Server–based Active GridLink data source can be configured to use SDP by changing the JDBC connection string, such as in the following example:

```
jdbc:oracle:thin:@(DESCRIPTION=(ADDRESS=(PROTOCOL=tcp)(HOST=192.x.x.x)(PORT=
1522))(CONNECT_DATA=(SERVICE_NAME=myservice)))
```

can be changed to this (changes in boldface):

```
jdbc:oracle:thin:@(DESCRIPTION=(ADDRESS=(PROTOCOL=SDP)(HOST=192.x.x.x)(PORT=
1522))(CONNECT_DATA=(SERVICE_NAME=myservice)))
```

To ensure that this features works, you will need to enable SDP listeners on the Exadata nodes. On the Exadata node, first enable SDP by following the steps:

1. Open /etc/infiniband/openib.conf in a text editor, and add the following:

   ```
   set: SDP_LOAD=yes
   ```

   Then save the file and close.

2. Open the /etc/ofed/libsdp.conf file in a text editor, and change the following two lines:

   ```
   use both server *:
   use both client *:
   ```

   can be changed to this (changes in boldface):

   ```
   use tcp server * *:*
   use tcp client * *:*
   ```

   Then save the file and close.

3. Open /etc/modprobe.conf in a text editor, and add the following setting:

```
options ib_sdp sdp_zcopy_thresh=0 recv_poll=0
```

Then save the file and close.

4. Reboot all database nodes for the changes to take effect.

Next, create an SDP-based database listener on the InfiniBand network on Exadata:

1. Edit /etc/hosts on each node in the cluster to add the virtual IP addresses you will use for the InfiniBand network. Make sure that these IP addresses are not used elsewhere. The following is an example:

```
# Added for Listener over IB
192.168.10.21 dm01db01-ibvip.mycompany.com dm01db01-ibvip
192.168.10.22 dm01db02-ibvip.mycompany.com dm01db02-ibvip
```

2. On one of the database nodes, as the root user, create a network resource for the InfiniBand network, as in the following example:

```
# /u01/app/grid/product/11.2.0.2/bin/srvctl add network -k 2 -S 192.168.10.0/
255.255.255.0/bondib0
```

3. For each node in the cluster, add the virtual IP addresses on the network created:

```
srvctl add vip -n dm01db01 -A dm01db01-ibvip/255.255.255.0/bondib0 -k 2
srvctl add vip -n dm01db02 -A dm01db02-ibvip/255.255.255.0/bondib0 -k 2
```

4. As the oracle user (who owns the grid infrastructure home), add a listener that will listen on the VIP addresses created in step 3:

```
srvctl add listener -l LISTENER_IB -k 2 -p TCP:1522,/SDP:1522
```

5. For each database that will accept connections from the middle tier, modify the **listener_networks init** parameter to allow load balancing and fail-over across multiple networks (Ethernet and InfiniBand). You can either enter the full tnsnames syntax in the initialization parameter or create entries in tnsnames.ora in $ORACLE_HOME/ network/admin directory. The tnsnames.ora entries must exist in the GRID_HOME. First update tnsnames.ora and complete this step on each node in the cluster with the correct IP addresses for that node. LISTENER_IBREMOTE should list all other nodes that are in the cluster. DBM_IB should list all nodes in the cluster.

Special Application Scenarios that Leverage Exalogic-Based Optimizations

Exalogic's set of optimizations benefits every application that is deployed on it, but some applications provide more benefits than others. This section describes some of the application use cases that can benefit from optimization and describes how to build your applications better to leverage these optimizations and deliver higher performance and value.

Web Applications with a Large HTTP Session Object

Traditionally, web applications are built with the principle of maintaining application and user state (user session information) on server-side. As applications have become more complex, user state has also become larger. Developers have to strike a balance between client-side processing in terms of JavaScript, versus keeping the processing on the server-side, resulting in larger session objects. This has become a bigger issue with richer web applications such as portals that require lots of data to be held in session, as bigger session objects mean slower HTTP response from the servers, because it takes more time to perform session replication required for high availability. JVM heap size also increases as session objects grow in size, resulting in longer Java garbage collection pauses. All this has eroded application performance and resulted in IT wanting to make compromises on high availability by switching off session replication or changing the applications to be more fragmented (non-portal) deployments, thus requiring more back-end service calls and infrastructure.

With Exalogic-based optimizations, web applications can leverage 40 times the bandwidth at a 10 times faster data transfer rate than on typical 1GbE, making HTTP session replication no longer an issue. This allows very rich and complex web applications to run up to 10 times faster at required levels of high availability and resilience.

One such application is ATG Web Commerce server. It was virtually impossible to run an ATG application with more than a million products in a catalog with a refresh rate of 100,000 price changes a second on commodity hardware, because this required a high rate of database interaction and very large session objects. When deployed on Exalogic, the ATG-based application is able to run at a rate of 50 pages rendered per second per core and with subsecond response times, with a high level of price changes on a large catalog. As a consequence, the ATG application infrastructure can scale to support 18,000 pages per second to a million concurrent sessions on a single Exalogic machine.

Processing Large Messages

As you know, an InfiniBand network allows a WebLogic Server to use higher than normal MTU size such as 64K instead of normal 1.5K. This has a major impact on how large objects are transferred across compute notes and on Network File System (NFS), making processing large messages far more efficient and quicker.

Using an MTU size of 64K means that it would take nearly the same time to transfer and process a 1K object as it would a 64K object, as the packet size is 64K with a very low latency of approximately 1 microsecond. As a result, the application built to run on the Exalogic cloud can easily transfer large objects without seeing the drop in performance that would normally occur while running the application on Ethernet.

Some application use cases, such as those in which a large message is broken down into smaller messages to be written to a file or sent to a remote JVM or process, can be revisited to ensure the additional CPU time in splitting the message into smaller chunks is avoided. Large messages can be handled on Exalogic as easily and without performance impact, as the smaller but more numerous messages permit simpler logic and reduced overhead.

Large In-Memory Data Grid

An in-memory data grid achieves low response times for data access by keeping the information in memory and in the application's object form, and by sharing that information across multiple servers. The applications may be able to access the information that they require without any network communication and without any data transformation step such as object relationship mapping. When network communication is required, it can avoid introducing a single point of bottleneck (SPOB) by partitioning information across the grid, with each server responsible for managing its share of the total set of information. This is a widely used approach in many high-volume transactional systems, from trading, settlements, financial systems, to online booking, order processing, and so on. These data grids are normally achieved through the implementation of Oracle Coherence.

Oracle Coherence 3.7.1 leverages the Exabus technology exclusive to the Oracle Exalogic Elastic Cloud. It dramatically increases scalability and lowers the latency of data grid operations by using InfiniBand-based SDP combined with Remote Direct Memory Access (RDMA) for communication and using the highest MTU size available. Exabus technology and Oracle Coherence 3.7.1 provides the next generation of massively scalable, low-latency data and state management for middleware applications.

Oracle Coherence 3.7.1 Elastic Data advancements provide more efficient memory and disk-based storage and improve data access performance, offering greater flexibility, expanded capacity, and more efficiency of existing infrastructure. The Elastic Data feature of Oracle Coherence allows organizations to leverage both memory and disk-based devices for data grid storage, enabling near memory speed access to data, regardless of the storage medium, by using the following optimizations:

- Prioritize RAM availability to store the primary copies of data, by moving backup copies to or from RAM to flash when necessary

- Data overflow to flash devices by dramatically increasing concurrency

- Feature to trigger its internal garbage collection as its remaining RAM capacity approaches zero

- Optimizes the Elastic Data garbage collection to become less aggressive when the available capacity is plentiful

Some of the early benchmarks have shown that Coherence can maintain a large data grid with the following:

- A cluster of up to 300 cache servers

- A data grid size of up to 300GB with backup enabled

- Sustained throughput at a rate of 25 Gbp/s

- Data change rate of 20 Gbp/s, running over a long period without any degradation

Using SDP for Standalone Java Applications

Many applications require high performance computing with high throughput and low latency—such as an execution environment where applications process and transfer large amounts of data at minimal delay. These applications can be deployed on Exalogic along with Exalogic Elastic Cloud software, to make use of SDP to achieve high performance and zero copy data transfers. SDP bypasses the TCP mechanism and uses the InfiniBand network directly. SDP is a transport agnostic protocol that supports RDMA on the InfiniBand fabric, moving data directly from the memory of one compute node to another and bypassing the operating systems on both compute nodes.

No application code change is required to take advantage of SDP. WebLogic Server, if configured to use SDP, seamlessly uses SDP-based communication for your application.

TIP
To debug SDP communication,
*set **-Dcom.sun.sdp.debug=debug.log***
option at server startup.

Applications hosted on Exalogic can use SDP for two scenarios: HTTP session replication and communication with Exadata. Other scenarios may be supported in the future, but this shouldn't stop you from configuring compute nodes for your specific requirements using JDK 7 SDP.

In some scenarios, a Java application does not need to be deployed on an application server. This is normally true for applications in the finance and gaming sectors, where specialized applications are written in Java as standalone applications. If you want to run such applications in a standalone JVM that is not running on WebLogic applications hosted on Exalogic, you can still make use of SDP through the in-built support in JDK 7.

SDP support is disabled by default. To enable SDP support, set the **com.sun.sdp.conf** system property by providing the location of the configuration file. The following example starts an application named CustomApplication using a configuration file named sdp.conf:

```
# Use SDP when binding to 192.168.1.1
bind 192.168.1.1 *
# Use SDP when connecting to all application services on 192.169.1.*
connect 192.168.1.0/24    1024-*
```

```
# Use SDP when connecting to the http server or a database
connect application.mydomain.com    80
connect database.mydomain.com    1521
```

Now you can run your application with the following command with SDP support enabled:

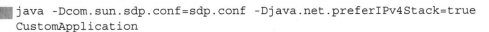

```
java -Dcom.sun.sdp.conf=sdp.conf -Djava.net.preferIPv4Stack=true
CustomApplication
```

NOTE
You should be aware of some technical issues when enabling SDP, most related to IPv6 stacks. Be sure to run the application with IPv4, using the Ipv4 preference option shown in the preceding code.

CustomApplication is a Java application that uses SDP over InfiniBand. JDK 7 classes support reads or writes to network sockets with SDP.

Using SDP to support high-performance computing in your custom non-WebLogic–based Java applications is as easy to implement as it is to deploy a Java Enterprise Edition (Java EE) application on a WebLogic Server on Exalogic. This section showed a non-intrusive way of configuring a standalone Java application to use SDP without making any code changes.

Summary

Building applications on Exalogic is a game changer because it allows a new way for IT to support SDLC for application development by ensuring that all the environments are identical and deployable with a click of a button. You saw how easy it is to deploy a private cloud based on Exalogic systems and Oracle Enterprise Manager. An organization can provision a cloud from scratch within a matter of days, not months or years. You also saw the many ways of building applications to take advantage of the Exalogic-based performance optimizations, demonstrating that Exalogic is not only about providing business agility, but also yielding value for your money by providing significant performance increases over commodity-based systems.

CHAPTER
8

Packaged
Applications
on Exalogic

t this point you should have a firm grasp of Oracle's vision for Exalogic, including its overall hardware and software architecture. We've discussed solution architectures, the deployment process, and data center requirements. Now it is time to discuss workloads that run on Exalogic.

This chapter covers the applications that can be run on Exalogic, including Oracle E-Business Suite, JD Edwards, PeopleSoft, SAP, Siebel, and others. This is not an exhaustive list, nor does it imply that other workloads are not suitable for Exalogic; as discussed previously, Exalogic has been designed to optimize the performance of many different types of Java workloads. These applications are, however, known to be extremely well suited for Exalogic, and several benchmarks have been developed to prove this.

Enterprise application development is not a core competency for most companies. Instead, many companies purchase enterprise applications and develop their own enterprise applications only when no existing product meets their needs. Enterprise applications serve important back-office and front-office functions that support a company's core business. Functions such as human resources (HR), financials (including accounts payable, general ledger, payroll, and so on), Supply Chain Management (SCM), Customer Relationship Management (CRM), and others, are handled by these enterprise applications, which are often labeled as *Enterprise Resource Planning (ERP)* applications.

These business-critical functions demand high availability and instant response times (For example, Amazon estimates that the company loses 1 percent of its customers for every 100ms delay in server response time.[1]) This places a high burden on the IT organization, which must manage the servers, operating systems, switches, cabling, storage devices, databases, and middleware components underlying these critical business applications. Business and IT are looking for ways to reduce costs and reduce the risk of system downtime, and their focus on consolidation is one of the drivers for the growth of cloud computing.

In most cases, moving to a public cloud would require changing the enterprise applications and/or organizational business practices. Some Software as a Service (SaaS) application providers require that applications be written in proprietary software languages, and most require that customers use their software "out of the box" with few, if any, customizations. In contrast, an engineered system allows companies to take advantage of an appliance-like platform for their enterprise applications without having to change the code of their existing enterprise application. This greatly reduces the complexity in the data center, which reduces the cost of maintaining the environment and the risk of system failure. The engineered systems also enable enterprise applications to improve performance greatly and provide scalability for the future. As discussed in previous chapters, Oracle Exadata and Exalogic work together in the data center to create a private cloud for the IT organization with all the associated benefits and the advantage of running existing applications.

This chapter describes specific benefits for running packaged applications such as Oracle E-Business Suite, Oracle PeopleSoft, SAP, and Oracle Siebel on Exalogic and Exadata. Since many of the application use cases involve both Exadata and Exalogic, we may refer to the systems as being deployed on the "Exa platform," with "Exa" referring to both Exadata and Exalogic.

All of the performance results that are discussed in this chapter have been previously published at conferences such as Oracle Open World and Collaborate, at smaller industry events dedicated to Exadata and Exalogic, and/or online. References to online information are provided in the book's appendices.

Application Sprawl and Consolidation

Application sprawl is not a new problem, nor is the use of consolidation a new solution. However, applying engineered systems as the consolidation solution of choice for enterprise applications is new.

Data centers today include many application instances running on different technology platforms that have been difficult to assemble and manage. Production application instances may also have other associated instances as well (development, test, user acceptance test, integration test, reporting, performance test, disaster recovery, and so on). Online transaction processing (OLTP) systems and data warehouses are usually separate. Batch tasks may also run in a separate instance to avoid interference with OLTP workloads. Mergers and acquisitions can result in additional applications running on different platforms in remote data centers. Entry into new markets can lead to new business requirements, which can be isolated into yet another separate instance. For example, order management instances may support a specific geography or a specific line of business. Some organizations have a separate application instance for every state in the United States for regulatory purposes. Each instance may be customized to meet specific local requirements, making consolidation difficult if local requirements must be supported. Enterprises can end up with a large number of servers hosting a large number of application instances with low utilization for each localized application. Furthermore, each system may have different peaks and troughs throughout the year. In old-style platforms, each host environment had to have capacity to meet the peak load, even though most of the year that excess capacity would be idle.

Exalogic supports consolidation by offering enterprise applications a standardized configuration that is a building block for data centers. Exalogic's optimized performance reduces the number of servers necessary to run enterprise applications, providing savings in space, power consumption, and cooling. Exalogic also supports multi-tenancy concerns around providing security and quality of service isolation for individual applications, comparable to what the applications would have had if deployed on separate hardware.

One example of Exadata and Exalogic consolidation is listed in the appendix and involves the United States Customs and Border Protection. They were able to consolidate 120 then-existing racks of servers into a dozen Exadata machines, with considerable savings on space, power consumption, and cooling—not to mention an improvement in manageability of approximately 60 percent.[2] Exalogic's support for open standards is a critical reason why different enterprise applications can take advantage of its capabilities as a platform.

Deployment on Exalogic and Exadata Benefits Different Applications Differently

Enterprise Applications have been developed over decades by different groups of engineers and targeted at different customer bases. Different technology choices were made in the development of enterprise applications. Some enterprise applications use Java, and others use C, C++, COBOL, and other languages. Some enterprise applications use a combination of several different programming languages. With regard to middleware, some enterprise applications use Java EE application servers such as WebLogic, and others are using Tuxedo or custom-built application servers.

However, they all share some features at the architecture level. Most of the applications discussed in this chapter are three-tiered or n-tiered, with a web tier, application server tier, and a database tier. Many applications separate OLTP from data warehouse reporting applications and online analytical processing (OLAP) to avoid back-office functions negatively impacting the front-office response times. Scaling is handled by vertically and horizontally scaling the individual tiers. For example, scaling the database tier can be accomplished by making the database run on a bigger machine (vertical scaling) or by using RAC or similar technologies to cluster the database (horizontal scaling).

Figure 8-1 shows an example architecture for a PeopleSoft enterprise application.

Exalogic provides the optimum platform for running the application server tier and other applications depicted in Figure 8-1. It is recommended that the database tier be run on Exadata. If Oracle Traffic Director is being used, it is recommended that the web server be put on the Exalogic machine to take advantage of Exalogic performance optimizations. If Oracle Traffic Director is not being used, it is recommended that the web server tier be run in front of Exalogic.

Application workloads may need additional middleware beyond an application server, such as WebLogic Server. There may be a need for integration via an enterprise service bus or Oracle SOA Suite, Business Intelligence, Identity Management, and Portal capabilities. Locating the Middleware components on the same Exalogic machine as the enterprise applications provides several benefits. The primary benefits are easier manageability and higher performance due to sharing the InfiniBand network fabric. Figure 8-2 shows an enterprise application deployed on Exalogic with additional middleware components.

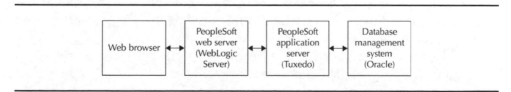

FIGURE 8-1.   *Example application architecture for a PeopleSoft enterprise application*

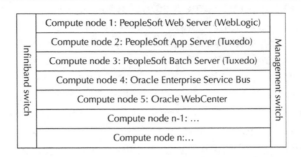

FIGURE 8-2. *Enterprise application deployed on Exalogic with middleware components*

As Figure 8-2 shows, there are great advantages to Exalogic consolidation. Oracle WebCenter and Oracle Enterprise Service Bus can easily share an Exalogic machine with Oracle PeopleSoft.

Benchmarks

Rigorous certification procedures must be followed before publishing a benchmark report. The figures and results described in this book are examples only and should not be considered a benchmark. Hyperlinks for published benchmarks for the Oracle applications described in this chapter can be found in the appendix.

Comparison hardware consisted of the latest generation servers and storage solutions (at the time of the test), optimized for the environment, but without any of the Exa advantages. So the comparable commodity hardware is similar to what a sophisticated IT department would set up to run the applications. However, there is no guarantee that the tuning performed for the tests described in this book is relevant to your environment. Every environment is different.

Unless explicitly stated otherwise, all tests in this chapter were conducted using Oracle Linux on Exalogic.

Configuration and Installation

In some cases, installing an application on Exalogic can be as simple as following the default installation process. In other cases, additional configuration is required to obtain the benefits from Exalogic optimizations.

For example, at the time of this writing, some applications support Sockets Direct Protocol (SDP) and Active GridLink for Java Database Connectivity (JDBC) communication between Exalogic and Exadata. However, the current installation software for a particular application may not have been updated to include these options. In that case, you would have to set up a regular multi-data source during installation and then manually configure SDP and Active GridLink afterward.

Oracle Applications

Oracle is continuing to innovate in the applications area, so other applications are supported beyond the applications described in this chapter. For the most recent list, please see the links in the appendix of this book. Table 8-1 shows certifications for E-Business Suite, JD Edwards, PeopleSoft, and Siebel.

Application Name	Application Versions	Application Server
E-Business Suite	12.0.6, 12.1.x	OC4J 10.1.3.5
JD Edwards EnterpriseOne	Applications: 8.11, 8.11 SP1, 8.12, 9.0 Tools: 8.98.4	WebLogic Server 10.3.2, 10.3.4
PeopleSoft Enterprise	Applications: 9.x PeopleTools: 8.50, 8.51	WebLogic Server 10.3.2, 10.3.3, 10.3.4
Siebel	8.1.1.4	Siebel Application Server 8.1.1.4 FP

TABLE 8-1. *Oracle Application Certifications for Exalogic*

Oracle PeopleSoft

As shown in Table 8-1, PeopleSoft 9.*x* applications are certified to run on Exalogic with PeopleTools 8.50 and 8.51. PeopleTools releases are certified with x86-64 based Oracle Linux.

PeopleSoft's runtime components leverage WebLogic Server, JRockit Java Virtual Machine, and Tuxedo. PeopleSoft's three-tier architecture includes the database server, application server (which includes the batch server and process scheduler), and client.

The application server is typically run on hardware separate from the database server, although it is positioned close to the database server from a networking perspective to reduce latency. The batch server can be run either on the same machine as the application server or on a separate machine, depending on load. Tuxedo acts as a transaction manager for the PeopleSoft applications. WebLogic Application Server, as shown in Figure 8-3, primarily acts as the Java servlet container for web interactions (and is often referred to as a "web server" in PeopleSoft architecture documents).

All of the WebLogic optimizations that were discussed in previous chapters will benefit PeopleSoft applications running on Exalogic. For example, WebLogic optimizes the way it passes data and messages between internal components, reducing the number of expensive data copying operations, thus increasing performance. PeopleSoft applications typically use large messages, so the data copy reductions will result in a substantial savings of CPU and memory that would have been otherwise spent on data creation and deletion.

Core components of PeopleSoft are coded in COBOL, which relies on Tuxedo in Exalogic. Tuxedo has been optimized to use SDP and Remote Direct Memory Access (RDMA) over InfiniBand instead of TCP/IP when communicating with components running on Exalogic or Exadata. SDP uses fewer CPU cycles, leaving more CPU cycles for other applications. With RDMA over InfiniBand, clients and servers on one node can talk directly to

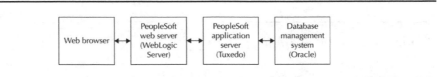

FIGURE 8-3. *Oracle PeopleSoft application architecture*

servers on another node without going through the Tuxedo bridge process, thereby reducing communication latency. Internal test results have shown dramatic improvement in throughput. In this manner, PeopleSoft applications benefit tremendously from these Tuxedo optimizations.

Exalogic Optimizations Benefit PeopleSoft

Internal testing has shown that Exalogic optimizations benefit PeopleSoft from a performance and scalability perspective. The scenario described next used a half rack of Exalogic Elastic Cloud and a quarter rack of Exadata Database Machine. Although a half rack of Exalogic was available, the tests actually used only seven to nine compute nodes (approximately the equivalent of a quarter rack, which has eight compute nodes). Figure 8-4 shows a test case scenario using eight nodes on Exalogic.

Although Oracle PeopleSoft has many functions expected in an ERP suite, it is widely used by organizations for HR tasks. An internal test scenario for PeopleSoft on Exadata and Exalogic was developed for an organization with 600,000 employees. For the test case, it was assumed that 40,000 users were online concurrently (or approximately 6.75 percent of the organization's user base). The 40,000 concurrent users were split into 24,000 employees (60 percent), 8000 managers (20 percent), and 8000 administrators (29 percent). A 30-minute steady state test run was developed with 240,000 transactions (six 5-minute transactions per concurrent user in a 30-minute period).

Compute node 1: PeopleSoft Web Server (WebLogic)
Compute node 2: PeopleSoft Web Server (WebLogic)
Compute node 3: PeopleSoft Web Server (WebLogic)
Compute node 4: PeopleSoft App Server (Tuxedo)
Compute node 5: PeopleSoft App Server (Tuxedo)
Compute node 6: PeopleSoft App Server (Tuxedo)
Compute node 7: PeopleSoft App Server (Tuxedo)
Compute node 8: PeopleSoft App Server (Tuxedo)

FIGURE 8-4. *Oracle PeopleSoft on Exalogic*

Each concurrent simulated user would log into PeopleSoft, navigate, perform a single transaction, and then log out within a 5-minute period. The concurrent users were assigned transactions that are typical for an organization of this size. For employees, self-service transactions included view paycheck (78 percent), view benefits summary (10 percent), update home address (3 percent), update home phone (3 percent), update beneficiary (2 percent), update direct deposit (2 percent), and add profile (2 percent). For managers, self-service transactions included view employee info (50 percent), initiate salary change (20 percent), initiate termination (20 percent), and initiate promotion (10 percent). For administrators, self-service transactions included add a job (40 percent), hire a person (40 percent), and add a person (20 percent).

For the test scenario, multiple tests were run with a varying quantity of compute nodes assigned to WebLogic Server and Tuxedo. For the tests, five or six compute nodes of Exalogic Elastic Cloud were assigned for the PeopleSoft application server (Tuxedo). Then two or three compute nodes of Exalogic were assigned for the PeopleSoft web server (WebLogic Server). Two nodes of Exadata ran the PeopleSoft database.

The test resulted in a ten-times scalability improvement for HR self-service (ten times the number of users could be supported, the largest scale performance test ever at the time of the test). Response time was improved three times relative to comparable commodity hardware (same generation hardware as the Exa systems).

Oracle E-Business Suite

Oracle E-Business Suite (EBS) is a modern ERP suite that is designed to perform many essential business processes. Individual modules can be implemented to handle an organization's financials (Global Ledger, Accounts Payable, Payroll, and so on), projects, procurement, supply chain management, human capital management, customer and master data management, and more. EBS includes global support for currencies, languages, business practices, locality requirements, and different industries.

EBS Release 12 is certified on Exalogic running Oracle Linux 5 (EBS versions 12.0.6+ 12.1+, and subsequent versions can run on Exalogic). Customers on EBS Release 12 can migrate their existing environments to Exalogic via the Rapid Clone methodology, upgrade from a previous E-Business Suite 11i version on an older system to Exalogic, or install a new Release 12 instance using the Rapid Install wizard. For Exadata, EBS supports versions 11.5.10, R12, and subsequent versions.

EBS applications run on Oracle Fusion Middleware and the Oracle Database. EBS application architecture is a three-tier architecture comprising the database, application, and client tiers, as shown in Figure 8-5.

EBS Release 12 application tier components include Oracle Fusion Middleware 10*g* components such as forms and reports, and Oracle Containers for Java (OC4J). E-Business Suite applications products are installed on this same tier. The application tier is typically scaled horizontally over multiple machines for better utilization and load-balancing purposes. The E-Business Suite user interface comprises Oracle Forms and HTML-only applications that are rendered to desktop and mobile devices.

Exalogic Optimizations Benefit E-Business Suite

Since EBS runs on Oracle Fusion Middleware 10*g*, the Exalogic optimizations described in Chapters 3 and 7, such as Active GridLink for RAC, do not apply to EBS. However, IP-over-InfiniBand (IPoIB) still provides performance enhancements for EBS when deployed on Exalogic.

Internal testing has shown that Exalogic benefits EBS from a performance and scalability perspective. For self-service applications, the performance increase resulted in eight times faster response time, thereby improving user productivity. For Order to Cash forms, the performance increase resulted in two to three times faster response times, thereby improving customer satisfaction (and potentially reducing customers lost due to slow response times). Twice as many users per core can be supported on Exalogic than

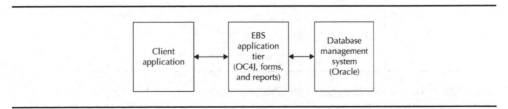

FIGURE 8-5.   *Oracle E-Business Suite application architecture*

commodity hardware, resulting in higher throughput, requirements for less hardware, and better response time. For backup and cloning, performance optimizations resulted in these tasks being 15 times faster, which not only greatly reduced the impact of backups on IT operations, but made creating new environments (for test, user training, and so on) a vastly more functional option. For Advanced Supply Chain Planning batch jobs, there was a 60 percent reduction in processing time, resulting in quicker answers and more agile supply chains. Figure 8-6 below shows EBS on Exadata and Exalogic.

An OLTP workload was simulated for EBS, in which 1200 concurrent users were used in a 50-minute steady-state test run (the 50 minutes excluded user ramp-up and ramp-down time). Performance test software automated the scripts for simulated users interacting with Oracle Forms. In the test, 400 users were simulated creating sales orders; then 200 users were simulated for each of the following activities, including releasing sales orders, order shipping, creating invoices, and ordering summary reports.

Exalogic and Exadata significantly outperformed comparable commodity hardware. Creating the sales order was 2.5 times faster. Releasing the sales order was 1.3 times faster. Shipping the order was 1.2 times faster (note that this is the EBS business process for shipping, physical shipment was not simulated). Creating the invoice was 3.5 times faster. Creating the order summary report was 1.2 times faster. Exalogic and Exadata processed 4 times the transactions of the comparable commodity hardware, resulting in 4x throughput.

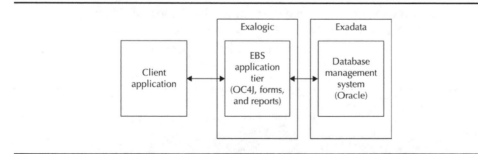

FIGURE 8-6.   *Oracle E-Business Suite on Exadata and Exalogic*

Oracle JD Edwards

Oracle's JD Edwards EnterpriseOne is an integrated ERP software package that offers more than 70 application modules to support business operations for customers of different sizes, industries, and geographies.

The JD Edwards EnterpriseOne three-tier architecture includes a Java EE tier for presentation and integration, a logic tier for the runtime kernel and business logic, and a database tier for storing system data and business logic. The Java EE tier and the logic tier would be consolidated onto the Exalogic machine, while the database tier would be consolidated onto an Exadata machine. Figure 8-7 shows the JD Edwards EnterpriseOne architecture.

As shown in Figure 8-7, the enterprise server provides the core runtime kernels, security, and business logic execution. The HTML server provides a presentation layer to end user (web browser) clients and Java logic execution. The business services server provides web-service–based integrations, both inbound and outbound, to third-party systems either directly or through services provided by the Oracle SOA Suite. The transaction server provides outbound notification of JD Edwards EnterpriseOne transaction events to a JMS queue. The portal is based on Oracle WebCenter Framework or WebCenter Spaces and provides the end user with access to JD Edwards EnterpriseOne applications via portlets.

From a certification standpoint, the JD Edwards EnterpriseOne server components align with the Oracle Exalogic architecture. JD Edwards EnterpriseOne servers are certified to run with Oracle Linux 5.5. JD Edwards EnterpriseOne components that run within a Java EE container are certified to run with Oracle WebLogic Server. Recommended releases are JD Edwards EnterpriseOne Applications 9.0 Update 2 and Tools 8.98 Update 4.

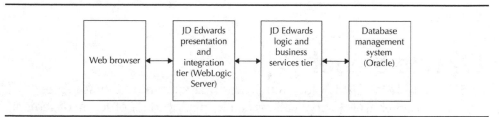

FIGURE 8-7. *JD Edwards EnterpriseOne application architecture*

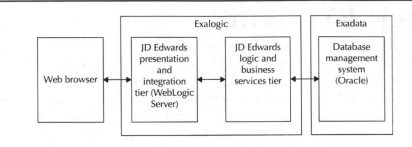

FIGURE 8-8. *JD Edwards EnterpriseOne on Exalogic and Exadata*

Exalogic Optimizations Benefit JD Edwards

The JD Edwards EnterpriseOne architecture can take advantage of several Exalogic optimizations, as shown in Figure 8-8. End user transactions (interactive queries, data entries, and system responses) are managed by Java processes running within a WebLogic Server container and can benefit from the Exalogic optimizations. JD Edwards EnterpriseOne transactions, both interactive and batch, require significant intercommunication between the logic server, the HTML server, and the database server. Exalogic's InfiniBand networking eliminates bottlenecks and latency from these communication paths, shortening the duration of transactions.

A three-tier test configuration (enterprise, HTML, and database servers) utilizing three Exalogic compute nodes was run simulating 900 concurrent users in an interactive scenario, and separately with a batch load consisting of 34 jobs running concurrently with the 900-user load. The user interactions were simulated with load-generation test tools and resulted in an average response time of just 0.16 second for pure interactive load, while the addition of the batch processing maintained an average response time of under a second.

Oracle Siebel

Oracle Siebel is a CRM solution that was first known mainly for sales applications. Siebel CRM applications can be deployed for order management, tracking services, managing activities, and other customer-centric activities.

Banks, financial institutions, telecommunications companies, pharmaceutical companies, government agencies, and other organizations use Oracle Siebel to track customer touch-points. Siebel applications can be used by call center agents and other front-office users to service customer interactions, but often CRM applications need to connect to back-office applications.

Siebel relies upon a distributed architecture, and Siebel applications are designed to integrate with finance, billing, and supply chain ERP applications. For example, a call center order booking applet in Siebel can look up a back-office inventory application to determine whether an order can be booked.

Siebel has a n-tiered architecture, with client, web server, Siebel application server, and Siebel database server tiers, as shown in Figure 8-9.

As shown in Figure 8-9, the web server directs requests to the Siebel application server tier. The business logic resides in the Siebel application server tier.

The Siebel n-tiered architecture allows horizontal and vertical scalability for large-scale deployments by load balancing across web servers and Siebel application servers with the database using Oracle RAC. Siebel applications versions that support Oracle Linux 5.5 are supported and validated to run on Oracle Exalogic. Siebel applications 8.1.1.4 onwards are supported on Exalogic. Siebel applications 8.0 and subsequent applications are supported on Exadata.

Transactions traverse the Siebel application components, going from web server to Siebel server, to database. When multiple Siebel servers are deployed on Exalogic for scaling, the InfiniBand fabric provides a fast pipe for inter-server communication among Siebel servers across Exalogic compute nodes.

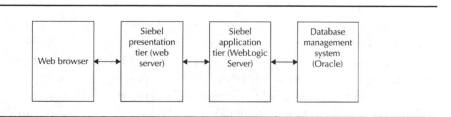

FIGURE 8-9. *Oracle Siebel application architecture*

Often other applications will coexist with Siebel on Exalogic. An enterprise service bus can be used to integrate Siebel and other applications while benefiting from the Exalogic performance improvements. A business intelligence application such as Oracle Business Intelligence Enterprise Edition (OBIEE) can also be used with Siebel, and customers may adopt some Fusion application modules and elect to host them on the same machine. All these application components can be integrated via Fusion Middleware.

Oracle Fusion Applications

Oracle Fusion Applications are based on Oracle Fusion Middleware. Oracle Fusion Applications can take full advantage of the optimizations built into Exalogic and Exadata.

Oracle ATG Web Commerce

Oracle ATG Web Commerce is a retail e-commerce application that lets companies sell retail products to consumers over the Web. ATG can be used for business-to-customer (B2C) commerce, business-to-business (B2B) commerce, and customer-to-customer (C2C) commerce. ATG supports several different interaction channels, including the web, mobile, and video game consoles, and has advanced social networking capabilities to link online customer profiles with their buying habits to create customized interactive experiences.

ATG uses a n-tiered architecture, with a Java EE application server (such as WebLogic Server) and a relational database (such as the Oracle 11g database). Figure 8-10 shows the ATG Web Commerce architecture on an Oracle stack.

ATG has been deployed in environments with requirements to support millions of end customers concurrently and thousands of page views per second. ATG applications are I/O intensive and can take advantage of some key Exalogic optimization enhancements. The high performance offered by the InfiniBand network and reduced overhead of the Exabus can significantly reduce I/O bottlenecks, thereby decreasing response time and improving the end user experience.

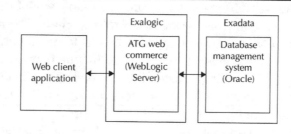

FIGURE 8-10. *Oracle ATG Web Commerce architecture on an Oracle stack*

Exalogic Optimizations Benefit Oracle ATG Web Commerce

Internal testing has shown that deploying ATG on Exalogic results in approximately three times better performance and three times better throughput compared to running ATG on commodity hardware. Testing results for performance and throughput varied based on the application, testing scripts, and testing methodology.

The most compelling reason for a retailer to consider Exalogic would be the increased revenue that an e-commerce application deployed on Exalogic can generate due to the reduced latency and greater throughput. The conversion rate is the percentage of people who enter a store (whether a physical bricks-and-mortar store or a virtual e-commerce store) and also buy something. Several studies have indicated that response time is critical for e-commerce conversion rates. According to Google, a 500ms delay in response time results in a 20 percent drop in web traffic[3]. With that impact in mind, Exalogic performance optimizations can help ATG applications increase customer satisfaction and conversion rates.

Oracle Utilities Global Business Unit on Exalogic and Exadata

Oracle Utilities Global Business Unit (UGBU) provides a suite of software products with capabilities including customer care, billing, meter data management, load forecasting, settlement, and transactions management for utilities.

Internal testing was performed on meter data management using a one-rack Exadata Database Machine and a one-rack Exalogic Elastic Cloud. A common household or business smart meter can be read electronically on a 15-minute interval versus traditional meters that were read manually once a month by a meter reader physically visiting a meter. Smart meters can quickly generate an enormous amount of data for even a moderately sized utility. After loading the information from all of the meter readings and applying business rules for validation, editing, and estimation, it was possible to process 1.4 billion meter readings per hour with this configuration. This compares very favorably to 300 million meter readings per hour on comparable commodity hardware. There is approximately a five times performance enhancement with Exalogic and Exadata.

Internal testing was also performed on the billing application for utilities deployed on Exadata and Exalogic. This configuration was capable of processing billing for 20 million households in one hour. In contrast, comparable commodity hardware was able to process billing for 2.75 million households in an hour. The result of the comparison between Exadata and Exalogic versus commodity hardware is approximately a seven times performance increase.

Oracle TimesTen In-Memory Database

The Oracle TimesTen In-Memory Database (TimesTen) is a relational database technology that has been optimized to store data in the memory of a computer instead of in traditional data storage systems. TimesTen is targeted to run in the application tier, close to performance-critical applications and can be used as the database or as a relational cache in combination with an Oracle 11*g* database. TimesTen is typically used with real-time applications and other applications that have high performance requirements. And it has been certified for deployment on Oracle Exalogic Elastic Cloud. Figure 8-11 shows Oracle TimesTen deployed on Exalogic.

Several tests with varying workloads have shown that TimesTen performance increases significantly when deployed on Exalogic versus comparable commodity hardware. In these tests, TimesTen is deployed to the same compute nodes where the application is deployed. Each individual compute node uses its own local instance of TimesTen.

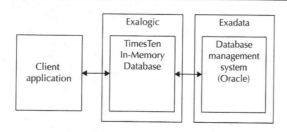

FIGURE 8-11. *Oracle TimesTen In-Memory Database on Exalogic architecture*

The Exalogic test server was configured with a quarter rack consisting of eight compute nodes. The prepaid mobile and online banking application workload included several different types of transactions, including authenticate user and account status; check account balance; update account profile; refill, credit, or debit account; and search accounts with a low balance. Throughput reached 8.7 million transactions per second on a quarter-rack Exalogic machine.

In an alternative scenario using a workload with 80 percent reads, 10 percent updates, 5 percent inserts, and 5 percent deletes, a peak throughput of 1.6 million transactions per second per compute node was achieved. Each compute node included 12 cores, with 10 concurrent processes running the application. The remaining 2 cores were used for the TimesTen data manager and persisting transactions to the disk on the shared storage server.

SAP on Oracle Exalogic

Running SAP software on Oracle Exalogic Elastic Cloud is officially supported by SAP. This section discusses architectural considerations when deploying SAP on Exalogic and Exadata. Only SAP NetWeaver 7.*x* or higher is supported, including SAP products that are based on SAP NetWeaver 7.*x*. Also, only Unicode implementations are supported. When running SAP NetWeaver on Oracle Exalogic, SAP uses an Oracle database running on an Oracle Exadata database machine, as shown in Figure 8-12.

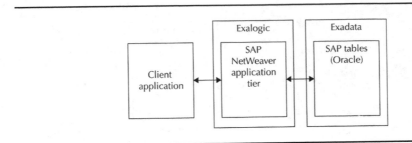

FIGURE 8-12. *SAP with Oracle Exadata and Oracle Exalogic*

Figure 8-12 illustrates the relationship between the SAP components, Exadata, and Exalogic in a three-tier configuration. It shows SAP application servers running the Advanced Business Application Programming (ABAP) stack use Oracle Net through Oracle Instant Client to connect to the Oracle database. This enables them to use SDP easily over InfiniBand for low latency, bypassing the traditional TCP/IP stack.

Summary

At the end of the day, the decision by businesses to deploy application workloads on Exalogic tends to not be driven by the cost advantages and/or the extreme performance offered by Exalogic. The decision tends to be driven by business desires to reduce the risk of custom platform development. This is the same desire that is driving the push to move to cloud services, which are usually championed by the business units. The cost advantages and extreme performance are additional benefits for those businesses that select an engineered system such as Exalogic for their mission-critical business applications.

In conclusion, Oracle Exalogic Elastic Cloud and Oracle Exadata Machine are the premiere platforms for deploying Java applications in general and Oracle application workloads specifically. They reduce the risk in implementing new applications and in maintaining the data center infrastructure, while lowering operations and maintenance costs substantially. If your organization does not have requirements that force a choice of another platform, the competitive advantages offered by Exalogic and Exadata are compelling.

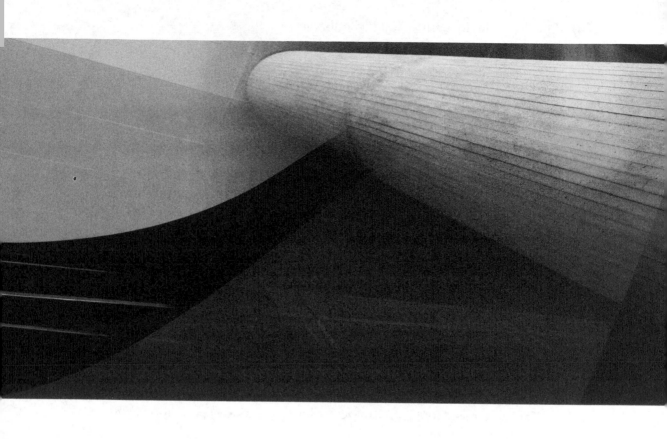

Conclusion

ne book cannot cover everything. For that reason, we have included an extensive list of resources to aid the reader in further research in this area, including URLs where you'll find additional information. We have also included end notes in Appendix B for the information we quoted in the various chapters of this book.

Oracle Exalogic Elastic Cloud is expected to change and evolve over the next few years to meet changes in customer demand. We expect that subsequent editions of this book will be written to update this content to cover the latest changes.

Among the topics that we wanted to write more pages on, but didn't have the time, are the following:

- Exalogic Control

- Oracle Virtual Assembly Builder

- Rehosting mainframe applications on Exalogic with Tuxedo

- Use cases for using Exalogic with MapReduce applications and the Big Data Appliance

- Complex Event Processing (CEP) on Exalogic

- Optimizations for Service-Oriented Architecture (SOA) on Exalogic

- Running databases on Exalogic instead of Exadata

- Comparing and contrasting Exalogic with SPARC SuperCluster

And the list goes on.

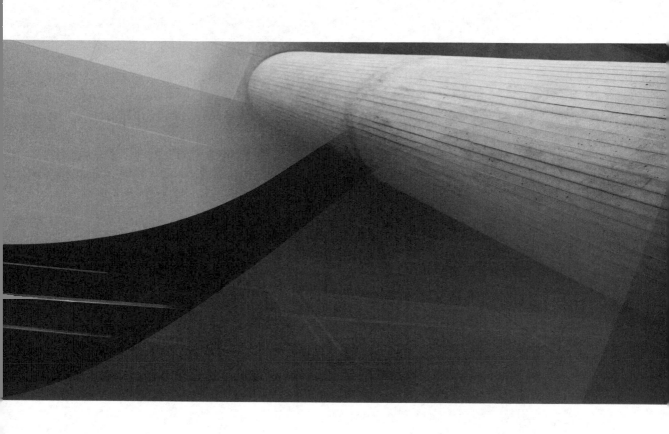

PART
III

Appendixes

APPENDIX
A

Additional Resources

Additional Reading: Books

Nearly every Oracle product is relevant to Exalogic, including books on Exadata, WebLogic, Java, Oracle Applications, and other topics. Some books that are particularly relevant include:

- *Oracle WebLogic Server 11g Administration Handbook*, by Sam Alapati (Oracle Press, 2011)

- *Professional Oracle WebLogic Server*, by Robert Patrick, Gregory Nyberg, and Philip Aston (Wiley, 2010)

Exalogic Web Sites, White Papers, and Documentation

- Exalogic web site: www.oracle.com/exalogic

- Exalogic on Twitter: http://twitter.com/OracleExalogic

- Exalogic on Facebook: http://facebook.com/Exalogic

- Exalogic channel on YouTube: http://youtube.com/exalogictv

- Exalogic playlist on the Oracle Media Network: http://medianetwork.oracle.com/search/results?q=exalogic

- Exalogic documentation: http://download.oracle.com/docs/cd/E18476_01/index.htm

- "Oracle Exalogic Elastic Cloud: A Brief Introduction": www.oracle.com/us/products/middleware/exalogic-wp-173449.pdf

- "Oracle Exalogic Elastic Cloud: Software Overview": www.oracle.com/us/products/middleware/exalogic-software-overview-345527.pdf

- "Oracle Exalogic Elastic Cloud: X2-2 Hardware Overview": www.oracle.com/us/products/middleware//exalogic-hardware-overview-345531.pdf

- Oracle A-Team blog on Exalogic and Cloud Application Foundation: https://blogs.oracle.com/ATeamExalogic/

■ Oracle Exalogic Elastic Cloud data sheet: www.oracle.com/us/ products/middleware/exalogic/exalogic-elastic-cloud-x2-2-ds-1367805.pdf

■ "Disaster Recovery for Oracle Exalogic Elastic Cloud": www.oracle.com/technetwork/database/focus-areas/availability/ maa-exalogic-dr-401789.pdf

■ "Oracle Exalogic Elastic Cloud: Datacenter Network Integration": www.oracle.com/us/products/middleware/exalogic/eec-datacenter-network-integration-1405367.pdf

■ "What Oracle Solaris Brings to Oracle Exalogic Elastic Cloud": www.oracle.com/technetwork/server-storage/solaris11/ documentation/wp-solaris-on-exalogic-cloud-345932.pdf

■ Oracle Exalogic Machine Owner's Guide: http://docs.oracle.com/cd/ E18476_01/doc.220/e18478/toc.htm

■ Oracle Fusion Middleware Exalogic Machine Multirack Cabling Guide: http://docs.oracle.com/cd/E18476_01/doc.220/e18481/ toc.htm

■ Oracle Fusion Middleware Exalogic Enterprise Deployment Guide: http://docs.oracle.com/cd/E18476_01/doc.220/e18479/toc.htm

■ Sun Rack II and PDU documentation: http://docs.oracle.com/cd/ E19657-01/index.html

■ Sun Fire Server documentation: http://docs.oracle.com/cd/E19762-01/index.html

■ Sun ZFS Storage Appliance documentation: http://docs.oracle.com/ cd/E22471_01/index.html

■ Sun Network QDR InfiniBand Gateway Switch Firmware documentation: http://docs.oracle.com/cd/E19671-01/index.html

■ Oracle Integrated Lights Out Manager (ILOM) documentation: http://docs.oracle.com/cd/E19860-01/index.html

Exalogic Educational Resources

Oracle University offers online and on-site training. For classroom training, visit http://education.oracle.com.

The Exalogic curriculum currently consists of the following courses:

- Oracle Exalogic Elastic Cloud Overview Seminar
- Oracle Exalogic Elastic Cloud Administration

Exadata Web Sites, White Papers, and Documentation

- Exadata web site: http://www.oracle.com/exadata
- Oracle Exadata technology portal on OTN: http://www.oracle.com/technology/products/bi/db/exadata

WebLogic Server Web Sites, White Papers, and Documentation

- WebLogic Server documentation: www.oracle.com/technetwork/middleware/weblogic/documentation/index.html
- Oracle WebLogic Server documentation library: http://download.oracle.com/docs/cd/E14571_01/wls.htm
- Oracle Fusion Middleware Supported Systems Configurations: www.oracle.com/technetwork/middleware/ias/downloads/fusion-certification-100350.html
- Enterprise Deployment Guides for Fusion Middleware 11*g* products: http://download.oracle.com/docs/cd/E17904_01/edg.htm
- "WebLogic Server Performance and Tuning": http://download.oracle.com/docs/cd/E12840_01/wls/docs103/perform/intro.html
- WebLogic Server YouTube channel: www.youtube.com/oracleweblogic

- WebLogic Server 12c - 5 Mins with the Zip File Distribution: www.youtube.com/watch?v=Ny1nd0BTCf4&list= UUrEIV9YO17leE9aJWamKEPw&index=8&feature=plcp

- WebLogic 12c Maven Plugin Demo: www.youtube.com/watch?v= hagaMr6UL6U&list=UUrEIV9YO17leE9aJWamKEPw&index= 2&feature=plcp

- "Java EE 6 Using WebLogic Server 12c and NetBeans": www.youtube.com/watch?v=WkxgrVqZ7D0&list= UUrEIV9YO17leE9aJWamKEPw&index=3&feature=plcp

- JRockit Mission Control: www.youtube.com/watch?v= kkyyIzx0xy4&feature=related

- Oracle WebLogic Active GridLink for RAC Demo: www.youtube .com/watch?v=8D6cf6Y5z94&feature=related:

- Patching a WebLogic Domain with Enterprise Manager 12c Cloud Control: www.youtube.com/watch?v=ZfwQ2oBKqk4&feature= plcp&context=C4e764afVDvjVQa1PpcFM-1oBty_ 321atztEtdaSv8FihT9hQInFE%3D

WebLogic Educational Resources

Oracle University offers online and on-site training. For classroom training, see http://education.oracle.com/pls/web_prod-plq-dad/db_ pages.getlppage?page_id=212&path=OWLA

Weeklong courses include the following:

- Oracle WebLogic Server 11*g*: Administration Essentials

- Oracle WebLogic Server 11*g*: Advanced Administration

- Oracle WebLogic Server 11*g*: Diagnostics and Troubleshooting

- Oracle WebLogic Server 11*g*: Monitoring and Performance Tuning

From a course perspective, administrators typically take the admin and/ or advanced admin course. The troubleshooting and tuning courses are typically taken by people who specialize in those tasks.

Coherence Web Sites and Documentation

- Coherence and Coherence*Web documentation library: http:// docs.oracle.com/cd/E24290_01/index.htm

- Exalogic Optimizations for Coherence: http://docs.oracle.com/cd/ E24290_01/coh.371/e22623/technotes.htm#sthref8

Web Tier Documentation

- Web Tier Components documentation library: http:// docs.oracle.com/cd/E23943_01/webtier.htm

- Traffic Director documentation library: http://docs.oracle.com/cd/ E23389_01/index.htm

Enterprise Manager Documentation

- Grid Control, Cloud Control, and Ops Center documentation library: http://docs.oracle.com/cd/E11857_01/nav/overview.htm

Tuxedo Web Sites and Documentation

- Tuxedo main web site: www.oracle.com/technetwork/middleware/ tuxedo/overview/index.html

- "Tuxedo is now optimized for Exalogic," Tuxedo Tidbits blog: https:// blogs.oracle.com/Tuxedo/entry/tuxedo_is_now_optimized_for

Oracle Applications Web Sites, White Papers, and Documentation

■ Oracle Benchmarks: www.oracle.com/us/solutions/benchmark/apps-benchmark

■ "Consolidating Oracle Applications on Exalogic" white paper, May 2011: www.oracle.com/us/products/middleware/app-consolidation-exalogic-395610.pdf

■ Support document 1302529.1 has the latest list of Oracle Applications supported on Oracle Exalogic. My Oracle Support site: Doc ID:1302529.1. Details for EBS, Siebel, PSFT & JDE. This document can be accessed on myoracle.support.com: https://support.oracle.com/CSP/main/article?cmd=show&type=NOT&doctype=BULLETIN&id=1302529.1

Oracle PeopleSoft Web Sites, White Papers, and Documentation

■ "Oracle PeopleSoft on Oracle Exadata Database Machine: Oracle Maximum Availability Architecture White Paper," February 2011: www.oracle.com/technetwork/database/features/availability/maa-wp-peoplesoft-on-exadata-321604.pdf

■ Hosted & Mobile PeopleBooks—PeopleTools PeopleBooks are available in three formats: hosted PeopleBooks, PDFs, and Amazon's Kindle format: www.oracle.com/technetwork/documentation/psftent-090284.html

■ Doc Home Pages—Constantly updated direct links to PeopleBooks, PeopleBook updates, release notes, installation and upgrade guides, and other useful product documentation from My Oracle Support. PeopleTools 8.52 Doc Home Page: https://support.oracle.com/CSP/main/article?cmd=show&type=NOT&doctype=REFERENCE&id=1356456.1

- Information Portal—Locate the documentation, training, and other info needed to help with your implementation process. Customers searching for this information should make this their first online destination: www.oracle.com/us/products/applications/054275.html

- Cumulative Feature Overview (CFO)—Provides concise descriptions of new and enhanced solutions and functionality that have become available starting with the 8.4 release through the 8.52 release: https://support.oracle.com/CSP/main/article?cmd=show&type=NOT&doctype=SYSTEMDOC&id=793143.1

- Upgrade Resource Report Tools—Helps you find all the documentation, scripts, and files you need for your upgrade project: https://support.oracle.com/CSP/main/article?cmd=show&type=NOT&doctype=SYSTEMDOC&id=1117047.1

Oracle E-Business Suite Web Sites, White Papers, and Documentation

- "E-Business Suite on Exadata: Oracle Maximum Availability Architecture White Paper," December, 2010: www.oracle.com/technetwork/database/features/availability/maa-ebs-exadata-197298.pdf

- Oracle E-Business Suite Online Documentation Library: www.oracle.com/technetwork/documentation/applications-167706.html

- MAA Best Practices—Oracle Applications: www.oracle.com/technetwork/database/features/availability/oracle-applications-maa-155388.html

- Sogeti Consolidates E-Business Suite on Exadata: http://medianetwork.oracle.com/media/show/16033

- "Rapid Clone methodology for Migrating EBS R12 to Exalogic," My Oracle Support Note 406982.1

- *Installing a New R12 instance: Oracle E-Business Suite Upgrade Guide, Release 11i to 12.1.3*

- *Oracle E-Business Suite Installation Guide: Using Rapid Install*

Oracle Siebel Web Sites, White Papers, and Documentation

- "A Technical Overview of the Oracle Exadata Database Machine and Exadata Storage Server" white paper: www.oracle.com/ technetwork/server-storage/engineered-systems/exadata/exadata-technical-whitepaper-134575.pdf

- MAA OTN Site: www.oracle.com/goto/maa

- "Oracle Exadata Tipe, Tricks, and Best Practices for Migrating to the Oracle Exadata": www.oracle.com/technetwork/database/features/ availability/s316822-175935.pdf

- "Siebel Maximum Availability Architecture" white paper: www.oracle.com/technetwork/database/features/availability/ siebelmaa-131211.pdf

- "Siebel on Exadata" white paper: www.oracle.com/technetwork/ database/features/availability/maa-wp-siebel-exadata-177506.pdf

Oracle JD Edwards White Paper

- "JDE on Exalogic Performance" white paper: https://support .oracle.com/CSP/main/article?cmd=show&type=NOT&id= 1322463.1

SAP on Oracle Exalogic Web Sites, White Papers, and Documentation

- "Using SAP NetWeaver with the Oracle Exadata Database Machine" white paper: www.oracle.com/us/products/database/sap-exadata-wp-409603.pdf

- SAP Note 1617188: https://service.sap.com/sap/support/notes/1617188

- SAP Product Availability Matrix: www.service.sap.com/PAM

Security Links

- STIGs: http://iase.disa.mil/stigs/

- Center for Internet Security: www.cisecurity.org/

- Tenable Network Security: www.tenable.com

- Qualys: www.qualys.com

OEM 12c YouTube Demos

- Oracle learning video on Enterprise Manager 12c that shows how to go from zero to Cloud in Under 5 Minutes (PaaS Edition): http://www.youtube.com/watch?v=A1_pLKlvKI0

- Oracle learning video on Enterprise Manager 12c: Setup and Use Chargeback: http://www.youtube.com/watch?v=0UbZsTVgQu0

- Oracle learning video on Enterprise Manager 12c: Setup the Cloud Servers: http://www.youtube.com/watch?v=WmeCaYYVJwg

- Oracle learning video on Managing Exalogic from Application to Disk: http://www.youtube.com/watch?v=CZ-HJhFw9vk

- Oracle learning video on Enterprise Manager 12c: Exalogic Management Overview: http://www.youtube.com/watch?v=L7BIJvVbrkA

APPENDIX B

End Notes

Chapter 1

1. On Mohamad Afshar's blog, http://moafshar.blogspot.com/2011/02/why-engineered-systems-its-been-barely.html, he shares a list of 19 steps that a traditional IT customer might follow when performing do-it-yourself platform development.

2. Lyrics to the Johnny Cash song "One Piece at a Time" can be found at http://www.azlyrics.com/lyrics/johnnycash/onepieceatatime.html.

3. *Information Week*'s Global CIO column described "The Surge to Optimized Systems" as the "Global CIO #1 Story Of The Year [2010], http://www.informationweek.com/news/global-cio/interviews/228700448?pgno=1&queryText=&isPrev=.

4. See http://en.wikipedia.org/wiki/Internet_traffic. See also "Minnesota Internet Traffic Studies showing annual growth rates of 50% or more in internet traffic," http://www.dtc.umn.edu/mints/home.php.

5. See the "One Day Installation Challenge" video on YouTube, http://www.youtube.com/watch?v=aWHPC188tus.

6. See Gartner 2010 Worldwide Application Server "Market Share, All Software Markets Worldwide 2010," March 30, 2011, by Colleen Graham, et al., http://my.gartner.com/portal/server.pt?open=512&objID=249&mode=2&PageID=864059&resId=1611814&ref=Browse.

7. See http://www.spec.org/jEnterprise2010/results/res2011q1 and http://www.spec.org/jAppServer2004/results/.

8. NIST draft definition of cloud computing v15.

9. "Privatizing the Cloud: 2010 IOUG Survey on Cloud Computing," produced by IOUG ResearchWire and Unisphere Research, is the source for the data.

Chapter 8

1. Greg Linden, Make Data Useful, slide 15, http://www.scribd.com/doc/4970486/Make-Data-Useful-by-Greg-Linden-Amazoncom.

2. Presentation by Kenneth M. Ritchhart, Deputy Assistant Commissioner and DCIO Customs & Border Protection (CBP), Department of Homeland Security (DHS) at the ACT/IAC on January 10. 2011; downloaded on June 21, 2011, http://www.actgov.org/knowledgebank/documentsandpresentations/Documents/Program%20Events/Executive%20Session%20featuring%20Ken%20Ritchhart,%20CBP%201-12-11.pdf.

3. Greg Linden, Make Data Useful, slide 15, http://www.scribd.com/doc/4970486/Make-Data-Useful-by-Greg-Linden-Amazoncom.

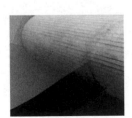

Index

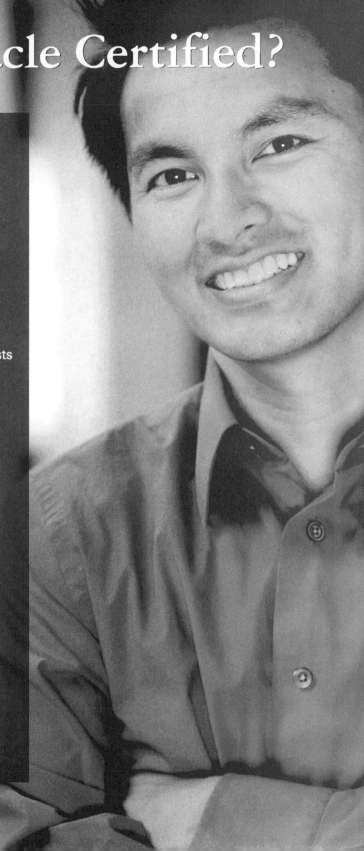

GET YOUR FREE SUBSCRIPTION TO *ORACLE MAGAZINE*

Oracle Magazine is essential gear for today's information technology professionals. Stay informed and increase your productivity with every issue of *Oracle Magazine*. Inside each free bimonthly issue you'll get:

- Up-to-date information on Oracle Database, Oracle Application Server, Web development, enterprise grid computing, database technology, and business trends

- Third-party news and announcements

- Technical articles on Oracle and partner products, technologies, and operating environments

- Development and administration tips

- Real-world customer stories

If there are other Oracle users at your location who would like to receive their own subscription to *Oracle Magazine*, please photo-copy this form and pass it along.

Three easy ways to subscribe:

① **Web**
Visit our Web site at **oracle.com/oraclemagazine**
You'll find a subscription form there, plus much more

② **Fax**
Complete the questionnaire on the back of this card
and fax the questionnaire side only to **+1.847.763.9638**

③ **Mail**
Complete the questionnaire on the back of this card
and mail it to **P.O. Box 1263, Skokie, IL 60076-8263**

ORACLE®

Want your own FREE subscription?

To receive a free subscription to *Oracle Magazine*, you must fill out the entire card, sign it, and date it (incomplete cards cannot be processed or acknowledged). You can also fax your application to +1.847.763.9638. **Or subscribe at our Web site at oracle.com/oraclemagazine**

○ **Yes, please send me a FREE subscription** *Oracle Magazine*. ○ No.

○ From time to time, Oracle Publishing allows our partners exclusive access to our e-mail addresses for special promotions and announcements. To be included in this program, please check this circle. If you do not wish to be included, you will only receive notices about your subscription via e-mail.

○ Oracle Publishing allows sharing of our postal mailing list with selected third parties. If you prefer your mailing address not to be included in this program, please check this circle.

If at any time you would like to be removed from either mailing list, please contact Customer Service at +1.847.763.9635 or send an e-mail to oracle@halldata.com. If you opt in to the sharing of information, Oracle may also provide you with e-mail related to Oracle products, services, and events. If you want to completely unsubscribe from any e-mail communication from Oracle, please send an e-mail to: unsubscribe@oracle-mail.com with the following in the subject line: REMOVE [your e-mail address]. For complete information on Oracle Publishing's privacy practices, please visit oracle.com/html/privacy/html

X _____

signature (required)   date

name   title

company   e-mail address

street/p.o. box

city/state/zip or postal code   telephone

country   fax

Would you like to receive your free subscription in digital format instead of print if it becomes available? ○ Yes ○ No

---

YOU MUST ANSWER ALL 10 QUESTIONS BELOW.

① WHAT IS THE PRIMARY BUSINESS ACTIVITY OF YOUR FIRM AT THIS LOCATION? (check one only)

- ☐ 01 Aerospace and Defense Manufacturing
- ☐ 02 Application Service Provider
- ☐ 03 Automotive Manufacturing
- ☐ 04 Chemicals
- ☐ 05 Media and Entertainment
- ☐ 06 Construction/Engineering
- ☐ 07 Consumer Sector/Consumer Packaged Goods
- ☐ 08 Education
- ☐ 09 Financial Services/Insurance
- ☐ 10 Health Care
- ☐ 11 High Technology Manufacturing, OEM
- ☐ 12 Industrial Manufacturing
- ☐ 13 Independent Software Vendor
- ☐ 14 Life Sciences (biotech, pharmaceuticals)
- ☐ 15 Natural Resources
- ☐ 16 Oil and Gas
- ☐ 17 Professional Services
- ☐ 18 Public Sector (government)
- ☐ 19 Research
- ☐ 20 Retail/Wholesale/Distribution
- ☐ 21 Systems Integrator, VAR/VAD
- ☐ 22 Telecommunications
- ☐ 23 Travel and Transportation
- ☐ 24 Utilities (electric, gas, sanitation, water)
- ☐ 98 Other Business and Services _____

② WHICH OF THE FOLLOWING BEST DESCRIBES YOUR PRIMARY JOB FUNCTION? (check one only)

CORPORATE MANAGEMENT/STAFF
- ☐ 01 Executive Management (President, Chair, CEO, CFO, Owner, Partner, Principal)
- ☐ 02 Finance/Administrative Management (VP/Director/ Manager/Controller, Purchasing, Administration)
- ☐ 03 Sales/Marketing Management (VP/Director/Manager)
- ☐ 04 Computer Systems/Operations Management (CIO/VP/Director/Manager MIS/IS/IT, Ops)

IS/IT STAFF
- ☐ 05 Application Development/Programming Management
- ☐ 06 Application Development/Programming Staff
- ☐ 07 Consulting
- ☐ 08 DBA/Systems Administrator
- ☐ 09 Education/Training
- ☐ 10 Technical Support Director/Manager
- ☐ 11 Other Technical Management/Staff
- ☐ 98 Other

③ WHAT IS YOUR CURRENT PRIMARY OPERATING PLATFORM (check all that apply)

- ☐ 01 Digital Equipment Corp UNIX/VAX/VMS
- ☐ 02 HP UNIX
- ☐ 03 IBM AIX
- ☐ 04 IBM UNIX
- ☐ 05 Linux (Red Hat)
- ☐ 06 Linux (SUSE)
- ☐ 07 Linux (Oracle Enterprise)
- ☐ 08 Linux (other)
- ☐ 09 Macintosh
- ☐ 10 MVS
- ☐ 11 Netware
- ☐ 12 Network Computing
- ☐ 13 SCO UNIX
- ☐ 14 Sun Solaris/SunOS
- ☐ 15 Windows
- ☐ 16 Other UNIX
- ☐ 98 Other
- 99 ☐ None of the Above

④ DO YOU EVALUATE, SPECIFY, RECOMMEND, OR AUTHORIZE THE PURCHASE OF ANY OF THE FOLLOWING? (check all that apply)

- ☐ 01 Hardware
- ☐ 02 Business Applications (ERP, CRM, etc.)
- ☐ 03 Application Development Tools
- ☐ 04 Database Products
- ☐ 05 Internet or Intranet Products
- ☐ 06 Other Software
- ☐ 07 Middleware Products
- 99 ☐ None of the Above

⑤ IN YOUR JOB, DO YOU USE OR PLAN TO PURCHASE ANY OF THE FOLLOWING PRODUCTS? (check all that apply)

SOFTWARE
- ☐ 01 CAD/CAE/CAM
- ☐ 02 Collaboration Software
- ☐ 03 Communications
- ☐ 04 Database Management
- ☐ 05 File Management
- ☐ 06 Finance
- ☐ 07 Java
- ☐ 08 Multimedia Authoring
- ☐ 09 Networking
- ☐ 10 Programming
- ☐ 11 Project Management
- ☐ 12 Scientific and Engineering
- ☐ 13 Systems Management
- ☐ 14 Workflow

HARDWARE
- ☐ 15 Macintosh
- ☐ 16 Mainframe
- ☐ 17 Massively Parallel Processing
- ☐ 18 Minicomputer
- ☐ 19 Intel x86(32)
- ☐ 20 Intel x86(64)
- ☐ 21 Network Computer
- ☐ 22 Symmetric Multiprocessing
- ☐ 23 Workstation Services

SERVICES
- ☐ 24 Consulting
- ☐ 25 Education/Training
- ☐ 26 Maintenance
- ☐ 27 Online Database
- ☐ 28 Support
- ☐ 29 Technology-Based Training
- ☐ 30 Other
- 99 ☐ None of the Above

⑥ WHAT IS YOUR COMPANY'S SIZE? (check one only)

- ☐ 01 More than 25,000 Employees
- ☐ 02 10,001 to 25,000 Employees
- ☐ 03 5,001 to 10,000 Employees
- ☐ 04 1,001 to 5,000 Employees
- ☐ 05 101 to 1,000 Employees
- ☐ 06 Fewer than 100 Employees

⑦ DURING THE NEXT 12 MONTHS, HOW MUCH DO YOU ANTICIPATE YOUR ORGANIZATION WILL SPEND ON COMPUTER HARDWARE, SOFTWARE, PERIPHERALS, AND SERVICES FOR YOUR LOCATION? (check one only)

- ☐ 01 Less than $10,000
- ☐ 02 $10,000 to $49,999
- ☐ 03 $50,000 to $99,999
- ☐ 04 $100,000 to $499,999
- ☐ 05 $500,000 to $999,999
- ☐ 06 $1,000,000 and Over

⑧ WHAT IS YOUR COMPANY'S YEARLY SALES REVENUE? (check one only)

- ☐ 01 $500, 000, 000 and above
- ☐ 02 $100, 000, 000 to $500, 000, 000
- ☐ 03 $50, 000, 000 to $100, 000, 000
- ☐ 04 $5, 000, 000 to $50, 000, 000
- ☐ 05 $1, 000, 000 to $5, 000, 000

⑨ WHAT LANGUAGES AND FRAMEWORKS DO YOU USE? (check all that apply)

- ☐ 01 Ajax
- ☐ 02 C
- ☐ 03 C++
- ☐ 04 C#
- ☐ 05 Hibernate
- ☐ 06 J++/J#
- ☐ 07 Java
- ☐ 08 JSP
- ☐ 09 .NET
- ☐ 10 Perl
- ☐ 11 PHP
- ☐ 12 PL/SQL
- ☐ 13 Python
- ☐ 14 Ruby/Rails
- ☐ 15 Spring
- ☐ 16 Struts
- ☐ 17 SQL
- ☐ 18 Visual Basic
- ☐ 98 Other

⑩ WHAT ORACLE PRODUCTS ARE IN USE AT YOUR SITE? (check all that apply)

ORACLE DATABASE
- ☐ 01 Oracle Database 11*g*
- ☐ 02 Oracle Database 10*g*
- ☐ 03 Oracle9*i* Database
- ☐ 04 Oracle Embedded Database (Oracle Lite, Times Ten, Berkeley DB)
- ☐ 05 Other Oracle Database Release

ORACLE FUSION MIDDLEWARE
- ☐ 06 Oracle Application Server
- ☐ 07 Oracle Portal
- ☐ 08 Oracle Enterprise Manager
- ☐ 09 Oracle BPEL Process Manager
- ☐ 10 Oracle Identity Management
- ☐ 11 Oracle SOA Suite
- ☐ 12 Oracle Data Hubs

ORACLE DEVELOPMENT TOOLS
- ☐ 13 Oracle JDeveloper
- ☐ 14 Oracle Forms
- ☐ 15 Oracle Reports
- ☐ 16 Oracle Designer
- ☐ 17 Oracle Discoverer
- ☐ 18 Oracle BI Beans
- ☐ 19 Oracle Warehouse Builder
- ☐ 20 Oracle WebCenter
- ☐ 21 Oracle Application Express

ORACLE APPLICATIONS
- ☐ 22 Oracle E-Business Suite
- ☐ 23 PeopleSoft Enterprise
- ☐ 24 JD Edwards EnterpriseOne
- ☐ 25 JD Edwards World
- ☐ 26 Oracle Fusion
- ☐ 27 Hyperion
- ☐ 28 Siebel CRM

ORACLE SERVICES
- ☐ 28 Oracle E-Business Suite On Demand
- ☐ 29 Oracle Technology On Demand
- ☐ 30 Siebel CRM On Demand
- ☐ 31 Oracle Consulting
- ☐ 32 Oracle Education
- ☐ 33 Oracle Support
- ☐ 98 Other
- 99 ☐ None of the Above